A Workbook Companion

Commentaries on the
Workbook for Students
from
A Course in Miracles

Volume II, Lessons 121 to 243

by Allen Watson and Robert Perry

Number 20 in a series based on
A Course in Miracles

This is the twentieth book in a series, each of which deals with the modern spiritual teaching, *A Course in Miracles*®. If you would like to receive future books or booklets directly from the publisher, or would like to receive the newsletter that accompanies this series, please write us at the address below.

The Circle of Atonement
Teaching and Healing Center
P.O. Box 4238
West Sedona, AZ 86340
(520) 282-0790, Fax (520) 282-0523
http://nen.sedona.net/circleofa/

All references are given for the Second Edition of the Course and are listed according to the numbering in the Course, rather than according to page numbers. Each reference begins with a letter, which denotes the particular volume of the Course (T=Text, W=Workbook, M=Manual for Teachers, C=Clarification of Terms, P=Psychotherapy pamphlet, S=Song of Prayer). After this letter comes a series of numbers, which differ from volume to volume:

T, P or **S-**	chapter.section.paragraph:sentence
W-	part(I or II).lesson.paragraph:sentence
M or **C-**	section.paragraph:sentence

ISBN 1–886602–10–7

Published by The Circle of Atonement: Teaching and Healing Center
Printed in the United States of America

Typesetting by Allen Watson
Cover design by Diane Goulder

TABLE OF CONTENTS

Tear-out card with Practice Instructions in back of book

A WORKBOOK COMPANION

INTRODUCTION

by Allen Watson

In this Introduction to Volume II, I want to repeat the most important thing I have to say about *A Workbook Companion:* it is definitely not intended as a replacement for the *Workbook for Students* that comes as part of *A Course in Miracles*. It is meant, rather, as a companion to the Workbook, to encourage students in practicing the exercises of the Workbook as we believe the author intended for us to do them.

Actually following the structured program presented in the Workbook is what can train our minds to think along the lines the text sets forth. Mere study alone cannot accomplish that (although study of the Text is also a necessary part of the training). Nor can simply reading through the Workbook lessons. What trains our minds is actually *doing the exercises. A Workbook Companion* is designed to help you to understand and practice the exercises—nothing more than that.

Each day's lesson in *A Workbook Companion* contains two parts: a Practice Summary (written by Robert Perry), which extracts and condenses the actual instructions for practice given in the Workbook, and a Commentary (written by myself), which attempts to highlight and clarify some of the teaching given in the lessons. The commentary does not, in most cases, attempt to comment on everything in the lessons; that could take dozens of volumes instead of just three.

Robert Perry's overview comments on practice, scattered throughout, will give you a better sense for how the Workbook is presenting a coherent, overall training program with specific objectives.

How should you use this book in conjunction with the *Workbook for Students*? I recommend reading the lesson for the day from the Workbook and then, if time permits, reading the corresponding section from *A Workbook Companion* before carrying out the instructions in the lesson. The *Companion* comments on the actual practice instructions, often clarifying them and helping your practice to be more focused and meaningful. If, however, you must choose between taking time to read the commentary and taking that same time to actually do the practice, by all means skip the commentary and do the practice. Read the commentary later in the day, whenever you find time.

A few notes on some formatting details in the book. I have chosen to include a date at the top of each lesson; this shows the day of the year the lesson will fall on if you begin with Lesson 1 on January 1. This is purely a convenience for people who choose to do the Workbook in synchronization with the calendar. There is nothing in the Workbook itself to suggest that this is necessary or even desirable. You can start the Workbook on any day of the year you choose

Although it isn't necessary to follow the calendar if you are working alone, it can greatly facilitate doing the Workbook along with a group of friends. The distribution of these commentaries by electronic mail resulted in hundreds of people doing the same lessons each day. Here in Sedona, in our local Course community, we have chosen to do the same thing. We have found that doing so adds enormously to our ability to support one another, to encourage one another in doing the Workbook, and to discuss the lessons together.

I highly recommend that anyone setting out to follow the Workbook program also obtain a copy of *The Workbook as a Spiritual Practice*, by Robert Perry (available from The Circle of Atonement), a booklet that gives a wealth of practical advice about making these lessons a part of a consistent, daily spiritual practice.

I will not repeat here the history of how these commentaries came into being; see the Introduction to Volume I if you are interested in that.

The Internet distribution of these commentaries still continues as of this writing (January, 1998), without much further effort on my part. The specific instructions for receiving these messages are, however, about to change. If you have Internet access and would like to receive the commentaries via Email on a daily basis, please do so via our web site, which will have the latest instructions (uppercase letters in the file name must be exact):

`http://nen.sedona.net/circleofa/EmailSignup.html`

My prayer is that these daily readings will encourage you to put the daily thoughts offered by the Workbook into practice, filling your mind with them until you begin to experience the inner peace and joy promised by *A Course in Miracles*.

Your companion on the journey,
Allen Watson
Sedona, Arizona, January, 1998
Email: circleofa@sedona.net

Note: A Course in Miracles, *which includes the Workbook for Students on which these commentaries are based, is published by Viking Books (Penguin Publishers), $29.95 for the three-in-one-volume, hard cover edition. It can be purchased at any major bookstore.*

Lesson 121—May 1

"Forgiveness is the key to happiness."

PRACTICE SUMMARY

Purpose: To learn to take and use the key to happiness.

Longer: Two times, morning and evening for ten minutes.

- Think of someone you dislike or despise or overlook or find irritable. The one that has already come to your mind will do.
- Close eyes and look at him a while in your mind. Try to find some little spark of light somewhere in him. Once you find it, let this light expand until it covers your picture of him. Look at this changed picture a while.
- Now think of one you call a friend. Try to transfer the light you saw around your "enemy" to this friend. Let that light reveal him as more than friend, as your savior.
- Then let your friend and "enemy" unite and offer you the light you offered them. Let them bless you with the forgiveness you gave to them. Now you are united with them.

Shorter: Every hour—do not forget.

Say: "Forgiveness is the key to happiness. I will awaken from the dream that I am mortal, fallible and full of sin, and know I am the perfect Son of God."

COMMENTARY

The longer I study the Course the more this lesson makes sense. When I first read it, it seemed unlikely to me that forgiveness was *the* key to happiness. I could see it being *a* key but not *the* key. As the Course's explanation of the root of our problems began to sink in, however, I began to see that in one way or another, unforgiveness was behind every problem. Then it began to make sense that forgiveness would solve them all.

Look at the litany of ills that comprise this description of "the unforgiving mind" (2:1–5:5):

- Fear.
- A cramped, constricted mind-set that offers no room for love to grow and thrive.
- Sadness, suffering, doubt, confusion, anger.
- The pairs of conflicting fears; the one that speaks to me most eloquently is: "afraid of every sound, yet more afraid of stillness" (3:1).
- The distortion of perception that results from unforgiveness, making us unable to see mistakes as what they are, and perceiving sins instead.

- Babbling terror of our own projections (4:2).

I recognize myself, or at least memories of myself, in so many of these phrases: "It wants to live, yet wishes it were dead. It wants forgiveness, yet it sees no hope" (4:3–4). I've felt like that. These paragraphs describe us all. I think that if someone does not recognize themselves somewhere in here, they are not being honest with themselves. And the most awful thought of all is, "It thinks it cannot change" (5:3). Hasn't that fear struck at your own heart at one time or another? I know it has struck at mine.

When we admit to ourselves that these descriptions fit us, that we find ourselves in one or another of these states of mind, the very word "forgiveness" sounds like an oasis in the Sahara. Cool, soothing and refreshing. As we were told in Lesson 79, we have to recognize the problem before we realize what the solution really is.

"Forgiveness is acquired. It is not inherent in the mind..." (6:1–2). This states a fundamental principle that explains much of the methodology of the Course, and explains why some sort of transition is necessary between where we think we are and where we already are in truth. If we are already perfect, as God created us, why do we have to learn anything at all? Because the solution to the problem of guilt is forgiveness, and forgiveness was *not* part of our mind as God created it. There was no need for it. Without a thought of sin the concept of forgiveness is meaningless. Because we taught ourselves the idea of sin, now we must be taught the antidote, forgiveness. Forgiveness has to be *acquired.*

But the unforgiving mind cannot teach itself forgiveness. It believes in the reality of sin, and with that as a basis, forgiveness is impossible. Everything it perceives in the world proves that "all its sins are real" (3:3). Caught in unforgiveness, we are convinced of the correctness of our perception of things. We do not question it. From that perspective there is no way our minds can even conceive of true forgiveness. This is why we need the Holy Spirit: "a Teacher other than yourself, Who represents the other Self in you" (6:3). There has to be a "higher Power" Who represents a different frame of mind. The source of our redemption has to be outside of the ego mind-set, apart from it, untainted by it. And so He is.

He teaches us to forgive, and through forgiveness, our mind is returned to our Self, "Who can never sin" (6:5). Each person "outside" of us, each representative of that unforgiving mind crowd, "presents you with an opportunity to teach your own [mind] how to forgive itself" (7:1). Our brothers and sisters, manifesting their egos, full of the fear, pain, turmoil and confusion of the world, snapping at us in their terror, are our saviors. In forgiving them we forgive ourselves in proxy. As we teach salvation we learn it. As we release others from hell, we release ourselves. As we give, we receive.

This is what the Course is all about. As we practice today, let's realize that we are engaging in the central exercise of the Course; we are learning "the key to happiness." And let's not think we already know forgiveness; let us come with humility, ready to be taught by One Who knows.

Lesson 122—May 2

"Forgiveness offers everything I want."

PRACTICE SUMMARY

Longer: Two times, morning and evening, for fifteen minutes.

Sink into the happiness, peace and joy that forgiveness offers you.

Remarks: You have reached the turning point in the road, after which it becomes far easier. You are near the end of the journey. Practice in the hope and faith that salvation will be yours today. Seek it earnestly and gladly, aware you hold the key, aware the end is guaranteed. The light you receive today will cause this world to fade away and another to rise in its place.

Shorter: Every fifteen minutes, for one minute—at least.

Say: "Forgiveness offers everything I want. Today I have accepted this as true. Today I have received the gifts of God."

Remarks: Do not let the gifts you receive in the longer exercise recede and be forgotten as you go through the day. Hold them firmly in mind by doing the shorter exercises.

COMMENTARY

There is a phrase near the end of this lesson that never fails to stand out to me. It speaks of how forgiveness enables me to "see the changeless in the heart of change" (13:4). For me, this phrase has become a whole other way to look at what forgiveness is.

Behind every appearance lies something that does not change. Appearances change, and rapidly. This is true both physically and in more subtle perceptions. But the spirit within us does not change, having been created by the eternal. Forgiveness is a way of looking past the appearances to the unchanging reality. It disregards the temporary picture of the ego's mistakes and sees the Son of God. As Mother Teresa said of each one she helped, we see "Christ, in his distressing disguises."

> Forgiveness lets the veil be lifted up that hides the face of Christ from those who look with unforgiving eyes upon the world (3:1).

Forgiveness is giving up all the reasons we have built up for withholding love. The veil of all our judgments is lifted, and we behold something marvelous, something wonderful, something indescribable. "What you will remember then can never be described" (8:4). (So I won't try!) When forgiveness has removed the blocks to our awareness of love's presence, we see love everywhere. Love is unchanging and unchangeable. There is no wonder, then, that forgiveness offers everything we want, bringing peace, happiness, quietness, certainty, and "a sense of worth and beauty that transcends the world" (1:4). When you see the changeless in the heart of change, distress drains right out of your heart because there is no reason for it.

Why are our moods and feelings such a problem to us? Because we identify with them, because as the moods and feelings change we believe we have changed. The Course is teaching us to learn to identify with something beyond change, with the Mind of Christ within ourselves that never changes and never will. Here is a very simple rule of thumb: *What changes is not me.* My Self is unchanged, unchanging and unchangeable (W-pI.190.6:5).

This is starting to take better shape in my mind as I began to see that forgiveness is simply to "see the changeless in the heart of change" (13:4). It is to recognize that the only thing that needs to be changed is the thought that it is possible to change the Mind of the Son of God. It is to realize that all my ego "thoughts" have changed nothing, and all my brother's ego "thoughts" also change nothing. It is to realize that what is changeable is not me; to cease to identify with that which changes, and to cease to believe that my brother *is* my changing perceptions of him. Forgiveness means looking beyond what is changeable to that which is changeless.

Our pain comes from identifying with the ephemeral. Our peace comes from identifying with the eternal. Nothing that changes is created by God. Nothing that changes is really me. What is changeable is threatened by change, and "nothing real can be threatened" (T-In.2:2). Therefore, nothing that changes is real.

All that changes is nothing but a passing landmark on the journey to the eternal. It is nothing to be held on to. Think of a line of stones by which you cross a creek; you do not cling to each stone as you pass it. You appreciate its value in moving you toward the other side, but you do not lament its passing. Your goal is the other side. That is the only value of things in this world, things which include our own bodies and the bodies of our loved ones as well as material things, or even concepts in our thought system. Changing things are to be valued only as stepping stones to that which is eternal, to be gently released as we take the next step toward the changeless, which is always with us, always the reality of our being, even as we appear to journey towards it.

Lesson 123—May 3

"I thank my Father for His gifts to me."

PRACTICE SUMMARY

Purpose: To give thanks to God and so gain insight into the gains you have made, which are greater than you realize. You have come to smoother roads now. You have some ambivalence, but your direction is set; you will not turn back.

Longer: Two times, morning and evening for fifteen minutes.

Give thanks to God that He still loves you and always will, has not abandoned you, has saved you, has given you a function, and has given you a Friend that speaks His saving Word to you. And receive God's thanks, for He will give yours back to you, multiplied a hundred thousand times. He thanks you for becoming His messenger who listened to His Word and let It echo round the world.

Remarks: By receiving God's thanks you will understand how much He loves and cares for you. God will give this half hour back to you with each second turned into years, enabling you to save the world eons more quickly.

Shorter: Every hour.

Remember to think of God and thank Him for everything He gave you.

COMMENTARY

Today's lesson causes me to reflect on all my Father's gifts to me, personally. I think that is what it is intended to do for each of us, sort of a day to count your blessings. So bear with me as I share some of my personal reflections with you, and take it as inspiration to do the same for yourself.

I think I've been on a spiritual journey most of my life, perhaps all of it. I can remember certain incidents as a very young boy that seem to say my direction was already set, way back then. I wrote a poem once for my babysitter; I think I was in second grade at the time. I can still recall the words:

> Thank Thee for the sun and fields,
> Thank Thee for the bush and tree,
> Thank Thee for the things we eat.
> Thank Thee, Lord, Thank Thee.

I remember one Monday after school, when I was about ten, gathering three of my friends around me on a street corner and trying to explain to them why I was so impressed with the Sunday School lesson I'd heard the day before. It was a lesson on Ecclesiastes 11:1, "Cast thy bread upon the waters, for thou shalt find it after many days." I was so struck by the principle involved, that what you give comes back to you, and that our wealth could be measured by how much we give, rather than what we acquire. It is a message that I heard again, very clearly, many years later in the Course.

I had a deep spiritual hunger and desire for God all through childhood, although I veered off in other directions for some time, getting into trouble for youthful pranks, even police trouble, and being horribly embarrassed at being caught shoplifting by a store owner who had offered me a summer job (which of course I did not get). I had experiences of what I would now call a holy instant several times, a sense of the nearness of God, and yet I couldn't seem to find Him most of the time.

At sixteen I had a "born again" experience, and I became, for the next twenty-two years, a fundamentalist Christian, although never firmly aligned with any religious denomination. Something kept me breaking out of all the molds people tried to cast me into. I read the mystics, I read the heretics, as well as the Bible. I didn't want anyone to draw me a map of the New Jerusalem; I wanted to walk its streets for myself. I spent years in a typical Western religious pattern, "fighting against sin" as Jesus calls it in the Course (T-18.VII.4:7). As he says in that sentence, "It is extremely difficult to reach Atonement" that way!

All through those twenty-two years, I hungered for God. All through those twenty-two years, I was miserable most of the time, disgusted with myself. All through those twenty-two years, I wondered if I would ever "make it." Finally, at the end of those years, I gave up. I laid aside my Bible and let it gather dust. I decided that Christianity was, for me, a dead end. I despaired of ever "crossing Jordan" and "entering the promised land." I decided I was just going to have to accept life as it was, and learn to live with it.

About six years went by. I was still seeking something, but no longer seeking anything spiritual. Or so I told myself. My relationship with God was in a holding pattern, and we weren't talking. I read psychology. I did the est training. I read Zen books and tried meditating a bit. I studied Science of Mind. I also enjoyed the world thoroughly, as I'd never allowed myself to do before, including some great sex, and making more money than I'd ever had in my life. I began to realize that the things which spoke to me in the psychology, secular philosophies, and Eastern religious writings that I was studying were all exactly the same things that had really spoken to me in Christianity. There was a "perennial philosophy," as Aldous Huxley called it, that ran through everything, a central core of truths that everyone who ever "made it," regardless of their religious background or lack of one, seemed to agree on. And the more I got clear about it, the more I realized it was all stuff I'd always known somehow. Like "cast your bread upon the waters."

Then, in January, 1985, I found *A Course in Miracles*. Ever since, I've been reading and studying these books, and practicing as best I can what they say. And as I look at my life today, I can see that somewhere along the line my life underwent a major shift. I moved from a gloomy certainty that I would never find real happiness to a steady conviction that I *have* found it.

So as I read today's lesson, a deep sense of gratitude washed over me. As I read the first paragraph, I felt I could honestly say it applied to me very well:

> There is no thought of turning back, and no implacable resistance to the truth. A bit of wavering remains, some small objections and a little hesitance, but you can well be grateful for your gains, which are far greater than you realize (W-pI.123.1:3–4).

A few days ago (in 1995) a friend of ours, Allan Greene, passed away at 51. He was a quadriplegic who moved to Sedona just over a year ago to take part in the ACIM classes and support groups of The Circle of Atonement. Our support group met in his home, since he was almost completely immobile. He could move nothing but his head and his shoulders, the latter just slightly. Within the last two years, a leg and a hand had to be amputated. He used to say that he was giving up his identification with his body piece by piece. Allan was a long-time student of the Course, one of the very few I know who actually knew the Course's scribe, Helen Schucman. He argued with it for a long time, but had settled in to a steady determination to realize all that it taught. Under adversity far greater than most of us can imagine, Allan maintained an amazing sense of humor and a joyful determination to heal his mind, whatever happened to his body. Miracles happened around him regularly; he took them as a matter of course. Last month, when he was having his gall bladder removed, he took no anesthesia because he had no feeling in his lower body at all, but a nurse held a screen during the operation so he would not have to watch himself being cut open. During the whole operation, Allan was conversing with the nurse about *A Course in Miracles*!

Last night (May 2, 1995) we had a memorial meeting for Allan. A very large number of people attended, and one after another shared how Allan had touched their lives, including a half dozen or so of the professional caretakers who had administered to him over the last year. It became evident that Allan's life had impacted scores and scores of people. I am sure *his* gains were, as our lesson tells us, far greater than he realized. I know Allan did not think of himself as particularly advanced. He lamented almost to the end about what a slow learner he was. He often argued with his caretakers, and had one or two walk out on him in a rage. He had his doubts. But from the evidence tonight in people whom he loved and people who loved him, he had advanced much farther than he thought.

I hope that is true of me; I believe it is true of all of us. We cannot know now, although I'm sure we shall at some point, all the positive impacts we have had on those around us with things as little as a smile, a small act of kindness, or a gentle, loving touch at the right moment.

Perhaps, as it often was with Allan, nothing more than our laughter, or making someone else laugh. Last Thursday, when Allan was in the hospital, we paused in our ACIM evening class and had a few minutes of silence for him. The next day, the day before he died, one of our students phoned him in the hospital and told him about our minutes of silence. Allan said, "It would have been more appropriate if you'd had a few minutes of telling jokes."

Let me then, today, take time to express my gratitude to God for all His gifts to me. I thank Him for this Course, which has become my certain way home. I thank Him for the relief from all those years of quiet desperation. I thank Him that, when I wandered off, He never deserted me. I am so grateful for His Spirit within me, my Guide and Teacher, and for all the loving friends and companions on the journey He has brought my way (especially, tonight, for Allan). I am so grateful for all of *you*, and for the opportunity He has given me to share with you all, and to receive from all of you. I thank Him that I am beginning to remember my Self. I thank Him for the steadily increasing assurance that I will find my way all the way home.

I thank my Father for His gifts to me!

Lesson 124—May 4

"Let me remember I am one with God."

PRACTICE SUMMARY

Purpose: To secure your peace by practicing your oneness with God. The first attempt at an extended practice period with no special rules or guidelines.

Longer: One time, whenever it seems best, for thirty minutes.

Devote the exercise to the thought that you are one with God. There is no other guideline. Abide with God, trust His Voice to speak, be certain He will do the rest.

Remarks: This holy half hour is a mirror framed in gold. Each minute is a diamond set around the mirror. You will look in the mirror and see in it your transfiguration, your perfect sinlessness. Even if you think nothing happens, the benefit will be the same. And sometime, somewhere, perhaps today, perhaps tomorrow, when you are ready, you will accept this benefit. You will recognize it when it comes and realize that no time was ever better spent. This half hour is your gift to God. His return will be a sense of love and joy too deep to comprehend. And yet sometime soon you will comprehend it.

Shorter: Hourly.

Repeat: "Let me remember I am one with God, at one with all my brothers and my Self, in everlasting holiness and peace."

COMMENTARY

This lesson holds forth a very high view; it comes from an elevated state of mind. Basically, in the first part of the lesson it seems to assume we are enlightened already. And, of course, from the perspective of this state of mind, we are. "Enlightenment is but a recognition, not a change at all" (W-pI.188.1:4). If it is not a change, then enlightenment must mean recognizing what is always so. This lesson, then, is simply stating the truth about us, the truth that we have been hiding from ourselves.

To pray, to give thanks for the truth as God sees it, the truth *about us* as He sees us, can be a very profitable exercise. Try taking a paragraph of this lesson (or the whole lesson) and turning it into thanksgiving, verbalizing your thanks as you read. For example, from the second paragraph, I might say:

> Thank You for the holiness of our minds! Thank You that everything I see reflects the holiness of my mind, which is at one with You, and at one with itself. Thank You for being my Companion as I walk this world; for the privilege of leaving behind shining

> footprints that point the way to truth for those who follow me.

This indeed *is* our calling; it is why we are here. Perhaps most of the time we don't remember our Identity in God. All the more reason to set aside a day given to remembering, for reminding ourselves. We could understand this lesson as a portrait of an advanced teacher of God. Everywhere she walks, light is left behind to illuminate the way for others. The teacher walks in constant awareness of God's Presence. She feels God within. God's thoughts fill her mind, and she perceives only the loving and the lovable. This teacher of God heals people in the past, the present and the future, at any distance.

Slip into that mind-set for a while today, my heart. Be the Christ; let all the obstacles to it that your mind throws up be brushed aside. *Practice* awareness of oneness with God.

In the latter part of the lesson it is clear that the author hasn't flipped out and isn't living in a dream world. He knows very well that we might sit for our half hour and get up thinking that nothing happened. He knows that, for most of us, what he is talking about is so far from our conscious awareness that we might devote thirty minutes to trying to recognize it and not find a glimmer of it. He doesn't care. He doesn't care because, from where *he* sits and how *he* sees, he knows with total certainty that what he is saying about us is the truth. And he tells us not to let it bother us:

> You may not be ready to accept the gain today. Yet sometime, somewhere, it will come to you, nor will you fail to recognize it when it dawns with certainty upon your mind (9:2–3).

Even though we experience nothing, he tells us that "no time was ever better spent" (10:3).

The practice for today of a single half hour given to remembering oneness is unusual in the Workbook. The routine goes back to two fifteen-minute periods, or three ten-minute periods, in the coming days. But what is more significant, actually, is the lack of "rules [and] special words to guide your meditation" (8:4). He's leaving us on our own today. If we have been doing the exercises all along, we should have a pretty good idea of some of the "techniques" we might want to use, and we can use any of them, or anything that comes to us. Actually he isn't leaving us "on our own"; he's leaving us in the hands of "God's Voice," our inner Guide. Ask how to spend this half hour of meditation, and listen to what comes to you.

> Abide with Him this half hour. He will do the rest (8:6–7).

You can be sure someday, perhaps today, perhaps tomorrow, you will understand and comprehend and see (11:3).

Lesson 125—May 5

"In quiet I receive God's Word today."

PRACTICE SUMMARY

Longer: Three times, at times best suited to silence, for ten minutes.

Be still and listen to the Voice for God, the Voice for your Self. Come in stillness and quiet listening, without your petty, meaningless thoughts, desires and judgments. Let God give you His holy Word, to spread across the world and usher in the quiet time of peace.

Shorter: Hourly for a moment.

Be still and in quiet receive God's Word. Remind yourself that this is your special purpose today.

COMMENTARY

All we are being asked to do today is to be quiet for ten minutes, three times during the day and for a moment each hour. Just to be quiet. "Only be quiet. You will need no rule but this..." (9:1). "Only be still and listen" (9:3). "His Voice awaits your silence, for His Word can not be heard until your mind is quiet for a while, and meaningless desires have been stilled" (6:2).

Isn't it amazing how much practice it takes to learn to be quiet? I can't tell you how many times I've sat down to meditate and be quiet only to find myself, sometimes only a few minutes later, so distracted by some passing thought that I open my eyes and start to get up to "do something" before I've even realized what I'm doing. I plop back down in my chair muttering "Good grief!" to myself at the distractedness of my mind. Draw a deep breath, think to myself, "Quiet, Allen. Quiet. Peace, be still."

The difficulties I have with being quiet, rather than standing as an insurmountable obstacle to me, have simply become indicators of how much I need this practice. Clearly, the Course is teaching us that a quiet mind is essential. "The memory of God comes to the quiet mind" (T-23.I.1:1). We can't hear His Voice until we are quiet for a while.

The Course describes the voice of the ego in various colorful phrases: "senseless shrieks," "raucous shrieks," "loud discordant shrieks," "the senseless noise of sounds that have no meaning," "frantic, riotous thoughts," "raucous screams and senseless ravings," "a loud, obscuring voice," "a frantic rush of thoughts that made no sense."[1]

Our ego is a constant noise machine trying to cover up the Voice for God; we need to learn to still our mind, to cease to pay attention to its

---

[1] References for the above descriptions of the ego's voice: T-25.V.3:5; W-pI.49.4:3; P-2.VI.2:6; T-31.I.6:1; W-pI.49.4:4; T-21.V.1:6; T-27.VI.1:2; W-pI.198.11:2.

loudness. The ego is noise; the Spirit is quiet. There is merit, then, simply in being quiet, even if nothing else seems to happen. Let me, then, remember to take this time to be quiet, to be still, and to listen.

Lesson 126—May 6

"All that I give is given to myself."

PRACTICE SUMMARY

Longer: Two times, for fifteen minutes.

Close your eyes and seek the quiet sanctuary within where thoughts are healed. Repeat the idea and ask the Holy Spirit to help you understand what it means. Be glad to let Him teach you. Give Him your faith; ask Him to practice with you.

Remarks: You will understand His words and recognize them as your own. If you get a tiny glimpse of the meaning of idea, it is a glorious day for the world. For this idea gives forgiveness its proper place, its meaning and its value.

Shorter: As often as you can—do not forget for long; a moment.

- Say: "All that I give is given to myself. The Help I need to learn that this is true is with me now. And I will trust in Him."
- Then in quiet, open your mind to His loving correction.

COMMENTARY

This is a lesson that clearly aims at thought reversal (1:1). It begins with the presumption that we have false ideas about forgiveness: "You do not understand forgiveness" (6:1). In the sixth paragraph it explains that our false understanding of forgiveness is the reason we cannot understand how forgiveness brings us peace, how it is a means for our release, nor how forgiveness can restore our awareness of unity with our brothers. Our misunderstanding of forgiveness is the reason that we may have had trouble really entering in to Lessons 121 and 122, which told us that forgiveness is the key to happiness and offers us everything we want.

The idea that, "All that I give is given to myself," is crucial to reversing our thought; understanding it would make forgiveness effortless. Paragraph 2 goes through a list of "what you do believe, in place of this idea." So, let's practice some thought reversal, and reverse the meaning of this paragraph to see what is implied by this key idea for the day.

If we understood that everything we give is given to ourselves, we would realize that other people are not apart from us. Their behavior does have bearing on our thoughts, and our behavior has bearing on their thoughts. Our attitudes affect other people. Their appeals for help are intimately related to our own. They cannot be seen as "sinners" without affecting our perception of ourselves. We cannot condemn their sin without condemning ourselves and losing our peace of mind.

If we understood all this and believed it, forgiveness would happen naturally. We would realize that judging someone as sinful causes our own guilt and loss of peace, and we would not choose to do it. We would realize that how we see the other person is how we see ourselves, and we would not want to see ourselves that way. We would learn very quickly to perceive that their ego actions are not sins but calls for help, closely tied to our own calls for help, and we would respond accordingly. We would know that our judgmental attitude has an adverse effect on the behavior of others, and would choose to change our attitude. We would adjust our thoughts so as to have a beneficial effect on their behavior instead of a detrimental effect. We would recognize that we are not separate and apart, but share in the same struggle with fears and doubts, as well as sharing in the release from those things.

Given all this we could understand how forgiveness is the key to happiness. We would see that if judging causes loss of peace, then forgiveness could bring us to peace again. We would understand how forgiveness restores our awareness of unity with one another. We could see how forgiveness can release us from what *seems* to be a problem with someone else.

The practice today is really a kind of thinking meditation. We are asked to come to the Holy Spirit with today's idea, "All that I give is given to myself," and to open ourselves to His Help in learning that it is true, "opening your mind to His correction and His love" (11:6). We are asking for help in understanding what today's idea means (10:2), and what forgiveness really means. We are reflecting on the ideas with His assistance, asking for new insights, new understandings.

Our behavior, our attitudes, and our painful experiences in this world are all evidence that we do need to have our thoughts corrected. If we truly believed what today's idea says, we would not be having these painful experiences. We must have false ideas still lodged in our minds, and we need to be healed. Perhaps we think we understand what is being said, and no doubt there is a part of us that resonates with them or we would not be studying these lessons. It is the other part we are concerned about, the hidden warriors, the contrary beliefs we have dissociated and even hidden from conscious awareness.

If we ask for help sincerely, help will be given (8:3). Today will bring new understanding. Perhaps it will come in the form of new insights as we meditate. Perhaps it will come in the laboratory of life, as circumstances shock us into awareness of how we still believe one or another of the ideas this lessons mentions in describing what we do believe in place of today's idea. But it will come.

> The help I need to learn that this is true is with me now. And I will trust in Him (11:4–5).

Lesson 127—May 7

"There is no love but God's."

PRACTICE SUMMARY

Purpose: To practice freeing your mind of the laws, limits and changes under which you think you must live. To leave the past behind and look upon a new future in which the world is reborn. To take the largest single step in your journey this course asks.

Longer: Two times, for fifteen minutes.

Open your mind and rest. Escape from every law of the world in which you believe. Withdraw all value you have given the world's worthless gifts and let the gift of God replace them all. Wherever you give up a false value or dark belief God will replace it with a spark of truth. Call to Him, certain He will answer. He will shine into your clean and open mind and teach you the meaning and the truth of love. He will abide with you and bless your practicing with His Love.

Remarks: Be glad to give some time today; there is no better use for it. For if you achieve even the barest inkling of what love means you will have advanced towards your goal in time and distance beyond measure.

Shorter: Three times per hour—at least.

Think of another who travels with you toward the same goal and give him this message from the Self you share: "I bless you, brother, with the Love of God, which I would share with you. For I would learn the joyous lesson that there is no love but God's and yours and mine and everyone's."

COMMENTARY

"Perhaps you think that different kinds of love are possible" (1:1). To my mind there is no "perhaps" about it; we all think that there are different kinds of love, varying from friend to family to children to lover, from person to animal to thing. The lesson asserts that there is only one Love—God's Love. To think that Love changes depending upon its object, says the lesson, is to miss the meaning of love entirely (2:1).

"It [Love] never alters with a person or a circumstance" (1:6). To us, this can seem to be a very intimidating description of love, because what we call love does not fit this picture. Our "love" comes and goes, waxes and wanes, varying with the person or the circumstance like a thermometer to the temperature. Love, as described in this lesson, is wholly unaffected by anything outside itself. This is truly unconditional love.

I am uplifted today by the idea that, if this is God's Love, and this is the only love there is, then His Love for me never alters, and has "no divergencies and no distinctions" (1:4). Nothing I do, or do not do, modifies His Love for me in the slightest. God's Love just *is*, eternally, endlessly. It has no opposite (3:7). It is the glue that holds everything together (3:8). It is the substance of the universe.

It can be comforting when we think of God's love for us being like this. It can be intimidating, however, when we realize that we are being asked to love one another in the same way. It seems beyond us, and if we are judged on whether or not we match up to this love, it would appear that we all "come short of the glory of God," as the Bible says in Romans 3:23. The lesson, however, meets this fear in us head on, and meets it with an incredible assertion:

"No course whose purpose is to teach you to remember what you really are could fail to emphasize that there can never be a difference in what you really are and what love is" (4:1). In short sentences, this is telling us: "Love is eternal, unconditional, and unalterable. You are that Love." You know this love we're talking about, that seems so foreign to us, so beyond our capabilities? Well, this is what you really are! It is the other image of yourself, incapable of such love, shifting and changing with every circumstance, that is the lie. This Love—this is the truth, this is you. There is absolutely no difference between this Love and what we are!

> What you are is what He is. There is no love but His,
> and what He is, is everything there is (4:3–4).

We aren't going to see this about ourselves by looking at the world (6:1). It isn't something that can be seen with the body's eyes; yet it is perfectly apparent to the eyes and ears that see and hear Love (what is called elsewhere the vision of Christ). That is the goal of today's lesson: to see that Love in ourselves, to catch even "the faintest glimmering of what love means" (7:1), to "understand the truth of love" (9:4). This attempt to quiet our minds, to free our minds of all the laws we think we must obey, all the limits we have placed on ourselves, and all the changes we believe we have made in ourselves, and to find our Self, Who is Love—this attempt is called "the largest single step this course requests in your advance towards its established goal" (6:5). If we succeed, we will "have advanced in distance without measure and in time beyond the count of years to your release" (7:1). This is no small thing! To be able, even in a very small degree, to perceive ourselves as this Love; to catch a hint of the fact that Love is everything there is, including ourselves. This is a quantum leap indeed! To spend a little time for this purpose is worth it. "There is no better use for time than this" (7:2).

As we begin to realize that Love is all there is, that this Love is everything including ourselves, we will realize that it includes everyone else as well. The only way Love can be everything is if it includes everyone! So we begin to see, not only ourselves, but the world, in a new way:

> The world in infancy is newly born (11:1).
>
> Now are they all made free, along with us. Now are they all our brothers in God's Love (11:3–4).
>
> ...we cannot leave a part of us outside our love if we would know our Self (12:1).

And so, three times an hour, we are asked to remember a brother or sister who is making this journey with us, and to mentally send them this message, as I now send it to you:

> I bless you, brother, with the Love of God,
> Which I would share with you. For I would learn
> The joyous lesson that there is no love
> But God's and yours and mine and everyone's (12:4–5).

Lesson 128—May 8

"The world I see holds nothing that I want."

PRACTICE SUMMARY

Longer: Three times, for ten minutes.

Pause, be still and rest. Let go all the value you have given the world. Hold it in mind as purposeless. Release your mind from the chains of this world and let it seek where it belongs. It knows the way home. Free its wings and it will gratefully fly there to rest safely within its Creator. Open your mind to Him.

Remarks: When you open your eyes you will not value anything here as much as you did before. Every time you practice thus, your whole perspective will shift just a little.

Response To Temptation: Protect your mind all day.

Whenever you think you see value in something in the world, refuse to chain your mind. Say with quiet certainty: "This will not tempt me to delay myself. The world I see holds nothing that I want."

COMMENTARY

The general thought of this lesson is similar to the first three of Buddha's Four Noble Truths: that life is suffering; that the cause of suffering is *tanha*, or desire for self at the expense of others; and that the way out of suffering is through the relinquishment of such desires.

"Believe this thought, and you are saved from years of misery…" (1:2). The lesson is asking us to give up all attachment to things of this world, to put an end to suffering by putting an end to craving anything the world offers. It can seem to be a harsh lesson, and yet it is eminently sensible: if you do not desire anything, you cannot be disappointed.

The things of the world act as chains when we value them (2:1). What is perhaps harder to grasp is that this is the purpose for which we made them: they "will serve no other end but this, For everything must serve the purpose you have given it, until you see a different purpose there (2:1–2). When we assign to the things of the world a purpose in time, usually some form of gratification or self-aggrandizement, we chain ourselves to this world. Inevitably, since everything in the world must have an end, this causes us untold pain. All our mistaken valuing accomplishes is to tie us to the world and to keep us from our final healing.

To the Holy Spirit, the only purpose of this world is the healing of God's Son (T-24.VI.4:1). There is nothing *in* the world worth striving for. "The only purpose worthy of your mind this world contains is that you pass it by, without delaying to perceive some hope where there is none" (2:3). This is similar to the statement in the Text: "The Holy Spirit interprets time's purpose as rendering the need for time unnecessary"

(T-13.IV.7:3). The Holy Spirit appropriates time, the world, and everything in the world for the purpose of salvation and the healing of our minds. To Him, nothing here has any other purpose.

Therefore, the world itself holds nothing that we want. All of it is, to borrow from the title of a book by Ram Dass, "grist for the mill." All of it becomes the means to an end—our awakening to life, our return to God. There is nothing in the world that is an end in itself.

When the lesson advises us, "Let nothing that relates to body thoughts delay your progress to salvation" (4:1), it is saying the same thing in other words. "Body thoughts" refers to our mistaken identification with our bodies. It is everything that stems from the idea, "I am a body, and to benefit and protect myself I must make taking care of my body a number one priority." Our cravings for bodily pleasure, bodily comfort, bodily protection, bodily longevity, and bodily beauty all fall into the category of body thoughts. Making such things our primary concern can only delay our progress.

The lesson is asking us to practice mentally letting go of all thoughts of values we have given to the world (5:1). We are asked to "loosen it [the world] from all we wish it were" (5:3). That is a tall order, isn't it? We spend so much of our time wishing things were different and trying to make them be that way. In fact, if we look at our lives honestly, wishing something or someone were different and trying to bring about that change is the activity that occupies most of our lives.

For the purposes of this lesson, then, practice taking a few minutes to let your mind rest from such activity: "Pause and be still a while, and see how far you rise above the world, when you release your mind from chains and let it seek the level where it finds itself at home" (6:1). Your mind, the lesson tells us, "knows where it belongs" (6:3). If you loosen the chains of your desires, it will "fly in sureness and in joy to join its holy purpose" (6:4). Each time you practice such an exercise for only ten minutes, "your whole perspective on the world will shift by just a little" (7:3). Let your mind rest, then, from its constant craving, and relax as its homing instinct takes over and brings you to where you really belong.

Throughout the day, the lesson is asking us to notice when we think we see some value in the world, and when we do, to mentally correct the notion with these words:

> This will not tempt me to delay myself. The world I see
> holds nothing that I want (8:3–4).

Lesson 129—May 9

"Beyond this world there is a world I want."

PRACTICE SUMMARY

Purpose: To have a day of grace in which you receive the world you really want. Through this you will realize that giving up the world you do not want is a giving up of nothing, not a sacrifice.

Longer: Three times—morning, evening and once in between, for ten minutes.

- Say: "Beyond this world there is a world I want. I choose to see that world instead of this, for here is nothing that I really want."
- Close your eyes on this world and in silent darkness watch the lights of the other world light one by one, until they blend together and cover all you see. Your eyes cannot see this light, but your mind can see and understand it.

Shorter: Hourly; for a moment.

Lay by your thoughts and dwell briefly on this: "The world I see holds nothing that I want. Beyond this world there is a world I want."

COMMENTARY

The Course is so down-to-earth sometimes! "You cannot stop with the idea the world is worthless, for unless you see that there is something else to hope for, you will only be depressed" (1:2). So true! The statement that "the world is worthless" is pretty blunt; there can't be much debate about what it means. And I have to confess that even after ten years of studying the Course and, over time, coming to agree with its ideas, I still find that wording a little jarring. I can almost hear myself replying, "Uhhh...that isn't exactly how I'd put it." Because there is still something in me that *wants* to find some value here, something worthwhile, something worth preserving and striving for.

The emphasis of the Course, however, isn't on "giving up the world, but on exchanging it for what is far more satisfying, filled with joy, and capable of offering you peace" (1:3). Well, that's not such a bad deal, is it?

It begins to look especially good if we take a hard look at the world we're trying to hang on to. Merciless, unstable, cruel, unconcerned with you, quick to avenge and pitiless with hate. Events such as the 1995 bombing of a government building in Oklahoma City, and the rabid rage against the bomber, are both testimony to this. The bomber was thought to be "avenging" the government's actions against David Koresh in Waco, and then people wanted vengeance on the bomber. The many wars motivated by racial, religious, or ethnic differences are vengeance cycles that have been going on for centuries. This *is* the way the world is. "No lasting love is found, for none is here. This is the world of time, where all things end" (2:5–6). That, perhaps, is the cruelest part of all about this world. Even when you *do* find love, it can't last forever.

So—wouldn't you rather find a world where *it is impossible to lose anything*? Where vengeance is meaningless? (3:1) "Is it a loss to find all things you really want, and know they have no ending and they will remain exactly as you want them throughout time?" (3:2) It's speaking here of what the Course calls "the real world," and the following sentence—"you go on from there to where words fail entirely" (3:3)—is talking about Heaven, a non-physical existence in eternity.

What is it talking about when it speaks of "all things you really want"? If they are things that have no ending and don't change over time, they can't be anything physical; certainly not bodies. It is speaking of Love Itself; it is speaking of our Self which is spirit, and which we share with everyone. We are here to find the changeless in the midst of the changeable, and to learn to value what is changeless and to let go of what is changeable.

When we choose the changeless, and value the real world of spirit instead of what changes and decays, it brings us very close to Heaven, and prepares us for it. Loosing our grasp on the world makes the transition to Heaven easy.

Holding on to the world brings loss. When you try to cling to the perishable you doom yourself to suffering. As we saw in yesterday's commentary, Buddhism has long taught a similar lesson.

Doing the practice exercises for today has a remarkable effect. When I say, "The world I see holds nothing that I want. Beyond this world there is a world I want," I find myself noticing all the attachments I still have to things in this world; I find myself noticing that my conception of what it is beyond this world that I "really want" is a bit vague. And so I bring that attachment and that unclarity to the Holy Spirit, and ask that He help me in those areas. I know He will.

Lesson 130—May 10

"It is impossible to see two worlds."

PRACTICE SUMMARY

Purpose: To learn that it is impossible to see two worlds. To learn each world is all of one piece because it stems from one emotion. To make no compromises with illusions; to leave them all behind and seek the truth. Another giant stride.

Longer: Six times for five minutes.

- Give these minutes gladly, in gratitude. Begin by remembering you are seeking the other world, the truth. And so empty your hands of illusions, of the world's petty treasures. Ask for God's strength to help you see the other world. Say: "It is impossible to see two worlds. Let me accept the strength God offers me and see no value in this world, that I may find my freedom and deliverance."
- You have called on God and He will be there, grateful to take this giant step with you. And you will see His gratitude expressed in new perception, which your eyes alone cannot see. You will not doubt this sight nor doubt that God's strength helped you in choosing it.

Response To Temptation: Whenever any part of hell tempts you to accept it as real, remember that the range of your choice is only Heaven or hell, and that whichever one you choose will fill your perception. Say: "It is impossible to see two worlds. I seek my freedom and deliverance, and this is not a part of what I want."

COMMENTARY

Today's lesson is extremely uncompromising. The first two paragraphs are as clear a statement of the Course's understanding of perception as there is in all three volumes. What we value we want to see; what we want to see determines our thinking; and what we see simply reflects our thinking. "No one can fail to look upon what he believes he wants" (1:6). Or as it is twice stated succinctly in the Text, "Projection makes perception" (T-13.V.3:5 and T-21.In.1:1).

On top of that, since we can't hate and love simultaneously, we can't project totally opposite worlds simultaneously. We project the world of fear or the world of love. And, "The world you see is proof you have already made a choice as all-embracing as its opposite" (6:2). In other words, the world we see proves that our minds have made an all-embracing choice for fear. "Fear has made everything you think you see" (4:1).

As I said, this is very uncompromising. It does not allow for any part of this world to be excluded from the category of "projection of fear."

The world we see is:

> ...quite consistent from the point of view from which you see it. It is all a piece because it stems from one emotion [fear], and reflects its source in everything you see (6:4–5).

If we try to exclude part of it from this portrait, maintaining that "Surely *this* part is good," we are trying to "accept a little part of hell as real" (11:1). It guarantees that the whole picture will be "hell indeed."

On the other hand, the Course does not try to foster any rejection of the world. It tells us that only the part of it we look upon with love is real (T-12.VI.3:2–3). Therefore we are urged to *love all of it equally*, and thus "make the world real unto yourself" (T-12.VI.3:6). Our attempts at salvaging "parts" of the world as real are mistaken in that they separate and make certain parts special, more loveable than the rest.

As we see it, through eyes of fear, this world is without any value whatsoever. Let us accept God's Strength and "see no value in the world." If we are willing to do this we will see another world, with sight that "is not the kind of seeing that your eyes alone have ever seen before" (9:4). "When you want only love you will see nothing else" (T-12.VII.8:1).

To be a little more practical for a moment: I have found the final words of this lesson to be an incredibly useful phrase in times of distress of all kinds: "This is not a part of what I want" (11:5). If I see only what I want to see, and I am seeing something distressing, let me affirm my choice to change my mind: "I don't want this any more." Although my application of it is still very inconsistent, I have seen this simple affirmation make separateness in a relationship evaporate. I have seen it make a sense of poverty evaporate. I have seen it change my body, and give it an energy I thought I had lost. I have watched it reverse impending illnesses. I recommend it highly to you all.

Lesson 131—May 11

"No one can fail who seeks to reach the truth."

PRACTICE SUMMARY

Longer: Three times, for ten minutes.

- Ask to see the real world rise in place of your foolish images, true ideas rise in place of your meaningless thoughts. Say: "I ask to see a different world, and think a different kind of thought from those I made. The world I seek I did not make alone, the thoughts I want to think are not my own."
- Close eyes and for several minutes watch your mind. Review the senseless world you think is real. Also review the thoughts which fit this world and which you believe.
- Then let these go. Sink below them. Beneath them lies a door which you have used to hide the holy place in your mind, but which you could not lock. Seek this door and find it.
- Before opening it repeat today's idea. Seeking the truth is now your only request, your only goal, the only thing you want.
- With this one intent, put out your hand and see how easily the door opens. Angels light your way. Darkness disappears as you stand in a light whose shining brilliance makes everything clear and understandable. You may at first be surprised, but then you will recall that the real world you now see reflects the truth you knew before the world.

Remarks: You cannot fail. The Holy Spirit has walked with you so He could help you pass this door some day. The goal of all your searching is that you would pass this door some day. Today is that day. Today God keeps His promises to you and you to Him.

Shorter: Often.

Remember that this day is one of special gladness, a time of grace for you and the world. Refrain from sadness and despair, for salvation has come.

Response To Temptation: If you forget gladness and fall into dismal thoughts and meaningless laments, say: "Today I seek and find all that I want. My single purpose offers it to me. No one can fail who seeks to reach the truth."

COMMENTARY

At times it seems to nearly everyone that the search for truth is one that will never succeed. It seems that we seek, and seek, and seek some more, and never arrive at certainty. Today's lesson comes as a welcome reassurance that the search for truth is the *only* search that will inevitably succeed.

"Searching is inevitable here" (3:1). It's the nature of the world, the nature of the predicament we've put ourselves into. Searching is why we came here, and so "you will surely do the thing you came for" (3:2). If we're going to search, then, we may as well search for something worth finding: "a goal that lies beyond the world and every worldly thought...an echo of a heritage forgot" (3:4). What we are searching for is Heaven, "a heritage forgot." What we are searching for is the home we left behind and almost put out of our minds, although to do so entirely is impossible. That's why we are driven to search. "Behind the search for every idol lies the yearning for completion" (T-30.III.3:1).

What we are seeking for is what we are; that is why finding it is inevitable. "No one can fail to want this goal and reach it in the end" (4:3).

Sometimes it may seem as though truth has deserted you. I think some experience of that is almost inescapable for all of us, a last-ditch effort of the ego to dissuade us from the search when we are getting too close. I know it has happened to me, and all I can tell you is, "Hang in there." Your search cannot fail, even though you may think it has *already* failed. I know I came through that dark period of my life. I don't know how I did because I didn't seem to have anything to do with it, which is part of what convinces me that my "coming out of it" is real and lasting. I still dip into despair from time to time, but I will never again live there. "No one can fail who seeks to reach the truth."

What we are looking for, and perhaps can find today, is something that is beneath all the thoughts in our minds that are compatible with this senseless world—"a door beneath them in your mind" (11:8). A door in our minds! Past that door is "a light so bright and clear that you can understand all things you see" (13:2). Today's exercise is wonderful for visualization, actually picturing that door, seeing ourselves standing before it, and with one intent, pushing it open to pass through, out of this world and into another, like the wardrobe doorway into Narnia in C. S. Lewis's fantasy books. These exercises are like rehearsals, and as we repeat them, they grow more and more real to us, engaging our minds and entraining them in a pattern that leads to real discovery of the real door, within our minds, to Heaven.

Lesson 132—May 12

"I loose the world from all I thought it was."

PRACTICE SUMMARY

Longer: Two times, for fifteen minutes.

- Say: "I who remain as God created me would loose the world from all I thought it was. For I am real because the world is not, and I would know my own reality."
- Then simply rest, alert but without strain. And in the quiet let your mind be changed.

Remarks: You will sense your own release, but you may not and need not realize that your release will also free the world, bringing healing to many brothers far and near. For you could never be released alone.

Response To Temptation: Throughout the day.

Whenever you doubt the power of your change of mind to free yourself and the world, say: "I loose the world from all I thought it was, and choose my own reality instead."

COMMENTARY

To me, today, the point of this lesson is: *I have the power to do that.* I can loose the world from all I thought it was, simply by changing my own mind.

This lesson contains what is perhaps the most startling statement in the Course:

> There is no world! This is the central thought the course attempts to teach (6:2–3).

The lesson admits that not everyone is ready to accept this idea, although it makes it clear that all of us will, eventually, accept it. (Such acceptance could take many lifetimes, I think, and doubtless we have gone through many already to get wherever we are; this is my own opinion, not necessarily that of the Course.)

In speaking of this in the analogy of a madman, the first paragraph says that no madman can be "swayed by questioning his thoughts' effects" (1:6). From the perspective of the Course, it is the *world* that is the effect of our thoughts. So the approach that will lead us, eventually, to understand that there is no world does not follow the path of directly questioning the reality of the world. That is a fruitless approach, as fruitless as trying to persuade a madman that his hallucinations are not real. The approach that bears fruit is raising the source to question—that is, in questioning the thoughts that produce the hallucinations.

"Change but your mind on what you want to see, and all the world must change accordingly" (5:2). As we begin to allow thoughts of healing to flow through us, we open ourselves to learn the lesson. "Their readiness will bring the lesson to them in some form which they can understand and recognize" (7:2). The focus for us, then, is not on denying the reality of the world, but on opening our minds to bring healing to the world we see. Doing so will bring us experiences that will convince us that the world is not as real as we supposed. We may have a near-death experience. We may undergo some experience of enlightenment that shows us an incontrovertible reality that contradicts all that we have believed to be reality up until that time. We may, in fact, experience something in doing today's exercises that will bring us our awakening.

The unreality of the world dawns upon us as we begin to grasp the reality of our Self: "To know your Self is the salvation of the world" (10:1). If we are as God created us, then what appears to change us cannot exist, it cannot be real; there cannot be a place where we can suffer, or time to bring change to us. The world is the effect of our thoughts, and nothing more: "You maintain the world within your mind in thought" (10:3). As we discover what we truly are by allowing love to move through us in healing, we realize that "If you are real the world you see is false, for God's creation is unlike the world in every way" (11:5). We release the world from what we thought it was by accepting our oneness with God, and realizing that the world, as we see it, cannot be real because it does not reflect this truth: "What He creates is not apart from Him, and nowhere does the Father end, the Son begin as something separate from Him" (12:4).

To "loose the world" is to heal it. The meditation for today is one in which we "send out these thoughts to bless the world" (16:1). "I loose the world" means, I extend healing to all the world, I free it from suffering, I absolve it from guilt, I heal it of sickness, I lift all thoughts of vengeance from it. It is taking this role as savior to the world that reveals our Self to us, and tranforms our thoughts and, in turn, the world that is their effect. This is "the power of your simple change of mind" (17:1).

Lesson 133—May 13

"I will not value what is valueless."

PRACTICE SUMMARY

Longer: Two times, for fifteen minutes.

- Say: "I will not value what is valueless, and only what has value do I seek, for only that do I desire to find."
- Now receive Heaven's gift. Hold in mind an honest willingness to not deceive yourself about what is valuable, and to instead value only what is truly valuable. Come with empty hands and open mind to the gate of Heaven, and it will swing open, offering you the gift of everything.

Response To Temptation: Whenever you feel a burden or think a difficult decision is facing you, immediately respond with this: I will not value what is valueless, for what is valuable belongs to me.

COMMENTARY

The laws that govern choice are two:

- There are only two alternatives: everything or nothing.
- There is no compromise; there is no in between.

The criteria for judging what is worth desiring are:

- Will it last forever? (If not it is nothing.)
- Is it a choice in which no one loses? (If not, you are left with nothing.)
- Is the purpose free of the ego's goals? (If not there is compromise.)
- Is the choice free of all guilt? (If not the real alternatives have been obscured.)

These are stringent rules! They are clear, but not easily learned. How can we know whether or not the ego's goals are intruding, for instance? Here it is easiest of all to be deceived (8:5). The ego masquerades in innocence. Yet the lesson asserts that the ego's camouflage is only a thin veneer, which could deceive but those who are content to be deceived. Its goals are obvious to anyone who cares to look for them (9:1–2). We need only to be willing to look, and the ego detector is quite simple: guilt. If you feel any guilt about your choice, you have allowed the ego's goals to come between the real alternatives (11:2).

If I apply these criteria for choice to the decisions in my life, it will be constantly revolutionized. The first criteria alone rules out absolutely every goal involving anything material, including bodies and ordinary human relationships. Will it last forever? What lasts forever in this world? Only love. And not all that we call love lasts forever; we've all demonstrated that for ourselves, in all likelihood, or seen it all around us. The assertion of the Course, by the way, is that if it doesn't last, it wasn't love to begin with.

> Where disillusionment is possible, there was not love but hate. For hate *is* an illusion, and what can change was never love (T-16.IV.4:3–4).

But there is a love not of this world; a light we cannot find *in* the world but which we can give *to* the world (see T-13.VI.11:1–2).

As Stephen Levine has written, we cannot own love, but we can be owned by it. And that is what is being said here.

We may think that most of our choices are not so monumental as all this. But they are all this very choice. In every moment we are choosing to give ourselves to love, to be taken over by it and used by it, or we are choosing to withhold ourselves from it, in fear. To choose love is the only guiltless choice.

It isn't complex; complexity is nothing but a screen of smoke, which hides the simple fact that no decision can be difficult (12:3). It is the decision, "Let me be love in this situation and nothing else." No, we don't know how to do that. That is why we must come with empty hands and open minds (13:1). Holding on to nothing, unencumbered (14:1) by any lesser values. And with no preconceptions about what being love means—open minds. In the words of a poem by the Christian poetess Amy Carmichael:

> Love through me, Love of God.
> Make me like Thy clear air,
> Through which, unhindered, colors pass
> As though it were not there.

Lesson 134—May 14

"Let me perceive forgiveness as it is."

PRACTICE SUMMARY

Purpose: To practice true forgiveness, that you may no longer delay joining the truth in you, and that your footsteps may light the way for those who follow you.

Longer: Two times, for fifteen minutes.

- Ask of the Holy Spirit, Who understands the meaning of forgiveness: "Let me perceive forgiveness as it is."
- Then choose a brother, under His direction.
- Now catalogue his "sins," one by one. Do not dwell on any one of them; realize you are merely using them to save the world from the belief in sin. After each one ask yourself: "Would I condemn myself for doing this?" For each time you condemn him, you do condemn yourself. Yet if you truly free him, you will free yourself. If you practice in willingness and honesty you will feel a lifting up, a deep relief, a lightening of weight on your chest.
- Spend the remainder experiencing the escape from the chains you tried to lay on your brother, but laid on yourself instead.

Shorter: In everything you do.

Remember: "No one is crucified alone, and yet no one can enter Heaven by himself."

Response To Temptation: Throughout the day.

Whenever you forget that your brother's sins are illusions, say: "Let me perceive forgiveness as it is. Would I accuse myself of doing this? I will not lay this chain upon myself."

COMMENTARY

This lesson contains a very focused discussion about what it means to "forgive." It deserves, not only careful practice as a Workbook lesson, but careful study, as a separate exercise when you have more time. Several of these longer Workbook lessons fall into that category.

The main teaching of this lesson is that forgiveness, to be true, must be fully justified. It applies only to what is false. Sin, if real, *cannot* be forgiven (5:3–4). True forgiveness sees the nothingness of sins. "It looks on them with quiet eyes, and merely says to them, 'My brother, what you think is not the truth'" (7:5).

The lesson itself explains that main idea very well. I want to focus instead on the *results* of forgiveness: the relief it brings to us. Forgiveness is "a deep relief to those who offer it" (6:1). It wakens us from our own dreams. Even if you don't understand all the Course theory behind forgiveness, when you forgive, when you let go of your grievances against someone, you can experience the lifting of a tremendous burden from your own heart. You may not understand why that happens, but you can know that it is true. As the lesson puts it: "You will begin to sense a lifting up, a lightening of weight across your chest, a deep and certain feeling of relief" (16:3).

Forgiving is a very happy feeling. Why is that? Because, without realizing it, when we condemn someone else for their sins we are secretly condemning ourselves. By condemning another, I am saying, "Sin is real and deserves to be punished." If I subscribe to that principle, then I must also believe that when I sin, I too deserve to be punished. My form of "sin" may not be the one I condemn in my brother; indeed, I may be accusing him, or her, of something I think I would never do, and I imagine that because I am free from that particular fault, somehow my condemnation of another will purchase my salvation. But I have supported the principle that sin is real and deserves punishment. Inevitably I know, deep within me, that I, too, have "sinned" in some way. And if I have, I have nothing to hope for but punishment. What I apply to my brother applies to me as well.

When we are tempted to condemn someone, the lesson advises us to ask ourselves, "Would I accuse myself of doing this?" (9:3) or "Would I condemn myself for doing this?" (15:3) The words "would I" are meant in the sense of "Do I want to?" The question is not, "If I did what this person has done, would I judge myself for it?" Because, if I am judging the other for it, I definitely *would* judge myself if I did the same thing. We usually reserve our sternest judgment for things we think we would never do, precisely because we *would* condemn ourselves for doing them. When we read this question, for instance, and think of a child molester, if we understand the question incorrectly we may answer, "I certainly would condemn myself if I did that!"

What the question is really asking is, "Do I want to make sin real and insist it must be punished? Because if I do, I am condemning myself to punishment also." We are laying chains of imprisonment on ourselves when we lay them on anyone (17:5; 16:4).

This is why releasing my brother from his chains brings relief to *me*. I am liberating myself from the principle that "sin is real and must be punished" when I liberate this other. And what a relief it is! The one who forgives, and offers escape to this other, now sees that escape is possible for himself as well:

> He does not have to fight to save himself. He does not have to kill the dragons which he thought pursued him. Nor need he erect the heavy walls of stone and iron doors he thought would make him safe. He can remove the ponderous and useless armor made to chain his mind to fear and misery. His step is light, and as he lifts his foot to stride ahead a star is left behind, to point the way to those who follow him (12:1–5).

Forgiveness is a deep relief.

Lesson 135—May 15

"If I defend myself I am attacked."

PRACTICE SUMMARY

Purpose: To come without defense and learn your part in God's plan. To anticipate with present confidence the time when your light, joined with the light of your followers, will light up the world with joy. A special day for learning; a giant stride for you; Eastertime in your salvation.

Longer: Two times, for fifteen minutes.

- Say: "If I defend myself I am attacked. But in defenselessness I will be strong, and I will learn what my defenses hide."
- Then rest from all planning and all thoughts that would block the truth from your mind. Without defense present yourself to your Creator. Receive from Him so that you may give. If there are plans, you will be told. They may not be the ones you expected, nor answer the problems you saw. They are answers to a crucial question that is yet unanswered.

Remarks: In light of simple trust, you will wonder why you ever raised defenses, which only defended against what you will receive today. The light of hope will be reborn in you, for you come without defense to learn your function. You will be sure that all you need for this function will be given you if you will just be defenseless and lay aside planning.

Response To Temptation: Throughout the day.

Whenever your defensiveness tempts you to weave plans, say: "This is my Eastertime. And I would keep it holy. I will not defend myself, because the Son of God needs no defense against the truth of his reality."

Remarks: Try not to shape and organize the day as you think would benefit you. Instead, learn the inconceivable happiness that comes from His plans, not yours. The world will celebrate your Eastertime with you.

COMMENTARY

"If I defend myself I am attacked." The general thought that heads this lesson states that all forms of defense are actually witnesses to attack, or to your belief in attack. If you see a need for a defense, you must be perceiving an attack.

The self you think you are is something so weak it needs defense; your true Self, which is mind or spirit, needs no defense. This lesson shows that when you make plans whose purpose is to defend your small "self" (the image you have made of yourself, comprised of your ego and its expression, the body), you are indirectly attacking your true Self, because you perceive that Self as attacking "you."

The Course continually teaches us that "all attack is self-attack" (T-10.II.5:1; line not in 1st Ed.). It says we constantly attack ourselves, but we are blind to the fact. We think the attack comes from somewhere outside ourselves, and never realize that it stems from our own thoughts of guilt. Over and over, the Course tells us to look at what we are doing and thinking, to recognize the self-attack, and to choose to let go of it.

Lesson 135 applies this general principle to a particular area of our lives that we have probably not thought of as self-attack: planning. First, it points out that all defenses are a form of self-attack because they make the illusion of threat real, and then attempt to handle them as if they were real. It asks us to look closely at what we think we are defending, how we defend it, and against what.

Second, it identifies our plans as a form of defense. Plans are a form of defense against anticipated future threats. If that is so, the reverse is true: All "Defenses are the plans you undertake to make against the truth" (17:1). In other words, defenses and plans are the same thing. When you set up a defense, you are making plans. All defenses are plans; and all self-initiated plans are defenses.

In sum, making plans is a form of defense, and all defenses are attacks on myself. Therefore, making plans is just another form of self-attack, to be noticed and abandoned.

Finally, the lesson discusses how "the healed mind" approaches life: not making plans, but receiving plans from the Holy Spirit, with full present trust in the guidance of the Holy Spirit, and with confidence in His plan. Only this approach allows for change, healing and miracles to take place in the present moment.

> A healed mind does not plan. It carries out the plans that it receives through listening to Wisdom that is not its own (11:1–2).

This does not mean that a healed mind does not follow a plan. It follows a plan; it just doesn't make the plan; it receives the plan through the guidance of the Holy Spirit.

In simple language, the healed mind listens to the Holy Spirit and does what He directs, instead of listening to the ego's plans, which are always based on fear and take a defensive posture. The ego's plans are always trying to protect and preserve the body; often, the plans of the Holy Spirit seem to be unconcerned about the body at all. The Holy Spirit has very different priorities.

When the Course is talking about "a healed mind" it is talking about the goal of the Course—the state your mind will be in after you graduate from the Course. This isn't something you simply step into after reading a few lessons; this is what you will be like after working with the Course and completely integrating it into your life.[2]

---

[2] The thoughts expressed above have been taken almost directly from a booklet I wrote, *A Healed Mind Does Not Plan*, published by The Circle of Atonement. This is a 48-page booklet that deals entirely with the subject of planning and decision-making as taught in the Course.

Lesson 136—May 16

"Sickness is a defense against the truth."

PRACTICE SUMMARY

Longer: Two times, for fifteen minutes.

- Begin with this healing prayer, to help you rise above defenses so that truth can come and set you free: "Sickness is a defense against the truth. I will accept the truth of what I am, and let my mind be wholly healed today."
- Open your mind and let healing flash across it. The light of truth will come to illuminate all the dark corners of sickness where dim figures pursued double purposes. Your mind will be healed of all the sick wishes it directed the body to obey.

Remarks: If you practice well your body will have no feeling at all, no feeling of illness or wellness, of pain or pleasure. It will have no power over the mind. Only its usefulness will remain. This releases the body from limits. Instead of being filled with needs for protection and sustenance, it will now be filled with continual strength to carry out its usefulness. But you must protect this with careful watching, responding quickly to any temptation to make the body real and so attack it with sickness.

Response To Temptation: Give instant remedy whenever you harbor attack thoughts, judgments or make plans. Say: "I have forgotten what I really am, for I mistook my body for myself. Sickness is a defense against the truth. But I am not a body. And my mind cannot attack. So I can not be sick."

COMMENTARY

This is another of those lessons that will repay careful study; there is a lot of good stuff in here!

The main thought is plainly stated: Sickness is a means we use to defend ourselves against the truth. It is a decision we make, chosen quite deliberately when truth gets too close for comfort, in order to distract ourselves and root ourselves once again in the body. On the bright side, then, when we get sick we can congratulate ourselves that we must have been letting in the truth in order for the ego to get this scared of it!

For instance, in 1995 Robert and I gave a weekend intensive on "We Are the Light of the World: Accepting Our Function." During that weekend I found myself being deeply impressed by the message the Course was conveying to us all. The day after the intensive I got diarrhea. Now, there is little that brings you down to a body level like having to run to the toilet all the time! But I actually found myself being amused by it. "How like my ego!" I thought. "What a predictable reaction!" Instead of having the desired (by the ego) effect, it had the opposite; it served to *remind* me of the truth instead of distracting me from it. And guess what? It very quickly went away. "Defenses that do not work at all are automatically discarded" (T-13.I.9:8).

Most people react to being told that they choose sickness by flatly denying it. This is not something that is easy to discover. The lesson says our choice is "doubly shielded by oblivion" (5:2). We choose first to hide the pesky truth that has been nibbling away at our delusions of separation and of the physical nature of our identity by making ourselves sick; that is the original decision we made. We then choose to forget we did it; the first shield of oblivion. Finally, we forget that we chose to forget, the second shield. All of this happens in a split second (see 3:4; 4:2–5:1). In that split second we are conscious of what we are doing, but the shields are up so quickly that the whole process *seems* to be unconscious (3:3).

We need to remember what we have forgotten, the deliberate forgetting of our choice. We *can* remember if we are willing "to reconsider the decision which is doubly shielded," that is, the decision to run away from the truth, the decision that truth is something against which we need to defend ourselves. This is why the exercise for the day is:

> Sickness is a defense against the truth. I will accept the truth of what I am, And let my mind be wholly healed today (15:6–7).

The antidote to the whole process is not attempting to heal the sick body, but to accept the truth about myself, to let my *mind* be healed. Sickness is a side effect of rejecting the truth about myself; the cure is to accept the truth instead, to reconsider the original decision which, although veiled from conscious awareness, *must* be there for sickness to have occurred.

The lesson warns us, in the final paragraph: "Do not be confused about what must be healed" (20:2). It isn't the body that needs healing; it is the mind. This agrees with the Text, which tells us:

"When the ego tempts you to sickness do not ask the Holy Spirit to heal the body, for this would merely be to accept the ego's belief that the body is the proper aim of healing. Ask, rather, that the Holy Spirit teach you the right *perception* of the body, for perception alone can be distorted" (T-8.IX.1:5–6). It is that original decision to reject the truth of what we are, because it seems to threaten what we *think* we are, that must be questioned and reversed.

The lesson says some rather incredible things about the body of a person whose mind is healed, and whose body has been accepted as nothing but a tool to be used to heal the world. The body's strength "will always be enough to serve all truly useful purposes. The body's health is fully guaranteed, because it is not limited by time, by weather or fatigue, by food and drink, or any laws you made it serve before" (18:2–

3). If a body is not limited by time it does not age. Not limited by weather means it needs no clothing or shelter. Not limited by fatigue, it needs no sleep. Not limited by food or drink, it does not need to eat. Who of us can say this is true of us?

Perhaps we have experienced a few glimmers of such brilliant light, fatigue thrown off, lack of food overlooked for a time. But no one I know is at this stage of perfect trust. We have a ways to go, you and I. So I do not think we need be surprised when a cold attacks, or the flu gets us down, or even if something "more serious" happens. We're still afraid of the truth—big surprise! Rather than thinking—"Oh, why did I do this to myself? What is wrong with me that I am still getting sick?"—let me say, "Ooops! I made a mistake. I forgot what I really am and mistook my body for myself. Silly me! I just need to remember that I am not a body; this isn't what I am." The "sickness" of the body can then become a catalyst for the healing of my mind, instead of a defense against the truth.

Lesson 137—May 17

"When I am healed I am not healed alone."

PRACTICE SUMMARY

Purpose: To let your mind be healed, that you may send healing to the world, aware that you and the world are healed as one.

Longer: Two times, morning and evening for ten minutes.

- Say: "When I am healed I am not healed alone. And I would share my healing with the world, that sickness may be banished from the mind of God's one Son, Who is my Self."
- Then rest in quiet. And as you rest, receive the Word of God to replace all your insane thoughts, and be prepared to give it to the world, to bless your brothers across the world.

Remarks: This exercise will prepare you for the hourly remembrances.

Shorter: Every hour on the hour for one minute.

Remember your function of letting your mind be healed so that you may extend healing to the world. Say: "When I am healed I am not healed alone. And I would bless my brothers, for I would be healed with them, as they are healed with me."

Remarks: Is it not worth a minute to receive the gift of everything?

COMMENTARY

Although this lesson has a great deal to say about healing in general, its primary message is that healing, which is our function in the world, is essentially a phenomenon that is shared, and that to heal *is* to share. Healing restores oneness. "Those who are healed become the instruments of healing" (11:1).

"Sickness is a retreat from others, and a shutting off of joining" (1:3). It is isolation (2:1). Healing reverses that; it is a move toward others, a joining, and a union. The healing being spoken of in this lesson is a healing of the mind, and not necessarily of the body. "Our function is to let our minds be healed, that we may carry healing to the world, exchanging ...separation for the peace of God" (13:1).

Whatever the state of my body, it cannot interfere with this function. My body cannot restrain or limit my mind. "Minds that were walled off within a body [become] free to join with other minds, to be forever strong" (8:6). My task today, and every day, is to allow my mind to be healed, and to allow healing to flow through my mind to other minds, carrying healing to the world. That can occur whatever state my body is in. I do not normally realize how powerful my mind is, and how extensive the effects of its healing can be. "And as you let yourself be healed, you see all those around you, or who cross your mind, or whom you touch or those who seem to have no contact with you, healed along with you" (10:1).

As I open my mind to healing today, I realize that whatever the state of my body, "what is opposed to God does not exist" (11:3). When I refuse to accept sickness as my reality, my mind "becomes a haven where the weary can remain to rest" (11:3). Sickness is just a special case of "I am my body." So what we are called on to do is not just to refuse the limitations of sickness, but to refuse the limits of the body altogether. Today, I choose to let "thoughts of healing...go forth from what is healed to what must yet be healed" (12:6). I set aside some time, ten minutes in the morning and evening, and a minute every hour, to give my mind over to its function of sharing healing thoughts with the world. "Reach out to all your brothers, and touch them with the touch of Christ" (T-13.VI.8:2).

Today, I want to let healing be through me (15:1). I want to be a channel, a channel of blessing to the world. What other purpose could bring me such joy?

Lesson 138—May 18

"Heaven is the decision I must make."

PRACTICE SUMMARY

Longer: Two times, the first and last moments of your day, for five minutes.

Make the choice for Heaven. Say: "Heaven is the decision I must make. I make it now, and will not change my mind, because it is the only thing I want." Realize you choose consciously between what is real and what only seems real. By bringing to light your unconscious illusion it will no longer seem enormous and fearful, but flimsy and transparent, a mere trivial mistake. You will not hesitate to choose Heaven when you see how worthless and powerless is its opposite.

Shorter: Hourly, a brief quiet time.

Maintain your sanity by declaring your choice again: "Heaven is the decision I must make. I make it now, and will not change my mind, because it is the only thing I want."

COMMENTARY

The lesson makes some stark contrasts between this world and creation. One is a realm of duality, in which "opposition is part of being 'real'" (2:2). The other is a realm of unity, of perfect oneness: "Creation knows no opposite" (2:1). This is a classic discussion about what can be called duality and non-duality.

Non-duality, or oneness, is what is real. Where there is only oneness there can be no choice, because there is nothing between which to choose. If oneness is reality, then choice, any choice, is an illusion and nothing more. Choice is impossible, inconceivable. That is the reality.

Within our dream, however, choice is not only possible; it is inevitable, it is life. Within this world, truth cannot enter because it would be met only with fear; the choicelessness of oneness seems the ultimate threat to a mind that thinks duality is all there is. Therefore, in this world, we are learning to make one, final choice. It is a choice to end all choices, the choice between illusion and reality. Time exists for nothing but this choice, to "give us time" to make it. We are being asked to choose Heaven instead of hell.

Years ago, before I encountered the Course, I had been through a lot of things, read a lot of books, and attended a lot of seminars. I sat down one day to try to distill, in writing, what I had learned from life. I was writing for my sons, then in their teens. I recall quite clearly that at that point in my life, I felt I was only sure of two things:

One, you can trust the Universe.

Two, happiness is a decision I make.

I won't bother to comment on the first item here, but the second was something very fundamental to the Course, the realization that nothing outside my mind makes me happy or unhappy; my happiness is entirely the result of my own choice.

When I first read this lesson in the Workbook I was stunned by the similarity of the concept, even the very words. "Heaven is the decision I must make." Perhaps the fact that I had arrived at this conclusion on my own was one of the reasons I took so rapidly to the Course; it confirmed what, to me, was the essence of my own personal wisdom, words that as far as I knew were entirely my own. Here was this book, saying the same thing. In saying that we must choose Heaven, and that this is "the decision" we have to make, the Course is saying that learning this is what life is all about. It is "the choice that time was made to help us make" (7:1). It is a choice, a decision, that accepts the total responsibility of the mind for the way it perceives reality.

But the lesson is saying far more than this. The discussion of duality and non-duality in this lesson explains clearly why so many of us, indeed most of us, experience such tearing, inner conflict over accepting the simple truth. We have become convinced that opposites and conflict are not simply part of life, they *are* life. They *are* reality to us. "Life is seen as conflict" (7:4). This belief shows up, for instance, in the somewhat frivolous objection that Heaven, where nothing changes and there are no opposites, sounds boring. We are addicted to the drama, devoted to the delicious agony of indecision. To be without choices, to us, seems like death. To finally and completely resolve the conflict appears to us like the end of life itself.

Yet that is what the Course promises and asks of us: the end of all conflict. When this truly dawns on our minds, we often recoil in mortal terror.

> These mad beliefs can gain unconscious hold of great intensity and grip the mind with terror and anxiety so strong that it will not relinquish its ideas about its own protection. It must be saved from salvation..." (8:1–2).

It is unconscious; we do not realize what is going on. But we literally run away from the truth, and shrink from total love, not knowing what we are doing. Virtually everyone who works with the Course over any length of time experiences something like this in their life. It seems as though we are being asked to die. And in a sense, we are: die to life *as we have known it.*

The only way out is through. Through fear to love. "Heaven is chosen consciously" (9:1). For a decision to be conscious, *both* alternatives must be seen clearly. We have to see hell in the plain light of day, as well as Heaven. Our fear of hell, our terror of destruction, our agony of guilt must be "raised to understanding, to be judged again, this time with Heaven's help" (9:3). It was our own mind's desire for an alternative to Heaven that made hell, and we must understand that duality is a beast of our own making—and that our desire had no *real* effect.

"Who can decide between the clearly seen and the unrecognized? Yet who can fail to make a choice between alternatives when only one is seen as valuable; the other as a wholly worthless thing, a but imagined source of guilt and pain?" (10:2–3) Our making of duality has seemed like such a monstrous thing; buried in our unconscious, it was "made enormous, vengeful, pitiless with hate," but when it is brought into conscious awareness, "Now it is recognized as but a foolish, trivial mistake" (11:4–5). Our guilt over it is all that holds it in place. When we look at it again, "this time with Heaven's help" (9:3), the choice to let it go becomes the only possible decision we can make. And in that decision, we are released.

Lesson 139—May 19

"I will accept Atonement for myself."

PRACTICE SUMMARY

Purpose: To accept the truth about yourself today, and go your way rejoicing in God's Love.

Longer: Two times, morning and evening for five minutes.

- Begin by reviewing your mission: "I will accept Atonement for myself. For I remain as God created me."
- Then accept the truth about yourself. You have not lost the knowledge of who you are. It is still in your memory, along with the knowledge of how dear your brothers are, how much a part of you. You can remember today for everyone, for all minds are one.

Shorter: Hourly, for several minutes.

Lay aside all thoughts that would distract you. Learn that the chains that would hide your Self from awareness are mere fragile cobwebs cluttering your mind, as you say: "I will accept Atonement for myself. For I remain as God created me."

COMMENTARY

What does it mean to accept the Atonement for myself? This lesson puts an end to any idea that this is a selfish notion, or that it means my only concern is myself, or my personal happiness. Nothing could be clearer than this: "It is more than just our happiness alone we came to gain. What we accept as what we are proclaims what everyone must be, along with us" (9:4–5).

To accept the Atonement for myself means to accept the truth of what I am, to decide to "accept ourselves as God created us" (1:2). And what am I? I already know, in my heart of hearts, but I resist knowing. This lesson is magnificent in its trenchant dissection of the insanity of the way we question our Identity. It questions all our questioning. It raises all our doubts to doubt. It denies the possibility of denial. It belittles our thoughts of littleness. How can we be anything except what we are? How can we *not know* what we are? "The only thing that can be surely known by any living thing is what it is" (2:3).

God created us as extensions of His Love. That is our mission; it is what we are. To accept the Atonement is to accept this truth about ourselves. To accept the Atonement is to begin to function as God's Love in the world.

Every time we refuse to see the magnificence in another we are denying our own. We look on others with less than love because we refuse to see how much *we* merit it. We are God's representatives on earth; accepting the Atonement is to accept our mission. We are here to restore the grandeur of what we all are to every mind—not just to our own. This grandness, this magnificent inclusiveness, this divine generosity is our very being. We are the open heart that embraces the world, remembering "how much a part of us is every mind" (11:6).

In us our Father's Love can contain them all. Our heart is big enough for all the world.

This is Who we are. Today, let me remember. Today, let me accept my holy aim. Today, let me know myself as part of this great throbbing, all-embracing Heart of God.

Lesson 140—May 20

"Only salvation can be said to cure."

PRACTICE SUMMARY

Purpose: To change your mind about the source of sickness. To not seek to cure the body but to seek in your mind the source of healing, the cure for all illusions. God placed it in your mind, so close that you cannot lose it.

Longer: Two times, beginning and end of day for five minutes.

- Let all your interfering thoughts be laid aside as one, for they are all equally meaningless.
- With open hands, lifted heart and listening mind, pray: "Only salvation can be said to cure. Speak to us, Father, that we may be healed."
- Then in stillness listen for only one voice, God's Voice of healing, Which will cure all ills, making no distinctions among them. Feel His salvation blanket you with protection and deep peace, allowing no illusion to disturb your holy mind.

Remarks: You will succeed to the degree you realize there are no meaningful distinctions among illusions. They are all unreal. That is why they can be cured.

Shorter: As the hour strikes, for a minute.

- Say your healing prayer: "Only salvation can be said to cure. Speak to us, Father, that we may be healed."
- Then listen in joyous silence, and hear God's answer.

COMMENTARY

The "cure" that the Course is talking about is a healing of the mind, not of the body.

> The body needs no healing. But the mind that thinks it is a body is sick indeed! (T-25.In.3:1–2)
>
> The lesson is the *mind* was sick that thought the body could be sick (T-28.II.11:7).

To seek a cure in the physical realm, by any means (even New Age means) is what the Course would call "magic." (Calling it "magic" doesn't mean we can't use it if our fear level requires it; the Course advocates a compromise approach in such circumstances. See T-2.IV.4–5 and 2.V.2, which I discuss a bit later.) The Atonement heals the mind that thinks the body can be sick. "This is no magic" (6:4).

This lesson applies to bodily sickness, but it applies equally to any apparent "problem" in this material world: financial lack, loneliness, and so on. These problems all occur within the dream, and finding "a magic formula" within the dream is never the solution (2:2). We are "curing" the symptom and not the disease. The root of the problem is within the mind. "Let us not try today to seek to cure what cannot suffer sickness" (7:1). Our problems are not physical in nature. "We will not be misled today by what appears to us as sick" (9:1). "So do we lay aside our amulets [crystals? religious medallions?], our charms and medicines, our chants and bits of magic in whatever form they take" (10:1).

Early in the Text, Jesus makes it clear that magic is not evil. It just doesn't really work. It is only a stop-gap, an attempt to rid ourselves of symptoms without really curing the disease. Yet sometimes that is the best we can do. We have a headache, and with a splitting headache it is often difficult to quiet the mind and peacefully meditate ourselves well. So we use magic. We take the aspirin; there is no shame in this. Only let us not deceive ourselves that we have really done anything to cure the disease; we have simply masked the symptom. "If you are afraid to use the mind to heal, you should not attempt to do so" (T-2.V.2:2). If our fear level is high, a "compromise approach" may be necessary (T-2.IV.4:4–7).

Only salvation can be said to cure. The magic of this world can mask symptoms but not cure. "The mind that brings illusions to the truth is really changed. There is no change but this" (7:4–5). Today we are asked to practice just this: bringing our illusions to the truth, allowing our guilt to be removed from our minds. *This* cures, and nothing else. "There is no place where He is not" (5:5), and this includes our minds. Sin would keep Him out, but since He is everywhere, sin cannot be anywhere (see 5:1–7); sin cannot be in our minds. "This is the thought that cures" (6:1). Sin, and therefore sickness, cannot be real because God is in us; He has not left us, and what we think is sin cannot be so. In our awareness of His presence, guilt disappears, and with it, the cause of sickness.

COMMENTS ON PRACTICE LESSONS 141–170

Review IV: Lessons 141–150

The practice for this review is surprisingly light: a couple of practices per day for five minutes or more and a quiet moment each hour. There are a few notable things about this, however:

- **The central thought**. This review begins the habit of the three final reviews in the Workbook: having all practice organized around one central thought, in this case, "My mind holds only what I think with God."
- **A kind of contemplative study practice.** The longer practice periods have two phases, and both are really just about unhurriedly dwelling on brief lines in the Course and soaking in the shining gift that God placed in those words.
- **Preparation for Part II**. Perhaps the most significant thing about this review is that it is the first time we are told that we are now getting ready for Part II of the Workbook. This means that the structure is starting to be taken away, the training wheels are beginning to come off, and we are getting ready to fly. The first hint of this was Lesson 124, with its unstructured holy half an hour. This theme of preparation for Part II will increase from this point on until, eighty lessons from now, we actually reach Part II.

Lesson 151: "All things are echoes of the Voice for God."

Teaching clarification: What does it mean that all things are echoes of the Voice for God? Does it mean that the Holy Spirit created the world? No. A careful reading will reveal that we are being urged to let the Holy Spirit interpret our identity and our life events for us. He will show us the truth behind the appearances, both by overlooking the appearances and by focusing on those appearances that reflect truth. In this way, we will hear His echo in all things.

Practice comment: The practice is a wonderful one of giving the Holy Spirit the thoughts that cross your mind and letting Him give them back to you in purified form. I find that this really works. It is an experience of the important principle from the Text that says He actually purifies our thoughts on an ongoing basis.

Lesson 152: "The power of decision is my own."

The morning and evening practice here are standard Workbook meditation, in which you leave your self-concepts and humbly open your mind to your true Identity. Hopefully, you are learning to spot the underlying unity of this meditation practice under the variety of different wordings.

Laying the Foundation for Full-Blown Practice

Lesson 153: "In my defenselessness my safety lies."

This is one of the most important shifts in the Workbook. Up until now we have been given various pieces:

- We have been instructed in longer practice periods that have slowly gravitated to morning and evening time slots. And we have learned several kinds of practice for these longer periods, meditation being perhaps the most frequent and notable.
- We have been instructed in hourly remembrances, beginning with Lesson 93. These have been anywhere from the demanding five minutes per hour of Lessons 93–110 to the brief moments spent with the idea in Lessons 121–152.
- We have been instructed in frequent reminders, beginning with that landmark Lesson 20 and its descendants, Lessons 27, 40 and 48, and then going into the intense frequency of the 60's and 70's.
- We have also been instructed in response to temptation, which has evolved enormously from its first appearance in Lesson 4. We started getting specific instructions for it in the 30's. We were trained in the crucial skill of letting related thoughts come in the 40's and 60's, a skill which we applied to response to temptation in the 80's. We got special lines to say in the 60's and 70's and were given particular temptations to respond to in the 130's.

Putting into place the bottom tiers of the pyramid.

We can look at these four types of practice as a series of tiers constituting a pyramid. The pyramid rests on the foundation of the morning and evening quiet times and extends up to the apex of response to temptation. Lesson 153 is a major step toward assembling the entire pyramid. It gives us forty-eight lessons in which to focus on putting the first two tiers solidly in place. This is a major step toward assembling the entire pyramid, which we will take with us into Part II of the Workbook.

The instructions for the next forty-eight lessons.

The instructions for this lesson begin by saying, "Today we will practice in a form we will maintain for quite a while." It does not mention that "quite a while" means nearly fifty lessons. Here are some comments on those instructions:

- **Morning and evening quiet time.** We are asked to give as much time as we can—at least five minutes and at best more than a half hour. This focus on duration drops away later, but for now it is important. We are still given some instruction in what to do in this time, but much of it is left up to us. We have enough experience in meditation, in listening for the Holy Spirit's Voice, in bringing our darkness to His light, and in waiting for an experience of vision from Him, that we are being increasingly left on our own.
- **Hourly remembrance.** This has reached its final form. Two things are notable about this final form of hourly remembrance:
    - Ideally we spend a couple of minutes or more, but given the nature of our days we spend however much we can. It is understood that we will often not be able to or will forget.
    - The hourly remembrance, both here and in its modified form in Lesson 193, focuses on putting to bed the previous hour and preparing us for the coming hour. The current instructions have us thanking God for the previous hour and asking for guidance for the coming one.
- **Response to temptation.** Though this practice is not mentioned as part of the instructions, it has become an assumed part of the practice of the Workbook. Hopefully, we know by now something of how to do this practice, how to watch our thoughts and use the idea to respond to egoic thoughts. Yet we will still occasionally get instructions for particular applications of certain lessons.

It either goes up from here or down from here.

The instructions for practice have been relatively relaxed lately, resting us up from that intense five minutes per hour of Lessons 93–110 and getting us ready for the leap forward of Lesson 153. If we are not ready to leap forward, chances are that we will start sliding down from here, for two reasons. First, the Workbook is asking for a lot of practice. Second, just as the Workbook is asking for more, it is also leaving us more and more on our own, giving us fewer and fewer instructions. We are thus being asked to practice more and do so under *our own motivation*. If we are not up to it, then just as the Workbook is trying to move us into the fullness of practice, we will be drifting away into less and less practice.

Lessons 153–170

There is not much I want to say about these lessons, since the basic practice regimen is the same. Perhaps the major theme is to receive an experience of Heaven or an experience of Christ's vision, and then give that to the world; express that in our function of extending to others.

There are a couple of the lessons, however, that contain unusual and important practice:

Lesson 157: "Into His Presence would I enter now."

A landmark lesson which is meant to usher in the direct experience of Heaven. This lesson claims that we are ready now to have this experience. And it says that the experience will usher in our ministry, sanctify our body, and begin a process in which we have this experience with increasing frequency, each time transforming our mind more and more, until we no longer return in this form. In Lessons 168 and 169 we also seek an experience of Heaven.

Lesson 161: "Give me your blessing, holy Son of God."

The last lesson in the Workbook in which we forgive a particular brother. It also contains important teaching on the psychological role of specifics or concretes.

Review IV—Introduction
May 21-30

REVIEW IV COMMENTARY

If you will recall, back in the Workbook Introduction we were told, "The workbook is divided into two main sections, the first dealing with the undoing of the way you see now, and the second with the acquisition of true perception" (W-In.3:1). Although Part II does not begin for another 80 lessons, Review IV announces that we are entering a transition stage of the Workbook, "preparing for the second part of learning how the truth can be applied." Part II of the Workbook, if you will look at it, consists of lessons that are a half page long, or less. They give very few specific practice instructions, and offer us a great deal more latitude in exactly how we practice. They are geared to students who have begun to make the truths of the Course their own, and who are ready to apply them independently. This review gives us some preliminary exercises in that kind of independent practice. In Lesson 153, shortly after we complete this review, there will be a major shift in practice, as we shall see, which will set the pattern for the practice during the rest of Part I of the Workbook.

Therefore, following the practice instructions for this review is quite important, if we want to be prepared for what is to come. You'll notice that the reviews give us nothing but the theme thought for the review and the two theme ideas being reviewed; there is no additional commentary. In a sense, we are meant to supply that commentary for ourselves. We are meant to take the ideas and let the Holy Spirit open their meaning in our own minds, without the prop of printed words to help us. "Let each word shine with the meaning God has given it, as it was given to you through His Voice" (7:4).

Perhaps you do not feel ready for this. I confess that when I first did the Workbook I pretty much lost interest after Part I; I did the lessons but really all I did was read them, think about them for a minute or two, and then forget them. The reviews such as this one seemed particularly pointless to me. Two or three sentences wasn't enough to stimulate my mind, and I was not ready, apparently, to allow the Holy Spirit to "let each word shine" in my mind. You may find yourself in the same boat. Still, I would say, try to follow the instructions. Take the few lines given for each day, and ruminate on them. Chew them over. Think about what you know of their meaning, and ask to be shown more. If it works for you, try to initiate a dialogue with the Holy Spirit about the ideas. Turn them into prayers. Think how they can apply to your life. Be still before God and let the *feeling* of the ideas wash over you. Do whatever seems to work for you.

Maybe you won't feel that you're doing very well, but what is the purpose of practice, if not to learn to do something you don't know how to do well?

Notice the theme thought for the review: "My mind holds only what I think with God." The instructions tell us to spend five minutes letting this one thought, and this alone, engage our minds, and remove all other thoughts. What we are doing is clearing the stage, making way for the Holy Spirit to teach us. The five minutes spent with this idea each day is our warm-up period. We are making ourselves ready to receive the thoughts of God, through His Holy Spirit. We are preparing ourselves to hold communion with God.

Only *after* this five-minute warm-up are we instructed to take the two thoughts for review, and let their meaning illuminate our minds. There is no time limit given here; we are to review them "slowly" and with "no hurry." Surely this will be more than a few seconds! More like several minutes, at the least. The best way is to be able to do this review without concern about time; if we take five minutes or twenty-five, it does not matter. The important thing is that we commune with God, and let His thoughts fill our minds. As the review says of our hourly review sessions, we should take "time enough to see the gifts that they [the two ideas] contain for you, and let them be received where they were meant to be" (8:2). The exact amount of time you spend is left to you.

Lesson 141—May 21

Review IV: "My mind holds only what I think with God."
(121) "Forgiveness is the key to happiness."
(122) "Forgiveness offers everything I want."

PRACTICE SUMMARY

Purpose: To prepare for Part II of the Workbook, by concentrating on readiness for it and by reviewing the last twenty lessons in a way that will facilitate that readiness.

Longer: Two times, beginning and ending of the day, for five minutes or more.

- Open your mind, clear it of all distracting thoughts. For five minutes let this thought alone occupy it, displacing all others: "My mind holds only what I think with God."
- Read the day's two ideas. Close eyes and repeat ideas slowly, without hurry, for this is what time was made for. Let each word shine with the meaning God gave it. Receive from each idea the gift God placed in it.

Remarks: Phase 1 will be enough to set your day along the lines God planned, making it a special time of blessing for you and for the world. It will be enough to place Him in charge of all your thoughts. Your thoughts will come from more than you. They will also come from Him and tell you of His Love. Thus will you, His completion, join with Him. And He, your completion, will join with you. He thanks you for your practicing. And as your day ends, His gratitude will surround you.

Shorter: Hourly, for a quiet moment.

- Say: "My mind holds only what I think with God." Spend a quiet moment with it.
- Then repeat the day's two ideas, slowly enough to see their gifts and receive their gifts.

COMMENTARY

Forgiveness really does offer us everything we want, and without true forgiveness, happiness just isn't possible. We may not consciously and completely believe this as yet, but our right mind believes it, and always has. Forgiveness operates not just on what I think the world did to me (in reality it did nothing to me), but also on what it *did not* do that I wanted it to. The older one gets, the more disillusioned one becomes about the world. We speak of people becoming "world-weary" and cynical as they age, because despite the high hopes we had when younger, despite the brilliant promises the world seemed to make to us, it disappointed us. It did not make us happy. We discover that the world isn't fair, that good people don't always succeed, that we don't always get what we want. And even when we do, it isn't as good as we had hoped.

Forgiveness involves recognizing that we are the ones who laid these expectations on the world, and we are the ones who made it to disappoint us. We asked the impossible; nothing in this world will ever satisfy us or make us happy. Happiness is to be found in our native state and there alone, that is, in union with God and with the Sonship. To forgive the world means to stop begrudging its imperfections. We cannot blame the world for our pain, nor can we blame it for its failure to make us happy. We cannot blame it at all. When at last our teeth unclench, our fists relax, and our breath eases as we release these deep-seated grievances, what we discover is our own inherent happiness, there all along, but masked by our unforgiveness.

Lesson 142—May 22

Review IV: "My mind holds only what I think with God."
(123) "I thank my Father for His gifts to me."
124) "Let me remember I am one with God."

PRACTICE SUMMARY

Purpose: To prepare for Part II of the Workbook, by concentrating on readiness for it and by reviewing the last twenty lessons in a way that will facilitate that readiness.

Longer: Two times, beginning and ending of the day, for five minutes or more.

- Open your mind, clear it of all distracting thoughts. For five minutes let this thought alone occupy it, displacing all others: "My mind holds only what I think with God."
- Read the day's two ideas. Close eyes and repeat ideas slowly, without hurry, for this is what time was made for. Let each word shine with the meaning God gave it. Receive from each idea the gift God placed in it.

Remarks: Phase 1 will be enough to set your day along the lines God planned, making it a special time of blessing for you and for the world. It will be enough to place Him in charge of all your thoughts. Your thoughts will come from more than you. They will also come from Him and tell you of His Love. Thus will you, His completion, join with Him. And He, your completion, will join with you. He thanks you for your practicing. And as your day ends, His gratitude will surround you.

Shorter: Hourly, for a quiet moment.

- Say: "My mind holds only what I think with God." Spend a quiet moment with it.
- Then repeat the day's two ideas, slowly enough to see their gifts and receive their gifts.

COMMENTARY

That my mind holds only what I think with God is not something I have to work at to attain. It is not a thought to be repeated like a purgative, to drive out opposing thoughts, with the undertone of "I have to *make* my mind have only God's thoughts in it." That my mind holds only what I think with God is "a fact, and represents the truth of What you are and What your Father is" (W-pII.rIV.2:3).

As we were told early in the Workbook, when we think that we are thinking without God, we are not really thinking at all; our mind is actually blank. "While thoughtless ideas preoccupy your mind, the truth is blocked. Recognizing that your mind has been merely blank, rather than believing that it is filled with real ideas, is the first step to opening the way to vision" (W-pI.8.3:2–3). "Now we are emphasizing that the presence of these 'thoughts' means that you are not thinking" (W-pI.10.3:2).

The Thoughts of God that fill my mind in reality are my Father's gift to me. I am opening my mind, today, to His Thoughts. What I ordinarily think of as thoughts that interfere or conflict with God's Thoughts are like the static on a radio that interferes with the actual signal. They are not thoughts; they are static, they are noise. The signal is still there; but the static needs to be tuned out so that the signal can come through. The truth about me is that I am one with God; His Mind is my mind, His Thoughts are my thoughts. I am not something other than what He is. This is "the truth of What you are and What your Father is" (W-pII.rIV.2:3).

To say that my mind holds only what I think with God can be a joyous affirmation of the truth. It can remind me of His gifts to me, and remind me that I am one with Him. That in me which seems contrary to God, distant from God, or opposed to God, is not who I am; it is not my reality. It is without meaning. There is nothing opposed to God in my mind. Another way of putting that is that what seems to be in me, opposing God, is actually nothing; it is an illusion or an hallucination, with no power and no strength of its own. It is empowered only when I believe in it. Today, I choose to deny that anything not of God has any power over me. I choose to remember what my reality is. I choose to remember that I am one with God.

Lesson 143—May 23

Review IV: "My mind holds only what I think with God."
(125) "In quiet I receive God's Word today."
(126) "All that I give is given to myself."

PRACTICE SUMMARY

Purpose: To prepare for Part II of the Workbook, by concentrating on readiness for it and by reviewing the last twenty lessons in a way that will facilitate that readiness.

Longer: Two times, beginning and ending of the day, for five minutes or more.

- Open your mind, clear it of all distracting thoughts. For five minutes let this thought alone occupy it, displacing all others: "My mind holds only what I think with God."
- Read the day's two ideas. Close eyes and repeat ideas slowly, without hurry, for this is what time was made for. Let each word shine with the meaning God gave it. Receive from each idea the gift God placed in it.

Remarks: Phase 1 will be enough to set your day along the lines God planned, making it a special time of blessing for you and for the world. It will be enough to place Him in charge of all your thoughts. Your thoughts will come from more than you. They will also come from Him and tell you of His Love. Thus will you, His completion, join with Him. And He, your completion, will join with you. He thanks you for your practicing. And as your day ends, His gratitude will surround you.

Shorter: Hourly, for a quiet moment.

- Say: "My mind holds only what I think with God." Spend a quiet moment with it.
- Then repeat the day's two ideas, slowly enough to see their gifts and receive their gifts.

COMMENTARY

God's Thought creates. We were created when God thought of us; His mind extended outward, and what was in His Mind extended into and became our mind. Speaking of the main theme thought, "My mind holds only what I think with God," the Review Introduction says, "It is this thought by which the Father gave creation to the Son, establishing the Son as co-creator with Himself" (W-rIV.In.2:4).

Our minds must therefore be like His, creating like His by extending our thoughts outward. We are God's Thoughts, and His Thoughts have His nature.

> As God's creative Thought proceeds from Him to you, so must your creative thought proceed from you to your creations. Only in this way can all creative power

> extend outward. God's accomplishments are not yours, but yours are like His. He created the Sonship and you increase it. You have the power to add to the Kingdom, though not to add to the Creator of the Kingdom. You claim this power when you become vigilant only for God and His Kingdom. By accepting this power as yours you have learned to remember what you are (T-7.I.2:3–9).

As we receive God's Word today, so we must give it. If we receive it we *will* give it, because what we receive is a thought of sharing. We were created by this sharing of thought, this extending of God's Self; sharing, or giving ourselves, is our heritage, the essence of what we are. In the first thought we review for today are the words, "I receive"; in the second thought are the words, "I give."

Accepting or remembering what we are means realizing we are beings who extend, who give, who share. Created by Love, we are lovers. This is why the Course places such stress on accepting our *function* as saviors of the world; in accepting this, we are accepting our Self as God created It. We are merely taking our place in the creative process, choosing no longer to block the flow of love from God to us, and through us to the world.

> To create is to love. Love extends outward simply because it cannot be contained (T-7.I.3:3–4).

In quiet today I receive God's Word, which is the affirmation of His love for all His creations. I open myself to acknowledge that love, receiving it for myself. And then I step forth to give as I have received, knowing that in giving to my sisters and my brothers, I am indeed giving that love to myself. My giving of it *is* my receiving of it. By my words, my thoughts, my expressions and my attitudes I communicate to all around me the Word I have received: "You, too, are loved. You, too, are loving. You, too, are the expression and channel of the love of God."

Lesson 144—May 24

Review IV: "My mind holds only what I think with God."
(127) "There is no love but God's."
(128) "The world I see holds nothing that I want."

PRACTICE SUMMARY

Purpose: To prepare for Part II of the Workbook, by concentrating on readiness for it and by reviewing the last twenty lessons in a way that will facilitate that readiness.

Longer: Two times, beginning and ending of the day, for five minutes or more.

- Open your mind, clear it of all distracting thoughts. For five minutes let this thought alone occupy it, displacing all others: "My mind holds only what I think with God."
- Read the day's two ideas. Close eyes and repeat ideas slowly, without hurry, for this is what time was made for. Let each word shine with the meaning God gave it. Receive from each idea the gift God placed in it.

Remarks: Phase 1 will be enough to set your day along the lines God planned, making it a special time of blessing for you and for the world. It will be enough to place Him in charge of all your thoughts. Your thoughts will come from more than you. They will also come from Him and tell you of His Love. Thus will you, His completion, join with Him. And He, your completion, will join with you. He thanks you for your practicing. And as your day ends, His gratitude will surround you.

Shorter: Hourly, for a quiet moment.

- Say: "My mind holds only what I think with God." Spend a quiet moment with it.
- Then repeat the day's two ideas, slowly enough to see their gifts and receive their gifts.

COMMENTARY

How is it that the theme thought for the review, that my mind holds only what I think with God, "fully guarantees salvation to the Son" (W-rIV.In.3:5)? It means that there is nothing in my mind that opposes God. It means that what seems to be contrary to God's thoughts, the things I see within myself that are ungodlike or unloving, are misperceptions of myself. It means that there is nothing in reality that can keep me from completion as God's offspring. The enemies and obstacles that seem to stand in the way—most especially the ones that seem to be part of me—are not real, and have no substance.

If there is no love but God's, and my mind holds only what I think with Him, then the emptiness I sometimes feel within myself, the lack of love, the longing for a fully satisfying love that never fails and is always there, something I can depend upon in every situation, will be fulfilled. Thinking that I am seeking for love in this world is simply a mistake. The love I am looking for is within me, right in my own mind. I am not looking for anything in this world, although I so often think I am. I am looking for something I already have, but have denied. And the way to find it is to give it. To *be* it.

Love is not something I can possess. Love is something that can possess me, and in that possession is satisfaction. The attempt to collect love, to possess it and to hoard it brings me pain. My joy can be found in pouring love out, sharing it, blessing the world with it. To recognize that my mind holds only this love, and to open it to the world, is all that I truly want. This, and only this, will bring me happiness.

The words, "The world I see holds nothing that I want," could be spoken in despair. The unspoken thought behind them might be, "Nothing here is good enough for me. Nothing here satisfies, and I will therefore never be satisfied." Or, these words can be spoken with joy. If I am driving a brand new car, exactly the kind I most want, equipped with every accessory I have ever desired, and I pass an auto junkyard, I can look at that junkyard and say, "That junkyard holds nothing that I want." I can speak the words with satisfaction. I can say the same thing as I pass a luxury car dealership, because I already have what I want. Likewise, if I already have what I want in God, there is no despair in the words, "This world holds nothing that I want." My wants are all filled.

If there is no love but God's, and He has imparted Himself, His very thought, to my mind, I can look calmly at the world and realize that there is nothing in it to compare with what I have. I have an Artesian well of love springing up in my heart. I can never lack for love. I am the very love, and I see that same love in every being around me, springing from the same Source.

Love is all around me and within me, if I am only willing to see it. Let me look for God's Love today in everything I see, and let me rejoice every time I find it. Let me acknowledge it in every smile. Let me give it every chance I have to do so. Let me encourage every spark of it in others, and in myself. This is where salvation lies. This is my function and my happiness. And it is guaranteed, because my mind holds only God's loving thoughts.

Lesson 145—May 25

Review IV: "My mind holds only what I think with God."
(129) "Beyond this world there is a world I want."
(130) "It is impossible to see two worlds."

PRACTICE SUMMARY

Purpose: To prepare for Part II of the Workbook, by concentrating on readiness for it and by reviewing the last twenty lessons in a way that will facilitate that readiness.

Longer: Two times, beginning and ending of the day, for five minutes or more.

- Open your mind, clear it of all distracting thoughts. For five minutes let this thought alone occupy it, displacing all others: "My mind holds only what I think with God."
- Read the day's two ideas. Close eyes and repeat ideas slowly, without hurry, for this is what time was made for. Let each word shine with the meaning God gave it. Receive from each idea the gift God placed in it.

Remarks: Phase 1 will be enough to set your day along the lines God planned, making it a special time of blessing for you and for the world. It will be enough to place Him in charge of all your thoughts. Your thoughts will come from more than you. They will also come from Him and tell you of His Love. Thus will you, His completion, join with Him. And He, your completion, will join with you. He thanks you for your practicing. And as your day ends, His gratitude will surround you.

Shorter: Hourly, for a quiet moment.

- Say: "My mind holds only what I think with God." Spend a quiet moment with it.
- Then repeat the day's two ideas, slowly enough to see their gifts and receive their gifts.

COMMENTARY

Though the mind of God's Son holds only what he thinks with God, "Lack of forgiveness blocks this thought from his awareness" (W-rIV.In.2:7). Therefore, the world I see is a world shown to me by unforgiveness. It is "the delusional system of those made mad by guilt" (T-13.In.2:2). The only thing that keeps up the illusion of this world's reality, with its seeming punishment, pain, sorrow, separation and death, is a lack of forgiveness. Why does my body seem to be what I am? Why does the pain I experience, mental, emotional and physical, seem so real? Why does loss seem so real? All of its reality originates and is sustained by a lack of forgiveness in my mind. This is why "Forgiveness is the key to happiness" (Lesson 121).

There is a world I truly want, a world that lies beyond this world. The Course calls it the real world. "The real world is the state of mind in which the only purpose of the world is seen to be forgiveness" (T-30.V.1:1). "The real world is attained simply by complete forgiveness of the old, the world you see without forgiveness" (T-17.II.5:1). My perception shifts from seeing the world of pain to seeing the real world by means of one thing: forgiveness.

This is why it is impossible to see two worlds. Either my mind is forgiving, or it is not. Either it condemns what it sees, or it accepts in merciful forgiveness. Let me begin within myself: how unkind I am to myself in the way I think of myself! How merciless I am in judging my mistakes! This harshness with myself is the origin of the harsh world I see.

There is within me, and within us all, a vast space of kindness, an enormity of heart that embraces everything in love. This is the Mind I share with God. Within me, too, is a fearful child, awash in pain, believing it has eternally damaged the universe. Let me turn with love to that hurt part of myself and open my arms in comfort and gentle loving-kindness. My heart is big enough to hold this pain instead of rejecting it. The love I share with God is vast enough to grant mercy to myself. Let me not shut myself out of my own heart any longer. Let me take myself in, in warmth and gentle welcome.

Let me look on the ones close to me, as well, with this same gentle, kind acceptance. Here is the cure for my loneliness and pain, for there is nothing so painful as a closed heart. Indeed there is no pain but this. Pain is constricting the heart. Pain is denying the love that I am. In this subtle, internal gesture of rejection lies the origin of the world I see. In the undoing of this contraction of pain is my salvation, and the salvation of the world. Here is the entry to the real world, a world bright with love, radiant with hope, certain in its joyfulness.

Beyond this world, there is a world I want, and the key to open the door is forgiveness.

Lesson 146—May 26

Review IV: "My mind holds only what I think with God."
(131) "No one can fail who seeks to reach the truth."
(132) "I loose the world from all I thought it was."

PRACTICE SUMMARY

Purpose: To prepare for Part II of the Workbook, by concentrating on readiness for it and by reviewing the last 20 lessons in a way that will facilitate that readiness.
Longer: Two times, beginning and ending of the day, for five minutes or more.

- Open your mind, clear it of all distracting thoughts. For five minutes let this thought alone occupy it, displacing all others: "My mind holds only what I think with God."
- Read the day's two ideas. Close eyes and repeat ideas slowly, without hurry, for this is what time was made for. Let each word shine with the meaning God gave it. Receive from each idea the gift God placed in it.

Remarks: Phase 1 will be enough to set your day along the lines God planned, making it a special time of blessing for you and for the world. It will be enough to place Him in charge of all your thoughts. Your thoughts will come from more than you. They will also come from Him and tell you of His Love. Thus will you, His completion, join with Him. And He, your completion, will join with you. He thanks you for your practicing. And as your day ends, His gratitude will surround you.
Shorter: Hourly, for a quiet moment.

- Say: "My mind holds only what I think with God." Spend a quiet moment with it.
- Then repeat the day's two ideas, slowly enough to see their gifts and receive their gifts.

COMMENTARY

Continuing to develop some ideas from the Review about the theme thought, I was struck by these words, from paragraphs 2 and 4:

> Yet it is forever true [that my mind holds only what I think with God] (W-rIV.In.2:8).
>
> And yet, your mind holds only what you think with God. Your self-deceptions cannot take the place of truth. No more than can a child who throws a stick into the ocean change the coming and the going of the tides, the warming of the water by the sun, the silver of the moon on it by night (W-rIV.In.4).

It is "forever true" that my mind holds only what it thinks with God. It was true when God created me. It will be true when the journey is over and I am home with God. And it is true *right now*. "Forever true." The third paragraph talks about the many forms of unforgiveness, the way unforgiveness is "carefully concealed" in my mind, the defenses of the ego, its illusions, its use of self-deception to keep the mindless game going. Yet, despite this, "My mind holds only what I think with God." Nothing I do affects this fact. All the self-deception in the world can only hide the truth, not change it. "Your self-deceptions cannot take the place of truth" (4:2).

The image of the child throwing a stick into the ocean is just perfect. I remember as a very young boy I used to go to Cape Cod. I would stand in the surf, with waves perhaps two or three feet high breaking before me, and I would punch the waves, battling with them, driving my fist through them. To me at the time, I was like a warrior, fighting against the ocean. I'm sure the ocean was deeply concerned! I'm sure my mighty efforts slowed down the tide a bit, at least. Sure they did. Right, of course.

Our "rebellion" against God has had about that much effect. In other words, none. The very idea that we could alter God's creation is as ludicrous as the child with the stick seriously believing he had damaged the ocean when he threw the stick in.

This is why, "No one can fail who seeks to reach the truth." Because the truth is right there, in my mind, where it always has been and forever will be. I can't fail to find it because I haven't lost it! I've still got it.

I have looked upon this world and believed it to be a place where God is not. I've seen what appears to be an outrageous lack of love. I've been deeply disappointed with the world. Well, "I loose the world from what I thought it was." I let all those impressions of the world drop away, because it can't be what I thought it was, not if all of our minds still hold only what we think with God. Something is wrong with this picture! Just when I thought I had begun to figure out the world, along comes the Course and says, "Not even warm." So I let my judgments about the world fall away, and open my mind to be taught anew. Maybe, just maybe, the way I've seen it had something to do with what I was thinking about myself, with my belief that my mind was at war with God. Maybe I've seen a world at war with God because that is how I imagine my mind to be, and I've projected that onto the world. And maybe, if I let go of my foolish ideas about myself, my image of the world will change, too. I'm willing to give it a try.

Lesson 147—May 27

Review IV: "My mind holds only what I think with God."
(133) "I will not value what is valueless."
(134) "Let me perceive forgiveness as it is."

PRACTICE SUMMARY

Purpose: To prepare for Part II of the Workbook, by concentrating on readiness for it and by reviewing the last 20 lessons in a way that will facilitate that readiness.

Longer: Two times, beginning and ending of the day, for five minutes or more.

- Open your mind, clear it of all distracting thoughts. For five minutes let this thought alone occupy it, displacing all others: "My mind holds only what I think with God."
- Read the day's two ideas. Close eyes and repeat ideas slowly, without hurry, for this is what time was made for. Let each word shine with the meaning God gave it. Receive from each idea the gift God placed in it.

Remarks: Phase 1 will be enough to set your day along the lines God planned, making it a special time of blessing for you and for the world. It will be enough to place Him in charge of all your thoughts. Your thoughts will come from more than you. They will also come from Him and tell you of His Love. Thus will you, His completion, join with Him. And He, your completion, will join with you. He thanks you for your practicing. And as your day ends, His gratitude will surround you.

Shorter: Hourly, for a quiet moment.

- Say: "My mind holds only what I think with God." Spend a quiet moment with it.
- Then repeat the day's two ideas, slowly enough to see their gifts and receive their gifts.

COMMENTARY

Let me, today, look at the things I value and reconsider them all. Why am I doing this particular thing? What is it I am valuing here? The things we value are often quite foolish when we look at them. For instance, when I have begun to experience the nourishing warmth of true intimacy in relationship, nothing seems worth the closing off of that warmth. I recall reading about a fundamentalist church that split up over the issue of whether or not it was sinful to plug in a guitar. How, I wondered, could anyone value *anything* like that enough to shut out from their hearts people who had once been close friends? So many relationships break up over issues that seem just as trivial.

Forgiveness sees that nothing is worth shutting another child of God out of my heart. We have so many absolutes in our consciousness, things we consider more important than love, more important than unity, more important than our own peace of mind. Have I come, yet, to value peace of mind above everything else? Have I come to the point where anything that interferes with the flow of love through me is quickly discarded?

We need to become aware of the source of our own pain. We ache when we close down our hearts. We ache when we refuse to forgive, when we latch on to the wrongs that have been done to us and fondle them over and over, refusing to let them go. "Love holds no grievances" (W-pI.68). Forgiveness is a gift to myself; it is a release from my own pain. What am I valuing above the free flow of love, the warmth of union with my brother or sister? Let me choose to no longer value this valueless thing, and choose to forgive.

Let me take five minutes this morning, and five minutes tonight, to open my mind and clear it of all thoughts that would deceive (W-pI.rIV.5:2). Let me brush aside lesser values, and remember that my mind holds God's own thoughts. Let me value these thoughts above all else. Let me rejoice in the congruence of my mind and God's Mind, and recognize that this blending of my mind with God's, this sharing of His thoughts, is all that is truly valuable to me.

Lesson 148—May 28

Review IV: "My mind holds only what I think with God."
(135) "If I defend myself I am attacked."
(136) "Sickness is a defense against the truth."

PRACTICE SUMMARY

Purpose: To prepare for Part II of the Workbook, by concentrating on readiness for it and by reviewing the last 20 lessons in a way that will facilitate that readiness.

Longer: Two times, beginning and ending of the day, for five minutes or more.

- Open your mind, clear it of all distracting thoughts. For five minutes let this thought alone occupy it, displacing all others: "My mind holds only what I think with God."
- Read the day's two ideas. Close eyes and repeat ideas slowly, without hurry, for this is what time was made for. Let each word shine with the meaning God gave it. Receive from each idea the gift God placed in it.

Remarks: Phase 1 will be enough to set your day along the lines God planned, making it a special time of blessing for you and for the world. It will be enough to place Him in charge of all your thoughts. Your thoughts will come from more than you. They will also come from Him and tell you of His Love. Thus will you, His completion, join with Him. And He, your completion, will join with you. He thanks you for your practicing. And as your day ends, His gratitude will surround you.

Shorter: Hourly, for a quiet moment.

- Say: "My mind holds only what I think with God." Spend a quiet moment with it.
- Then repeat the day's two ideas, slowly enough to see their gifts and receive their gifts.

COMMENTARY

What seem to me to be obstacles within my mind, out-of-control thoughts that hinder me on my spiritual path, are my defenses against the truth. Nothing enters my mind without my permission. No one is thinking thoughts in my mind except me (and God). As Lesson 26 taught us, my attack thoughts are attacking my own invulnerability. I may think I am attacking someone else, but I am really attacking my own Identity with God.

My ego has built up a clever, multi-layered defense system against the truth, and has hidden it in obscurity and disguise. The process the Course sets before me is one of uncovering these defenses, becoming aware of them, judging them as insane, and letting them go. All of them are false, and what is false cannot affect what is true. Beneath all the camouflage of the ego, my mind still holds only what I think with God.

The rest is elaborate illusion with no real power to cause any effects whatsoever.

Sickness is one very prominent and very effective defense system of the ego. In sickness, something my mind has caused appears to be an attack from the outside, a visible or invisible enemy with very visible effects on my body. It is something I must continually defend against, and fight with every resource when it strikes. As soon as one disease is conquered, another seems to arise with even more devastating effects. Most of mankind is not ready to accept that sickness is only of the mind. I have not fully accepted it myself; my level of fear is still too high. So there is every reason to continue to alleviate diseases in the ways we have been doing, yet we must realize that we are only muting the symptoms and not eradicating the cause. Only as more and more of us begin to realize that our minds hold only what we think with God, and that everything which seems to be other than from God is an illusion of our creation, will the need for the compromise approach of physical medicine begin to disappear.

Today in my practice I am contributing to the ultimate cure of every disease. As I search out my own inner defenses, which are actually forms of self-attack, and let them go, I am collaborating with the power of God to free mankind from disease, and not only disease, but every such ego-based system of defense against the truth. As I clear my mind of all thoughts that would deceive (W-pI.rIV.5:2), and place God's Mind in charge of the thoughts I receive (5:4), I am not working alone. "They [the thoughts] will not come from you alone, for they will all be shared with Him" (6:1).

Let me, then, take the assigned times today to remember the true Source of all my thoughts, and to allow the Holy Spirit to clear the cobwebs of deception from my mind. Let me take five minutes in the morning to "set the day along the lines which God appointed" (5:4). Each time I do so, each day I remember my practice, I bring myself and all the world nearer the day when all deception will vanish in the light.

Lesson 149—May 29

Review IV: "My mind holds only what I think with God."
(137) "When I am healed I am not healed alone."
(138) "Heaven is the decision I must make."

PRACTICE SUMMARY

Purpose: To prepare for Part II of the Workbook, by concentrating on readiness for it and by reviewing the last 20 lessons in a way that will facilitate that readiness.

Longer: Two times, beginning and ending of the day, for five minutes or more.

- Open your mind, clear it of all distracting thoughts. For five minutes let this thought alone occupy it, displacing all others: "My mind holds only what I think with God."
- Read the day's two ideas. Close eyes and repeat ideas slowly, without hurry, for this is what time was made for. Let each word shine with the meaning God gave it. Receive from each idea the gift God placed in it.

Remarks: Phase 1 will be enough to set your day along the lines God planned, making it a special time of blessing for you and for the world. It will be enough to place Him in charge of all your thoughts. Your thoughts will come from more than you. They will also come from Him and tell you of His Love. Thus will you, His completion, join with Him. And He, your completion, will join with you. He thanks you for your practicing. And as your day ends, His gratitude will surround you.

Shorter: Hourly, for a quiet moment.

- Say: "My mind holds only what I think with God." Spend a quiet moment with it.
- Then repeat the day's two ideas, slowly enough to see their gifts and receive their gifts.

COMMENTARY

More and more, as we progress through the Workbook, what we are being asked to do is really to commune with God. Or, to put it in more mundane terms, to get back into communication with Him.

> You taught yourself the most unnatural habit of not communicating with your Creator. Yet you remain in close communication with Him, and with everything that is within Him, as it is within yourself. Unlearn isolation through His loving guidance, and learn of all the happy communication that you have thrown away but could not lose (T-14.III.18:1–3).

As we clear our minds of lesser thoughts and tune in to the thoughts we share with God, thoughts will come to our minds, and they won't be from ourselves alone.

> And so each one will bring the message of His Love to you, returning messages of yours to Him. So will communion with the Lord of Hosts be yours, as He Himself has willed it be (W-pI.rIV.6:2–3).

Connecting in my mind with God connects me, as well, with my brothers and sisters, because all of us are connected to the Source. I am not healed alone.

I could use a "message of His Love" today; how about you? And I wouldn't mind returning my message of love to Him, as well. There are moments in a loving relationship where the love just seems to be ping-ponging back and forth so fast you can't follow it, you can't even be sure whose love is whose. It outstrips ping-ponging, in fact; it transcends the back-and-forth motion implied by that analogy and becomes a constant, cyclical current of love, going both ways simultaneously. You don't even feel as though you are *doing* anything; you are just caught in the current, possessed by love. Sort of the way you might feel when you look into your beloved's eyes and feel you are falling in, when the love coming back at you is almost too much to bear, and the love you are feeling threatens to blow your circuits. I'd like a moment like that today with my Beloved. Well, I'd like a moment like that *this year*. I've had such moments, but they are rare.

Why are they rare? Having those moments of communion, which is a foretaste of Heaven, is up to me. It's a decision I must make; no, *the* decision I must make.

> The instant in which magnitude dawns upon you is but as far away as your desire for it. As long as you desire it not and cherish littleness instead, by so much is it far from you. By so much as you want it will you bring it nearer (T-15.IV.2:2–4).

It is nearer than my own heart, so close. This ecstasy of love, this communion with God, is actually going on right now. My right mind has never ceased to be in perfect communication with Him (T-13.XI.8). "The part of your mind in which truth abides is in constant communication with God, whether you are aware of it or not" (W-pI.49.1:2).

So all that is necessary is to decide that I want it, and it is there. I just plug in to it. What is it that prevents me from choosing it? What keeps me from letting myself fall in love with God? What holds me back? Am I willing to be in love with everyone, or am I afraid of appearing too "mooshy"? Am I afraid of being out of control? Am I afraid of being too vulnerable? What holds me back? Let me look at myself today and ask myself, "Why am I not experiencing being in Heaven right now?"

When you realize that you could just "switch over" at any instant—and that you don't!—it is a sobering moment. All of a sudden you can't blame anyone or anything for expriencing anything less than Heaven.

You recognize that you are choosing it; "I am doing this to myself" (see T-27.VIII.10:1). There is literally nothing to prevent me from experiencing the holy instant right now. Nothing but my refusal to accept it; nothing but my fear. "So we begin today considering the choice that time was made to help us make" (W-pI.138.7:1). There is no rush; we have all of time to make this choice. But why wait? Why not now?

Lesson 150—May 30

Review IV: "My mind holds only what I think with God."
(139) "I will accept Atonement for myself."
(140) "Only salvation can be said to cure."

PRACTICE SUMMARY

Purpose: To prepare for Part II of the Workbook, by concentrating on readiness for it and by reviewing the last 20 lessons in a way that will facilitate that readiness.

Longer: Two times, beginning and ending of the day, for five minutes or more.

- Open your mind, clear it of all distracting thoughts. For five minutes let this thought alone occupy it, displacing all others: "My mind holds only what I think with God."
- Read the day's two ideas. Close eyes and repeat ideas slowly, without hurry, for this is what time was made for. Let each word shine with the meaning God gave it. Receive from each idea the gift God placed in it.

Remarks: Phase 1 will be enough to set your day along the lines God planned, making it a special time of blessing for you and for the world. It will be enough to place Him in charge of all your thoughts. Your thoughts will come from more than you. They will also come from Him and tell you of His Love. Thus will you, His completion, join with Him. And He, your completion, will join with you. He thanks you for your practicing. And as your day ends, His gratitude will surround you.

Shorter: Hourly, for a quiet moment.

- Say: "My mind holds only what I think with God." Spend a quiet moment with it.
- Then repeat the day's two ideas, slowly enough to see their gifts and receive their gifts.

COMMENTARY

Accepting Atonement for myself means, to me, allowing God to release me from all kinds of guilt. Letting go of all my judgments against myself, all my diminishing self-evaluations. It means accepting that I am not my thoughts and, above all, I am not my ego. I am not what I have thought I am. I am not what I am afraid I am. Accepting the Atonement for myself means that I can look upon my own ego without condemnation, recognizing it as no more than a foolish mistake about myself that can be corrected.

When I accept Atonement for myself, I stop measuring myself against arbitrary standards and accept myself just as I am. I am able to look upon myself with love, to view myself with merciful acceptance. In the holy instant, I accept the Atonement, and to enter such a moment it is not necessary that I have no thoughts that are not pure, only that I have no thoughts that I want to keep (T-15.IV.9:1–2). I recognize that I have made mistakes, but I am willing for every mistake to be corrected, and I accept no guilt concerning those mistakes. I do not allow my mistakes to keep me from the holy instant, because the holy instant is the place those mistakes can be corrected, and their consequences undone.

This is salvation. This is the undoing of errors, the correction of mistakes.

> Salvation is undoing in the sense that it does nothing, failing to support the world of dreams and malice. Thus it lets illusions go. By not supporting them, it merely lets them quietly go down to dust (W-pII.2.3:1–3).

This is the only thing that can be said to truly cure. Anything less than this is mere alleviation of symptoms, mere shifting of form without any change in content. The root cause of guilt must be undone. "The Holy Spirit knows that all salvation is escape from guilt" (T-14.III.13:4).

To know that my mind holds only what I think with God is to escape from guilt. To know that my mind holds only what I think with God is salvation, and truly cures my ills. Atonement is God's answer to everything within my mind that appears to be other than God. It erases every thought opposed to truth and leaves me with the clean, crisp truth of my own innocence. I can bring every impure thought, every unworthy thought, every guilty thought, every thought of isolation and separateness, every thought of pain and vengeance and despair to this miraculous place of Atonement, lay it there on the altar, and watch it disappear.

> This is the shift that true perception brings: What was projected out is seen within, and there forgiveness lets it disappear. For there the altar to the Son is set, and there his Father is remembered. Here are all illusions brought to truth and laid upon the altar. What is seen outside must lie beyond forgiveness, for it seems to be forever sinful. Where is hope while sin is seen as outside? What remedy can guilt expect? But seen within your mind, guilt and forgiveness for an instant lie together, side by side, upon one altar. There at last are sickness and its single remedy joined in one healing brightness. God has come to claim His Own. Forgiveness is complete (C-4.6:1–10).

Lesson 151—May 31

"All things are echoes of the Voice for God."

PRACTICE SUMMARY

Morning/Evening: One time, for five minutes.

- Repeat idea once, slowly.
- Then watch your thoughts. Give to the Holy Spirit each thought that comes to mind. He will evaluate it, retain the elements of truth and remove the elements of illusion. Then He will give it back as a miracle which does not contradict God's Will and proclaims your wholeness. Each thought will thus take on healing power that offers its perfection to everyone.

Remarks: Purifying your thoughts will begin your ministry. For everyone will share in the thoughts He has purified. Through your transformation the world is released from guilt and learns of its sanctity.

Hourly: Remember the Holy Spirit Who restored you to sanity. Lift your resurrected mind to Him in gratitude.

COMMENTARY

The world as we see it seems to bear unrelenting witness to separation, sin, death, hatred, and the transient nature of everything. The world seen with the vision of Christ, as the Holy Spirit sees it, bears witness to the truth, to unity, holiness, life, love and the eternal nature of everything. *Everything* is echoing the Voice for God, all the time, but we do not hear it. We hear the ego's voice with relentless consistency. The two views could not be more stark in their contrast. Why do we display such a prejudice for the ego's view?

The early part of this lesson points out that the reason the world so often seems so solidly real to us is because of our underlying doubt of its reality. It asks us to look at the fact that the ego goes too far in its stubborn insistence that what our eyes and ears show us is solidly reliable. It says that, although we know very well from our experience that our senses often deceive us, and our judgments are often wide of the mark, we irrationally continue to believe them down to the last detail. We show surprise whenever we discover that what we thought was true is not, in fact, true, even though we have had this experience hundreds or thousands of times. And it asks:

> Why would you trust them [your senses] so implicitly? Why but because of underlying doubt, which you would hide with show of certainty (2:5–6).

It is like the line in Shakespeare's *Hamlet*: "The lady doth protest too much, methinks." It is the behavior of someone who is trying to shout down their doubts with protestations of absolute certainty. So, to the Holy Spirit, our very "certainty" of the world's reality is a proof of underlying doubt! We are certain even when it is unreasonable to be certain, and that is a certain evidence of hidden uncertainty.

We who study the Course are used to the idea that we project our guilt and anger onto others. Here, however, the Course introduces the idea that there is a way in which our egos project themselves onto us. The ego doubts. The ego condemns itself. The ego alone feels guilt. Only the ego is in despair. (See 5:1–6.) But it projects all of these things onto us, and tries to convince us "its evil is your own" (6:2). It plays this trick on us by showing us the world through its eyes, and introducing the things of the world as witnesses to our evil, our guilt, our doubt and despair. The ego is desperate for us to see the world as it wants us to because the ego's world is what proves to us that we are identical with the ego. For instance, it leads us to evaluate our own spiritual progress and to find ourselves wanting; it induces us to despair. Why? Because *it* [the ego] is feeling despair. It knows (without admitting it) that it is going to lose. This is why spiritual despair so often strikes after a major spiritual advance. The ego feels despair, and projects that despair onto our minds, trying to convince us the despair is *ours* rather than *its*.

This is why the ego is so insistent on convincing us of the world's reality. It needs the world to build its case.

The lesson asks us to raise all our evaluations, which we have learned from the ego, to question, and to doubt the evidence of our senses. It asks us to let the Holy Spirit be the Judge of what we are, and of everything that seems to happen to us (6:2, 6:6). If we try to judge things by ourselves, we will be deceived by our own egos, and the way in which we see ourselves and the world will become a witness to the ego's reality. If, however, we let go of our judgments and accept the judgment of the Holy Spirit, He will bear witness to our beautiful creation as God's Son. Everything we see, if we look with Him, will show us God.

Read the 11th paragraph; it describes perfectly just how the Holy Spirit accomplishes this retranslation of everything. When we give Him our thoughts, He gives them back as miracles (14:1).

Let me, then, give my thoughts to Him today. Let me not hide my thoughts from Him, nor try to alter them myself before I expose them to His sight. Let me ask Him to work His alchemy on them, to transmute the lead into gold before my eyes. That is His job. Every thought has elements of truth in it, to which we have added falsehood and illusion. The Holy Spirit strips away the false, and leaves the golden kernel of truth. He does not attack our thoughts; He purifies them. He shows "the love beyond the hate, the constancy in change, the pure in sin" (11:3). He does this with our very thoughts, and so reveals to us the gentle face of Christ as our very Self.

Lesson 152—June 1

"The power of decision is my own."

PRACTICE SUMMARY

Morning/Evening: Five minutes.

- Encourage your frightened mind with this: "The power of decision is my own. This day I will accept myself as what my Father's Will created me to be."
- Then wait in silence. In true humility give up all your arrogant self-concepts, which say that you are a guilty, fearful sinner. Give up all your self-deceptions, which comprise the ephemeral physical world you made. Give up all your frantic thoughts.
- Humbly ask your Self to reveal Himself to you, in all His mightiness, changelessness and wholeness. Lift your heart in true humility to Him Who created you like Himself in purity, power and love. His Voice will then substitute your true Self for your self-concepts and self-deceptions.

Hourly: Invite your Self with these words: "The power of decision is my own. This day I will accept myself as what my Father's Will created me to be."

COMMENTARY

The central appeal of this lesson is to get me to "accept [my] rightful place as co-creator of the universe" (8:3). It attempts, through its logical arguments, to persuade me to accept the fact that I made the world I see (6:1). "Nothing occurs but represents your wish, and nothing is omitted that you choose" (1:5).

If that is true, and I accept it, then the main thought of the lesson makes sense: "The power of decision is my own." My choice makes the world. What grants our illusion of pain, sin and death such apparent solidity is that we believe it exists outside of our power; that we are *not* responsible for it. If, however, I can accept that I made it what it is, then I can recognize the possibility of exercising the same power of choice to make it disappear. If I deny that I made it I cannot unmake it.

If, however, I recognize that I have made the world I see, I am accepting at the same time that God did *not* make it. The absurdity of the idea that God created this world is clearly stated here.

> To think that God made chaos, contradicts His will, invented opposites to truth, and suffers death to triumph over life; all this is arrogance. Humility would see at once these things are not of him (7:1–2).

If they are not of Him, they must be of me—my fabrications, the results of my power of decision, and therefore things that I can undo.

Applied to myself, these ideas mean that I must be still whole, unchanged by mistakes.

> As God created you, you must remain unchangeable, with transitory states by definition false. And that includes all shifts in feeling, alterations in conditions of the body and the mind; in all awareness and in all response" (5:1–2).

I love those words, "transitory states by definition false." If it changes, it is not real. Wow! What does that do to any concerns I might have about mood swings? About aging? About sickness? About the level of my income? ("Transitory" seems so apropos in regard to income!) How about alterations in awareness? Transitory, therefore false. Alterations in my response to the Course? Transitory, therefore false. Truth is true, and only truth is true; any and all alterations are "contradictions introduced by [me]" (4:4).

I have begun to learn that when I feel bummed out, for any reason, I can remind myself that this feeling is transitory and therefore false; nothing to be concerned about. This doesn't always immediately dispel my feeling bummed out, but it *does* prevent me from feeling guilty about feeling bummed out, or feeling anxious that something is seriously wrong with me. As a result, the negative feeling does not last as long as it used to, because I am no longer adding additional layers of self-condemnation on top of the original feeling.

Such an attitude somehow distances me from the transitory feelings or shifts in my awareness. Instead of relating *from* the feeling I begin to relate *to* it, with gentleness and merciful forgiveness. Some have expressed the difference in words by saying things like, "My body is sick," instead of, "I am sick," or, "I am experiencing a depression," instead of saying, "I am depressed." Instead of the passing thought or feeling being mistaken for "me," I am aware of "me" over here, consistent and unchanging, but experiencing this transitory state of mind. "I" am distinct from, and not identified with, the passing show of my mind. And in that situation, I can recognize: "The power of decision is my own."

Lesson 153—June 2

"In my defenselessness my safety lies."

Special Note: The following Practice Summary instructions will apply for the most part to all lessons from Lesson 153 through Lesson 200. (See Robert's *Comment on Practice* about this lesson on pages 48–49 for more details.) Only a few variations in practice are given for the next forty-eight days. Rather than reprinting the exact same instructions for the next forty-eight lessons, we will print them only once here. Bound into the book, at the back, you will find a perforated card which has, on one side, the generic instructions for Lessons 153 to 200, and on the other side, the instructions for Part II of the Workbook, which starts with Lesson 221. You can tear this card out and use it as a bookmark, so that you have the instructions to refer to every day as needed.

In the daily practice summaries, only the daily variations will be noted, and you will be referred to the "Practice Card" for the overall Practice Summary.

PRACTICE SUMMARY

Morning/Evening Quiet Time: Five minutes, at least; ten is better; fifteen even better; thirty or more, best.

Let your weakness disappear as you remember that Christ's strength abides in you. Leave dreams and fearful thoughts behind as you recognize you need no defense, for you were created unassailable. You will stand secure, certain of your safety, salvation and your holy purpose of blessing the world.

Hourly Remembrance: As the hour strikes, for more than one minute (reduce if circumstances do not permit).

Sit quietly and wait on God. Thank Him for His gifts in the previous hour. And let His Voice tell you what He wants you to do in the coming hour.

(Suggestion for 181–200) Do a short version of morning/evening exercise.

Remarks: At times the business of the world will allow you only a minute or less, or no time at all. At other times you will forget. Yet whenever you can, do your hourly remembrance.

Frequent Reminder: Through the day, remind yourself God remains beside you, supporting your weakness with His strength.

Remarks: In time you will never cease to think of God, not even for a moment, not even while busy giving salvation to the world.

Response To Temptation: Whenever you feel tempted to defend yourself, call upon God's strength, pause a moment, and hear Him say: "I am here."

Overall Remarks: Your practice will begin to be infused with the earnestness of love, keeping your mind from wandering. Do not be afraid, you will reach your goal. God's Love and strength will make sure of it, for you are His minister.

COMMENTARY

In regard to our practice, notice that this lesson presents instructions that are to be followed "for quite a while" (15:1). Specifically, the form of practice given today continues for every lesson through Lesson 170. They are given this once and not referred to again except in brief mentions; we are supposed to remember the instructions from this lesson. Notice, too, that the instructions about what we are to do in this five to thirty-minute period each day are rather vague. Mostly they are summed up as "giving our attention to the daily thought as long as possible" (15:2). We are told that our "practicing will now begin to take the earnestness of love" (20:1). The longer practice periods have become "a time to spend with God" (15:5); we enjoy His loving Presence so much that half an hour seems too short! To some degree, by this time, our practicing has switched from sessions with a drill sergeant to a rendezvous with our Lover. If that hasn't happened for us yet, it will: "There can be no doubt that you will reach your final goal" (20:3).

The lesson opens by pointing out that this world is *not* a safe place: "It is rooted in attack" (1:2–3). Peace of mind in *this* world is impossible (1:5). On every side are things that provoke us to defensiveness (2:1–2). But defenses affect not only what is outside of us; they affect ourselves. They reinforce our sense of weakness (2:4), and since they ultimately do not work (2:4), they betray us. We are betrayed by the world outside and by our own defenses within (2:5–6).

> It is as if a circle held it [the mind] fast, wherein another circle bound it and another one in that, until escape no longer can be hoped for nor obtained (3:1).

We are trapped in concentric vicious circles of attack and defense; we find ourselves unable to break out of the attack-defense cycle (3:2–3).

We do not realize how profoundly our minds are threatened by the world around us. If we try as hard as we can to conceive of someone caught deep in a frenzy of intense fear, "The sense of threat the world encourages is so much deeper, and so far beyond the frenzy and intensity of which you can conceive, that you have no idea of all the devastation it has wrought" (4:2). All of us, the Course is saying, are living in blind panic masked by a superficial act of being calm. Panic is always there, just below the surface. Think of the things that threaten us constantly, and the attention that is paid to them in our personal lives and in the media. Nuclear holocaust. Street gangs. Drunk drivers. *All* drivers. Corrupt politicians. The greedy power structure. Threatening economic collapse. Food additives, depletion of the ozone layer, vitamin-depleted foods, growth hormones in our milk, nitrates in the bacon, cholesterol, saturated fat, sugar, polluted water supplies, drought, heat waves, blizzards, floods, hurricanes, tornados, earthquakes, alien invasion, lying news media, insects in our homes, aging bodies, untrustworthy love partners or business partners, AIDS, cancer, heart disease—the list could go on and on. And we have not begun to speak of the threat of foreign invasion or economic takeover, racial animosities, or religious intolerance.

We are slaves of the world's threat (5:1). "You do not know what you do, in fear of it. You do not understand how much you have been made to sacrifice, who feel its iron grip upon your heart" (5:2–3). Try to imagine, for a moment, what it would be like to be completely *without* any and all fear concerning the things we have mentioned. If you are like me, you can't even *imagine* it. We have become so accustomed to the subliminal hum of fear! Nor do we realize how much we have sabotaged our own peace by our stance of constant defensiveness (5:4).

The choice this lesson presents to us (6:3) is between two things: the "silly game" (6:4) of defensiveness, played by tired children too sleepy to remember what they want (a bit like how I feel right now!), and the "game that happy children play" (12:1), a joyous game that teaches us that the game of fear is gone. The happy game is "salvation," or functioning as a minister of God in the world, offering the light to all our brothers. In brief, we can spend our time trying to defend ourselves, or we can drop our defenses and reach out in love to the world. Those are the only options.

The game of defensiveness is a deadly one. In defensiveness "lies madness in a form so grim that hope of sanity seems but to be an idle dream, beyond the possible" (4:2). Defenses bind us into an attack-defense cycle that never ends.

Defenselessness is based on the reality of what we are. "We need no defense because we are created unassailable" (9:1). It witnesses to our strength. As God's ministers we are protected. We need no defense *because* we are "the ones who are among the chosen ones of God, by His election and [our] own as well" (10:6).

To choose defenselessness is to choose the strength of Christ, instead of our own weakness. To reach out to heal, instead of contracting inward in self-defense, puts us in an unassailable position. Our true safety lies, not in protecting what we have, but in giving it away, because this firmly identifies us with the Christ.

Lesson 154—June 3

"I am among the ministers of God."

PRACTICE SUMMARY

Generic Instructions: Morning and evening times, hourly remembrance, and frequent reminders in between. See Lesson 153 or Practice Card, and Robert's practice comments on pages 48–49.

Purpose: To give what you have received, and so recognize that it is yours. To give the Holy Spirit your voice, hands and feet.

Morning/Evening Quiet Time:

- Say: "I am among the ministers of God, and I am grateful that I have the means by which to recognize that I am free."
- Let the world recede from your mind, as your mind lights up with the realization that these holy words are true. Thus will the gifts of God spring to your awareness, so you can give them.

COMMENTARY

As I see it, this lesson has two main things to say to me:

1) My function on earth is to be a minister (or messenger) of God, and the specific form that function takes is determined, not by me, but by the Holy Spirit.

2) As a messenger, my function is to receive God's messages for myself, and then to give them away, as directed by the Holy Spirit. By giving away the messages I will recognize and understand the messages I have received.

The Holy Spirit knows me to the core. He knows my individual strengths and weaknesses; He knows the "larger plan" I cannot possibly know (1:5); He knows how best to use my particular strengths, "where they can best be applied, for what, to whom, and when" (2:2). Therefore, it is unwise to try to evaluate myself or to direct my own functioning in this world, and far wiser to place myself in His hands. Because of this, I will "choose no roles that are not given [me] by His authority" (7:3). He chooses my function for me, tells me what it is, gives me strength to do it and to succeed in everything related to it (3:2).

A major part of the training program in the Workbook is learning to hear His Voice and to submit to Its authority. Learning to hear His Voice isn't something that comes without any effort. Indeed, it takes effort and great willingness (T-5.II.3:9–10). I may feel at first that I don't know how to hear His Voice, but that is *exactly* why I need this practice. I don't know, as I begin, how to tell the Voice of the Holy Spirit apart from my own ego's voice; I need training in that discernment, and some of it will be trial and error. But if I will follow the instructions in this book, I will learn.

The second point is really an encouragement to take up the function given me by God, which in a generic sense is to be His messenger. "He needs our voice that He may speak through us. He needs our hands to hold His messages, and carry them to those whom He appoints. He needs our feet to bring us where He wills, that those who wait in misery may be at last delivered. And He needs our will united with His Own, that we may be the true receivers of the gifts He gives" (11:2–5). Clearly, He directs me very specifically, choosing where I go physically, whom I speak to, and what I say. Yet the main thing is that I accept this overall function of "messenger" for my life; if I accept that, the specifics will follow.

There is a three-step process clearly delineated in this lesson:

Receive — Give — Recognize

First, I receive the message for myself, accept it and apply it to my own life. I accept the Atonement for myself, seeing that the appearance of guilt within me is an illusion, and recognizing the innocence it hides. I accept my acceptance with God. I let go of my false and guilty self-concept.

Second, I give this message to those to whom the Holy Spirit sends me. This can be with words, with actions, or simply with the attitude of mercy and acceptance I show to those I meet. I give the message I have received. I show them the mercy God has shown to me. I see in them what I have begun to see in myself.

Third, as a result of giving, I recognize the reality of what I have received. "No one can receive and understand he has received until he gives" (8:6). Giving away the message cements it and validates it in my own mind. "We will not recognize what we receive until we give it" (12:1).

The second step is an essential part of the whole process. Without giving away the message, the cycle cannot be completed; my own recognition of salvation cannot become complete. It is not enough simply to receive the messages of God. "Yet another part of your appointed task is yet to be accomplished" (9:4). The messages must be given away, shared, in order to be fully received. I must take up my function as the messenger of God if I am to understand what I have been given.

Notice that the practice instructions are adapted from Lesson 153, where we were told "we practice in a form we will maintain for quite a while" (W-pI.153.15:1). These instructions will be followed until new ones are given in Lesson 171 (Review V), and apply to Lessons 181–200 as well.

Lesson 155—June 4

"I will step back and let Him lead the way."

PRACTICE SUMMARY

Generic Instructions: Morning and evening times, hourly remembrance, and response to temptation. See Lesson 153 (page 78) or the Practice Card, and also Robert's practice comments on pages 48–49.
Purpose: To give what you have received, and so recognize that it is yours. To give the Holy Spirit your voice, hands and feet.
Morning/Evening Quiet Time:
Practice gladly with this thought: "I will step back and let Him lead the way, for I would walk along the road to Him." Think of Him a while and let Him tell you of His limitless Love and trust in you.
Hourly Remembrance:
Practice gladly with this thought: "I will step back and let Him lead the way, for I would walk along the road to Him." Think of Him a while and let Him tell you of His limitless Love and trust in you.

COMMENTARY

"There is a way of living in this world that is not here, although it seems to be" (1:1). And to this way of living we all aspire. The remarkable thing about the Course is that it offers what might be called a middle way between renouncing the world and diving into it. Many, perhaps the majority, of spiritual seekers make the mistake of thinking that a spiritual life must somehow look different. Some dress differently; some abjure the modern conveniences; some find spirituality in vegetables; some fill their homes with incense; some live in poverty, or apart from normal worldly concourse.

This lesson is one of the clearest statements in the Course that a good Course student does not change appearance—except that perhaps he smiles more frequently. There are spiritual paths that demand a changed appearance—a shaved head, difference in dress—and this is not to put down these other paths. But they are not the way of the Course. One of the more difficult lessons for students of the Course, in my observation, seems to be learning to be normal. A true student of the Course is like anyone else, so much so that "those who have not yet perceived the way will...believe that you are like them, as you were before" (1:5).

Yet we are different. The difference is inward; we have stepped back, taken our hands off the controls of our lives, and we are letting our Inner Guide lead the way to God. Everyone, including ourselves, came to this world by choice, "seeking for a place where they can be illusions, and avoid their own reality" (2:2). But we have discovered that we cannot escape our reality, and we have chosen to place diminishing importance on the illusions, and to follow the truth. We have taken up our function, and we recognize that we are here now, not for ourselves alone, but to serve those around us as we serve ourselves (5:4). We walk to God, and we lead the world to God with us (12:1; 13:1). We step back, and let Him lead the way.

Lesson 156—June 5

"I walk with God in perfect holiness."

PRACTICE SUMMARY

Generic Instructions: Morning and evening times, hourly remembrance, and response to temptation. See Lesson 153 (page 78) or the Practice Card, and also Robert's practice comments on pages 48–49.
Morning/Evening Quiet Time: Repeat today's idea, and reflect on it as long as possible. Be aware that you spend the time in the Presence of your Companion.

COMMENTARY

"Ideas leave not their source" (1:3). When a mind thinks an idea, that idea stays in the mind; it does not become a separate thing, apart from the mind that thought it. And I am a thought of God; therefore, I cannot possibly be apart from Him. I have thought I was separate. Indeed, much of the time I still think and behave as though I were separate from God. But I am not; I cannot be.

To be apart from God is impossible. God *is* Being; He is Existence. Whatever exists is in Him. He is Life; whatever lives, lives in Him. "He is what your life is. Where you are He is. There is one life. That life you share with Him. Nothing can be apart from Him and live" (2:5–9).

God is also holy. If God is holy, and I am in him, I am holy, too. "What lives is holy as Himself" (3:3). Therefore, "I walk with God in perfect holiness." I could "no more be sinful than the sun could choose to be of ice" (3:3). This is not a feeble hope; it is a fact. It is the truth about me, and about you, and about everyone who lives.

Yet we have taught ourselves that this truth is not true. It fascinates me to see what contradictory ideas arise in my mind when I repeat this statement. It would be a useful exercise to write today's idea as an affirmation, ten times or more, and in a second column, write down the response of the mind to this idea. You might get things like this:

"I walk with God in perfect holiness." "I'm not so holy." "I walk with God in perfect holiness." "I have a long way to go to be holy." "I walk with God in perfect holiness." "I don't like being called holy." "I walk with God in perfect holiness." "Most of the time I walk alone."

And so on. What's interesting about such an exercise is that it reveals the train of thought that dominates my mind, that opposes today's idea and constantly counteracts it. It is this chain of negative thought that blocks the light in me. All the responses are some form of the idea, "I am a sinner," which I would probably vehemently deny that I believe, if anyone asked me. And yet, faced with the affirmation that I walk with God in perfect holiness, these forms of that idea arise "spontaneously." Where are they coming from? Obviously from a backlog of very careful mind-training by the ego, very effective brainwashing, so well done that I don't even realize my mind has been programmed.

Do I believe I am a sinner? "You have wasted many, many years on just this foolish thought" says the lesson (7:1). Yes, indeed I do. But when I am made aware of these negative thoughts about myself, I can let them go. I can "step back," and stop accusing myself. When I do, "The light in you steps forward and encompasses the world" (6:2).

How can we counter the programming of the ego? One way, clearly recommended by this lesson, is explicit counter-programming. It recommends that 1000 times a day we ask ourselves the question, "Who walks with me?" And then, that we answer it by hearing the Voice for God, saying for us:

> I walk with God in perfect holiness. I light the world, I light my mind and all the minds which God created one with me (8:5–6).

Certainty of our holiness does not come with a single repetition of today's idea. We need thousands of repetitions. We need to keep repeating it until we *are* certain of it. If we took this literally, repeating the idea 1000 times would mean repeating it a little more often than once per minute, all day long, assuming we are awake sixteen hours. That's a lot of repetition!

Let me today see the "quaint absurdity" (6:4) of the idea of sin, and laugh at the thought. Let me begin to absorb the wonderful teaching of the Course that sin "is a foolish thought, a silly dream, not frightening, ridiculous perhaps" (6:5). And let the wonder of it steal over me: "I walk with God in perfect holiness."

Lesson 157—June 6

"Into His Presence would I enter now."

PRACTICE SUMMARY

Generic Instructions: Morning and evening times, hourly remembrance, and response to temptation. See Lesson 153 (page 78) or the Practice Card, and also Robert's practice comments on pages 48–49.
Purpose: To usher in the experience of Heaven. This will shed a light on what you have learned and prepare you for what you will learn. A holy day, a special time of promise, a crucial turning point in the curriculum, the beginning of a new journey. It will transform your mind, usher in your ministry and sanctify your body. Your only purpose now will be to bring to the world the vision that reflects your experience. And you will be given power to touch everyone with that vision.
Morning/Evening Quiet Time:

Let your Self direct your practicing. Let today's idea light your mind and bring it to a state of quiet anticipation and joy. Your mind will then go to the highest reaches of learning, to the vision of Christ's shining face. And then you will transcend even that. You will forget the world and walk into eternity a while.
Remarks: You have come far enough to experience this today. And, as you faithfully practice each daily lesson, you will learn to experience this more and more. As a result, all goals but this will fade away. Each time you return from this experience, the world will be closer to the light, and you will see the light more sure and distinct. Eventually, you will not return in your current form.
Hourly Remembrance: Sit quietly and wait on Christ.

COMMENTARY

Experience and Vision

Today I'd like to share some thoughts based mainly on Lesson 157, but with some references to 158 also. This lesson introduces a series of lessons designed to lead us into the holy instant, which is a major goal of the Workbook. From this point on, "Every lesson, faithfully rehearsed, brings you more swiftly to this holy place" (3:3).

The Course talks here of both an *experience* and of *vision* which results from the experience. The holy instant contains a moment of knowledge—something beyond all perception—from which we return with the vision of Christ in our minds, which we can offer to everyone.

The experience spoken of here is simply entering the Presence of God. It is "a different kind of feeling and awareness" (1:4) in which we "learn to feel the joy of life" (1:6). It is called elsewhere the holy instant. Lesson 157 calls it "a touch of Heaven" (3:1) and a moment in which we are left to our Self. It is an instant in which "the world is quietly forgot, and Heaven is remembered for a while" (6:3). We leave time for a moment and walk into eternity (3:2). It is not something we do ourselves; the Holy Spirit, the "Giver of the happy dreams of life" and "Translator of perception into truth," will lead us (8:2).

The vision spoken of is the result of the experience. This is not "a vision," something that is seen, but "vision," a way of seeing. We are not talking of some trance state, some appearance within our minds of mystical sights. We are talking about a different way of seeing the world, a different mechanism of sight, something other than the physical senses. Eastern religion might talk about opening the Third Eye to indicate the same sort of thing.

In experiencing the holy instant, we have awakened a different way of seeing. That new sort of vision does not disappear when we "come back to the world," so to speak (7:1). It is only a figure of speech to say we come back. We never left. Or perhaps better, since Heaven is what is real and this world is the illusion, we never came here at all. What "comes back" with us, into the dream, is the remembrance of God and Heaven, the remembrance of what we saw in that holy instant. We continue to see glimpses of it beyond the sight of the world, seeing the "real world" beyond the world, and beyond that, Heaven.

Each (apparently separate) holy instant we experience strengthens this new vision, this new mechanism of seeing. This is the purpose of the Workbook's recommendations for daily morning and evening periods of meditation; they are practice sessions, exercises to develop our new vision. We are meant, of course, to exercise this vision constantly during the day, to have repeated holy instants all day long. If we compare this to learning a language, the meditation sessions are like language labs and grammar studies. The concentrated language exercises are not an end in themselves but are meant to prepare us and improve our speech and understanding as we go out and actually use the language. Likewise, meditation is not an end in itself. It is an exercise to strengthen spiritual vision, but the purpose is to go out into daily life and begin using that new vision as often as possible.

Lesson 157 says, "We cannot give experience like this directly. Yet it leaves a vision in our eyes which we can offer everyone" (6:2–3). I can't give you a holy instant directly. I can tell you about it, but you have to do the work yourself and have the experience yourself.

What I can give you or offer to you is the new vision, the new way of seeing the world. The vision we can all teach, as fledgling teachers of God, is that of forgiveness and love within the world. I can teach you that it is possible to see the invisible beyond the visible, to see the undimmed Truth behind the clouds of doubt, fear and defense. I can teach you to "see no one as a body. Greet him as the Son of God he is, acknowledging that he is one with you in holiness" (158.8:3). By seeing you without guilt I teach you that seeing without guilt is possible.

And in willingness to practice the vision, williingness to ask to be shown a different way of seeing, the experience of the holy instant comes.

Lesson 158—June 7

"Today I learn to give as I receive."

PRACTICE SUMMARY

Generic Instructions: Morning and evening times, hourly remembrance, and response to temptation. See Lesson 153 (page 78) or the Practice Card, and also Robert's practice comments on pages 48–49.
Purpose: To practice seeing with the eyes of Christ. To give the knowledge you have received by giving Christ's vision to your brothers, and thus letting that vision look on you as well.

COMMENTARY

This lesson has a lot of profound metaphysics in it, particularly the stuff about time. If you'd like to dig into the Course's concept of time, a terrific starting place is Ken Wapnick's book, "A Vast Illusion: Time in *A Course in Miracles*." I can't write a book tonight and you probably don't want to read one right now! So I'm going to skip over most of that stuff.

The practical point this lesson is trying to make is that "knowledge," which lies in the sphere of Heaven, is outside the scope of this Course. We *all* received knowledge when we were created; every living thing knows, inherently, that it is still connected to its Source: "a mind, in Mind and purely mind, sinless forever, wholly unafraid because you were created out of Love" (1:2). It may seem to us that this is something we do *not* have, and that it is this we are trying to give to others and to receive for ourselves. But we can't give it because everyone already has it. It exists outside of time entirely. The point in time at which the experience of this knowledge reveals itself to us is already determined, by our own minds (2:9). When it happens, it will happen.

Within time—which is an illusion—what we can give, and receive, is forgiveness. Forgiveness is the gift that reflects true knowledge "in a way so accurate its image shares its unseen holiness" (11:1–2). What we can give is a vision of sinlessness, "Christ's vision." We can look past the body and see a light; look past what can be touched and see an idea; look past the mistakes and fears in our brothers and sisters, and see their inherent purity. We can greet one another and in each one, "see him as the Son of God he is, acknowledging that he is one with you in holiness" (8:4).

We are not giving knowledge. When we meet someone, we can give them our vision of themselves as sinless. In the way that we perceive them, they can find a new perception of themselves, one they have not found on their own. As they respond to our merciful vision, they will reflect that vision back to us, enabling us to perceive the Love of God within ourselves. When we forgive another, we have simultaneously forgiven our own sins, because "in your brother you but see yourself" (10:3).

We cannot know when revelation of truth, the experience of our reality, will come to us. The time is set; the drama is being played out; there is not one step we take only by chance (3:1–3). And yet, each act of forgiveness brings the day nearer. Our concern, then, is not with the final experience, but with the practice of vision, seeing with the eyes of Christ. This is something we can attain; this is something we can do something about. And we can do so *today*. Right now.

"This can be taught; and must be taught by all who would achieve it" (8:1). The way to learn the vision of Christ is to give it. The way to achieve the vision of ourselves as Christ sees us is to practice seeing others with His eyes. We give it to have it. This is the whole plan of the Course.

Lesson 159—June 8

"I give the miracles I have received."

PRACTICE SUMMARY

Generic Instructions: Morning and evening times, hourly remembrance, and response to temptation. See Lesson 153 (page 78) or the Practice Card, and also Robert's practice comments on pages 48–49.
Purpose: To receive the miracle of Christ's vision by opening His storehouse in your mind, and then by giving His miracles and vision away.
Morning/Evening Quiet Time: Open the storehouse of your mind and receive the miracle of Christ's vision.

COMMENTARY

You might notice that today's lesson title is almost the same as yesterday's: "Today I learn to give as I receive." There is definitely a commonality of thought that runs through these two lessons, even extending two lessons back. They all talk of Christ's vision. They are all presenting a picture of the holy instant as a key part of our spiritual practice, although that term is not specifically mentioned in every lesson.

The general picture being presented is of our ongoing spiritual practice. It is this: We enter frequently into a holy instant. There, we experience a touch of eternity or Heaven, a taste of the knowledge of the truth. While we cannot carry this experience back with us to the world, we can carry back what that experience is like, translated into perception; this is called "the vision of Christ," which is manifested in forgiveness.

In this lesson, the holy instant is only hinted at by such phrases as, "Let us an instant dream with Him" (10:6), or, "Receive them now by opening the storehouse of your mind, where they are laid" (2:5). The Holy Instant is the "treasure house" we come to, the place in which we receive the gifts of Christ's vision. We must receive before we can give.

But we cannot recognize, or become fully aware of, what we have received until we give it away: "To give is how to recognize you have received. It is the proof that what you have is yours" (1:7–8). The extension of Christ's vision is an integral part of the plan of salvation presented by the Course. It is what brings us to certainty. This is quite similar to the principle taught by AA, that you stay sober by helping someone else to stay sober. Here,

> You understand that you are healed when you give healing. You accept forgiveness as accomplished in yourself when you forgive (2:1–2).

It is only as we bring the "lilies" of forgiveness from the holy instant, where we received them, and distribute them into the world that we truly know we are forgiven. It is in giving away miracles that we receive them.

Father, help me today to realize that I am rich. The storehouse of my mind is filled with miracles. I can come to this storehouse and, in this holy instant, receive them. You entrust them to me for the giving. Let me pause often today, to meet here with You, and then carry these treasures forth to offer them to the world. This is my whole purpose in life; this is why I am here.

Lesson 160—June 9

"I am at home. Fear is the stranger here."

PRACTICE SUMMARY

Generic Instructions: Morning and evening times, hourly remembrance, and response to temptation. See Lesson 153 (page 78) or the Practice Card, and also Robert's practice comments on pages 48–49.
Morning/Evening Quiet Time:
- Ask your Father: "Who is the stranger here?"
- Hear His Voice quietly assure you that you are not a stranger to your Father nor He to you, that you will always remain at one with Him, that no stranger can separate whom God has joined as one. Welcome the Christ Who has come to search the world for you who belong to God. Offer thanks to Him.

Response To Temptation:
- When tempted to be afraid, repeat idea or say: "This is my home. Here I belong, and will not leave because a madman says I must."
- When tempted to deny a brother and see him as a stranger, remember you will thus see your Self as a stranger. Instead, accept the gift of Christ's vision.

COMMENTARY

Fear in this lesson is virtually synonymous with "ego." The picture being given is that we have invited fear, personified as a stranger, into our house, and the stranger has taken over and declared that he is us. He has taken over our identity almost completely. And the insane part of it all is that we have gone along with the stranger. We have accepted that this stranger is really us, and we have given our home over to him completely. We have been dispossessed.

Who is the stranger? You, or the ego? It is so easy, when thoughts of fear occupy our minds, to believe that the fear is us. The anger is us. The loneliness is us. The sense of helplessness is us. We have habituated ourselves to identifying with our thoughts and feelings of fear; we believe they are us. The thrust of this lesson is that all of these manifestations of fear are an interloper, not a genuine part of us at all. You are not the ego; the ego is not you.

Stephen Levine, in several of his books, talks about relating *to* our fear rather than relating *from* it. The distinction he is making is between identifying with the fear (relating from it) or distinguishing our self from it (relating to it). When I relate from my fear, I am in its grips. The fear runs me; the fear is me. When I relate to my fear, however, I can look on it with dispassionate mercy. I can react to it with mercy, and heal instead of go into panic. It is the difference between saying, "I am afraid," and saying, "I am having thoughts of fear" or "I am experiencing fear." My thoughts are not me. I am the thinker who is thinking the thoughts, but I am not the thoughts.

When we can separate ourselves from the fear we feel, we already have identified with our true Self. Our Self is certain of Itself, and it operates to heal our minds, to call us home. As we give this Self welcome in our minds, we remember who we are.

Yet this new vision of ourselves, of necessity, includes everyone. It is as though God were offering us a pair of glasses and saying, "If you put these on, you will see your true Self." But when we discover that, in putting them on, we see not only ourselves in a new light, but everyone, we rebel. We want to see ourselves as innocent, but we are unwilling to see everyone that way. If we refuse to see those around us as innocent, we will put down the glasses, refuse the vision of Christ, and we will not be able to recognize ourselves (10:5). "You will not remember Him [God] until you look on all as He does" (10:4).

When thoughts of fear enter my mind today, let me recognize that they are the stranger, the interloper, and that I am the one who is at home—not fear. Fear does not belong. I do not need to accept it in my mind. But let me not fight against it; let me look on my own thoughts of fear with compassion and understanding, recognizing them as merely a mistake, and not a sin. There is no guilt in feeling fear, or there need not be. I can step back from these thoughts, step back into my Self, and see them as the illusions that they are. I can look upon myself with love. And from this same place of merciful awareness, I see all my brothers in the same light: caught in fear, mistaking the fear for themselves, and needing, not judgment and attack, but forgiveness, kindness, and mercy.

Lesson 161—June 10

"Give me your blessing, holy Son of God."

PRACTICE SUMMARY

Generic Instructions: Morning and evening times, hourly remembrance, and response to temptation. See Lesson 153 (page 78) or the Practice Card, and also Robert's practice comments on pages 48–49.
Purpose: To take a stand against our anger, that our fears may be removed and replaced by love.
Morning/Evening Quiet Time:

- Select one brother as a specific symbol for all brothers.
- Picture him as clearly as you can. See his face, hands, feet, clothing. Watch him smile and make his familiar gestures.
- Then realize that what you are seeing blocks the vision of your savior, the Christ in him, who can forgive all your sins and free you from crucifixion.
- Ask him to set you free. Say: "Give me your blessing, holy Son of God. I would behold you with the eyes of Christ, and see my perfect sinlessness in you."
- The Christ in him will answer you, for He will hear God's Voice in you calling on Him. Look on him whom you have seen as a specific body, a symbol of fear, and realize that Christ has come to you.

Remarks: These words are the Holy Spirit's answer. They have power to bring salvation, carry you past the world and on to Heaven.
Response To Temptation: Use the idea *instantly*, whenever you are tempted to perceive a brother as a symbol of your fear, justifying your anger and attack. And he will be instantly tranformed from seeming devil into the Christ.

COMMENTARY

[Today's comments are something I wrote several years back while I was working as a computer consultant in New York City. On this particular day, I had expected to be able to work from home, via modem, but my client had insisted I come into the office. This threw off my plans for a long "quiet time." The comments that follow were what came to me as I read over the lesson.]

"Today we...take a stand against our anger, that our fears may disappear and offer room to love" (1:1). How "coincidental" that I begin this lesson with flares of anger at having to rush off to work! When a brother or a circumstance seems to cause anger in me, instead of listening to the ego and agreeing that the brother or circumstance is the cause of my anger, let me see that the brother is giving me a blessing by revealing to me that I am angry, that I have dropped the hand of Jesus.

Think about it logically for a moment. If I am totally connected to the love of God in my heart, nothing will be able to disturb my peace. If something comes along that does (seemingly) disturb my peace, something must have happened beforehand. I must have disconnected from God's love first, in order to react as I do. That something, then, instead of causing my upset, is merely revealing it to me. I can therefore see my brother's action, or the circumstance, as a blessing, a message from God, a lesson God would have me learn.

"Complete abstraction is the natural condition of the mind" (2:1). Abstraction is the concern with content rather than form. It separates the inherent qualities or properties of something from the actual physical object to which they belong. The natural state of mind considers content "apart from concrete existence" (American Heritage Dictionary).

Part of the mind, says Jesus here, has become concrete and specific rather than abstract. It sees fragments of the whole, rather than the whole. This is the only way we could see "the world." "The purpose of all seeing is to show you what you wish to see" (2:5). If I am seeing something that "makes me" angry or upset, it is because I wish to see it. The mind, dealing in the abstract, has already separated from the love of God (or thinks it has, or wishes to, since that separation is inherently impossible). Therefore, it splinters reality, sees specific forms that seem to justify its separation, upset and anger. It creates illusions that seemingly give valid reasons for being upset.

It accomplishes this only by seeing fragments instead of the Whole. If I could see the whole picture, as God does, including things I cannot even imagine from my limited perspective, I would never be upset. I have made up those specifics. Since I have made them up, and am immersed in specifics that were made for the purpose of justifying my separation from God, "now it is specifics we must use in practicing" (3:1–2). The Holy Spirit will take the specific circumstances I have made as an attack on God and use them to bring me back. How?

> We give them to the Holy Spirit, that He may employ them for a purpose which is different from the one we gave to them. Yet He can use but what we made... (3:3–4)

(In other words, all we have to work with are the specifics we've made up, so He will use them.)

> ...to teach us from a different point of view, so we can see a different use in everything (3:4).

"The mind that taught itself to think specifically can no longer grasp abstraction in that sense that it is all-encompassing" (4:7). Ideas like "All minds are joined" and "One brother is every brother" mean absolutely nothing to us! We cannot grasp them. These abstract statements simply don't help us, immersed in the illusion as we are.

We cling to the specifics, to symbols like the body, because our egos want fear, and that is the only way fear can seem real. There is no reality to fear itself, but the symbol of fear can seem very real. So we focus on the symbols, the specifics, the body. We feel limited by our own body, and by other bodies; we see bodies as attacking us.

What I see, when I see a brother as a body attacking me, is my own fear external to myself, poised to attack (paragraph 8). We tend to think that when we project fear, we see people who are afraid; not so, what we see are people who seem to be *making us* afraid. We see a monster that "shrieks in wrath, and claws the air in frantic hope it can reach to its maker and devour him" (8:4). When I am upset and angry at my client for "forcing me" to come to in to the office, that external specific is actually revealing to me my own fear of God's love! It is giving me the opportunity to see beyond the apparent attack and to ask him for a blessing, to show me my own perfect sinlessness.

If I allow the Holy Spirit to show me my brother as he is, instead of how my fear has made him, what I see will be so awesome that I will hardly be able to keep from kneeling at his feet in adoration (9:3). And yet what he is, I am, and so I will, instead of kneeling, take his hand (9:4).

I call upon the Christ in him [my client] to bless me. I am seeing only a symbol of my own fear of God. I bring that fear to the Holy Spirit now. And as I do, I begin to feel a spark of true gratitude to my brother for offering me this salvation from fear. I feel the resentment about having to commute into the city melting away. This, too, is a lesson, and a very good one. Thank You, Jesus, for this lesson. And thank you, my brother.

Lesson 162—June 11

"I am as God created me."

PRACTICE SUMMARY

Generic Instructions: Morning and evening times, hourly remembrance, and response to temptation. See Lesson 153 (page 78) or the Practice Card, and also Robert's practice comments on pages 48–49.
Purpose: To accept the perfect holiness that is your right, to recognize the Son of God. And through doing so to bring this acceptance and recognition to everyone.
Morning/Evening Quiet Time:
You need no other words to guide your practicing than today's idea. For these words are mighty and by themselves can change your mind into a treasure house where God's gifts are stored and from which they are given to the world.

COMMENTARY

For the third time we encounter as the main thought of a lesson what may be the single most repeated thought in the Course. (The first two lessons were 94 and 110; the idea was featured in Lesson 93 as well.) The phrase "as God created" occurs 105 times in the Course. We will see it as a focus of our Workbook review period in another twenty lessons, 201–220.

Why is this idea so important and repeated so often? "This single thought, held firmly in the mind, would save the world" (1:1). In the Text, our entire spiritual journey is characterized in terms of this idea: "You but emerge from an illusion of what you are to the acceptance of yourself as God created you" (T-24.II.14:5). If these statements are true, it is reason enough to memorize this idea and repeat it over and over until it becomes part of our pattern of thought. We might say that the entire Course is aimed at nothing more, and nothing less, than bringing us to the point where we hold this thought firmly in our minds.

In paragraph 4 our practice for the day is described as a very simple practice. All we need are the words of the main idea: "They need no thoughts beyond themselves to change the mind of him who uses them" (4:2). The change of mind the Course aims at is simply the acceptance of ourselves as God created us. By focusing on this thought, meditating on it, repeating it, and chewing it over in our minds, we accelerate this change of mind. "And thus you learn to think with God. Christ's vision has restored your sight by salvaging your mind" (4:4–5).

In Lesson 93, there was a useful addition to the words that helped clarify their meaning for me:

> Salvation requires the acceptance of but one thought;—you are as God created you, not what you made of yourself. Whatever evil you may think you

> did, you are as God created you. Whatever mistakes you made, the truth about you is unchanged. Creation is eternal and unalterable (W-pI.93.7:1–4).

We are not what we made of ourselves. Our mistakes have not changed the truth about us. That is what accepting this idea means: the recognition that nothing we have done has been able to alter our relationship to God in the slightest, nor to change our nature, given us by God in creation. Our most shameful acts, the thoughts we would never want exposed to the world, have, none of them, changed God's creation in the slightest. There is no reason for guilt, no cause to shrink from God in fear; our imagined "sins" have had no effect. We are still safe, and complete, and healed, and whole.

How are we to use this thought? "Holy indeed is he who makes these words his own; arising with them in his mind, recalling them throughout the day, at night bringing them with him as he goes to sleep" (3:1). It reminds me of the words written about the words of God in the Old Testament: "And thou shalt teach them diligently unto thy children, and shalt talk of them when thou sittest in thine house, and when thou walkest by the way, and when thou liest down, and when thou risest up" (Deuteronomy 6:7). In other words, make them a part of your entire life, especially on rising in the morning and when going to bed.

To acknowledge that, "I am as God created me," is to recognize the Son of God. It is to be free of guilt. It is to know the innocence of every living thing. It is to acknowledge God as perfect Creator. It is to release the past. It is to forgive the world. In these words is everything we need: "I am as God created me."

Lesson 163—June 12

"There is no death. The Son of God is free."

PRACTICE SUMMARY

Generic Instructions: Morning and evening times, hourly remembrance, and response to temptation. See Lesson 153 (page 78) or the Practice Card, and also Robert's practice comments on pages 48–49.
Purpose: To make no compromise with death; to take a stand against every form of it; to look past it and see the life beyond. And thus to release its worshippers by showing them that death is an illusion.
Morning/Evening Quiet Time: Begin with the prayer, in which you ask to receive Christ's vision, and affirm that you abide in Heaven at one with God, and accept His Thought and His Will as yours.

COMMENTARY

When the Course says, "There is no death," it is not talking about the death of the body. In fact, elsewhere it states that the body does not die, for the simple reason that it never has lived (T-28.VI.2:4; T-6.V(A).1:4). To talk of physical immortality and to base it on ACIM is foolishness. How could what never lives live forever?

"Death," says the lesson, "is a thought" (1:1). Not an event in the physical world, but a thought. In its simplest form it is the thought, "Life ends." It is from this root thought that many different forms spring forth. Sadness is the thought of death. Fear is the thought of death. Anxiety is the thought of death. Lack of trust is the thought of death. Concern for the body is the thought of death. Even "all forms in which the wish to be as you are not" are really variants on the thought of death (1:2). My concern with my body and wishing to lose weight is a veiled form of a death thought. Part of the motivation to avoid being overweight is to "live longer." But if the body is not alive at all, what are we talking about?

Even the apparently spiritual thought of desiring to leave the body behind and to be free of it is a way of seeing physical death as some sort of salvation. "The body is a wholly neutral thing" (W-pII.294). It is neither a holy thing, destined to exist forever if we become sufficiently spiritual, nor is it a trap, prison, or real limitation on spirit. Being in a body does not keep me from being completely spiritual. Being in a body does not make me an ego. Rather, it is being an ego that makes the body!

In the world's way of thinking, death is the only certainty. Everything else is "too quickly lost however hard to gain" (3:1). As the Preacher of Ecclesiastes cries, "Vanity of vanities! All is vanity, futility and striving after wind" (Ec. 1:2,14, paraphrased). Wealth, luxury, family, friends, nothing satisfies, and nothing lasts forever. Death takes them all in the end. Death never fails to triumph over life.

The Course says that to accept this thought system—which we all do to a greater or lesser degree, and far more extensively than any of us recognize—is to proclaim the opposite of God (death) "as lord of all creation, stronger than God's Will for life" (4:3). Each apparent triumph of death is a witness that God is dead (5:1–3). He Whose Will is life could not stop this death, so He must be dead. And as we watch the deadly drama, we "whisper fearfully that it is so" (5:4).

We may respond by saying we don't want to believe it. We don't want to worship death; we don't want to die; we want to believe in God and believe in life. In fact, however, we do want to believe in death, at least in certain forms of it. We've already pointed out that anger is a death thought. In anger, we want something or someone to "go away" or "not be," which in its essence means we want them to die. We actually hold on to guilt because we think guilt is useful; we are afraid that without guilt everything would be chaos. Guilt or condemnation is a judgment that some certain aspect of things does not deserve to exist. It is a wish for death, death of part of ourselves or of another. And certainly we hold on tenaciously to "the wish to be as you are not" (1:2).

We try to compromise. We want to hold on to certain death thoughts while letting others go. The lesson says this is impossible. You can't "select a few [forms of the death thought] you would not cherish and avoid, while still believing in the rest" (6:1). Why? Because "...death is total. Either all things die, or else they live and cannot die. No compromise is possible" (6:2–4).

If death exists at all, it totally contradicts life. It is life's opposite; surely that is clear. The lesson says, "What contradicts one thought entirely can not be true, unless its opposite is proven false" (6:5). In concrete terms we could paraphrase these words in this way: Death contradicts life entirely, and cannot be true unless life is proven false. The reverse is also true: Life contradicts death entirely, and cannot be true, unless death is proven false.

If God is the Will to life, how can death exist? Something must be there contradicting His Will, something more powerful than God. Anything more powerful than what we call God must actually be God, the real God. So if we are saying death is real in any form—physical death, or anger, or envy, or fear—we are saying death is God, and the God of Life is dead.

Here again we find an echo of the profound words from the Text's Introduction: "Nothing real can be threatened. Nothing unreal exists." Life cannot be threatened. Death does not exist.

"The idea of the death of God is so preposterous that even the insane have difficulty in believing it" (7:1). It is absurd to believe that God died! Yet, the point the Course is making here is that this is what we *must* believe if we believe in death in any form.

"Death's worshippers may be afraid" (8:1). He's speaking about us, about you and me. We are afraid of death, let's be honest about that.

> And yet, can thoughts like these be fearful? If they saw that it is only this which they believe, they would be instantly released (8:2–3).

In other words, can the thought that God died be fearful? It is so patently absurd, so utterly ridiculous, so absolutely, obviously untrue. If we saw that this is what we are believing, when we believe in death in any of its myriad forms, we would be instantly released. We would laugh at ourselves!

Belief in death is just another form of the "tiny, mad idea" at which "the Son of God remembered not [i.e. forgot] to laugh" (T-27.VIII.6:2). If we truly saw that worry about physical death, sadness, anger, envy, anxiety, fear, doubt, mistrust, concern for bodies, and the desire for change are all just forms of the idea, "God is dead," we would laugh at them! We would see that all of this is no big deal, all of it is just a silly idea that is downright impossible and therefore nothing to worry about at all.

And so,

> There is no death, and we renounce it now in every form, for their salvation [those around us who believe in death] and our own as well. God made not death. Whatever form it takes must therefore be illusion. This is the stand we take today. And it is given us to look past death, and see the life beyond (8:5–9).

No one is saying this is easy. In the illusion of time it does not happen overnight. In practice, it takes countless repetitions, constant vigilance of the mind, until we learn to uproot and deny all the forms that denial of truth has taken in our minds. To believe in death in any form is to deny life and thus deny truth. Our function here is "to deny the denial of truth" (T-12.II.1:5). It is to recognize the thoughts based on death and see they are simply silly and meaningless.

When I find myself being worried, anxious or sad, I can ask myself, "Is God dead?" Somehow I find that helps me see the absurdity of it all. I lift a bag of groceries and the bottom falls out, spilling food all over the floor, and I am flushed with anger and deep sadness, in the form of feeling sorry for myself. Suppose in that moment I ask myself, "Is God dead?" For that is what my anger and sadness is proclaiming: God is dead. It suddenly seems so absurd for me to leap from spilled groceries to the death of God, so absurd I can laugh. And pick up the groceries.

More seriously, perhaps I experience "a great loss." My loved one dies, or perhaps I go through a wrenching divorce. The sorrow seems unending, and I feel as if life is over. "Is God dead?" In contrast to the magnitude of God my personal [and illusory] loss is as nothing. Do I really believe that what happens in my little life can destroy the reality of God? Of course not. Especially if what I believe happened isn't even real.

Naturally in such profoundly disturbing circumstances I don't recover as quickly as I might over a bag of spilled groceries. Yet the same thoughts suggested by this lesson can be of immense comfort. Nothing dies. Nothing real can be threatened. Whatever form death takes must be illusion. When a body "dies" nothing really dies. When a divorce rips a beloved body out of my experience, nothing has truly been lost. I've been attached to an illusion, but God is still alive.

The pain and agony of loss through death or divorce can continue for months. Denying what I feel is simply not healthy, and I do not mean to suggest that we should attempt to stuff our grief with idealistic affirmations that "Death isn't real" and "Nothing has been lost." Rather, as the Course so often suggests, I can simply look at what I am thinking and feeling and recognize that, however real it feels, it is based on a denial of the truth. I can remind myself, "I'm believing that death is real, and loss is real. I'm believing that God is dead, and that's just a foolish notion. This pain, which I am indeed feeling, is therefore not real and is nothing to be concerned about. I'm okay, and God is still alive."

You might call it lucid living, similar to lucid dreaming. Although the experience you are going through seems terribly real, and the grief and sadness are real in proportion to your belief in the reality of the loss, there is still a part of you that is aware that you are dreaming, that you are being fooled by an illusion. You are fooled by the illusion, you do suffer the grief and sadness, but part of you knows it isn't really real.

That's all the Course is asking us to do. We're not being asked to abrubtly jettison our feelings and our mis-thoughts. All the Course asks is that we recognize that they are based on a lie, that really they are proclaiming God is dead, and that simply isn't true. If we do that, the Holy Spirit will do the rest. Bit by bit, gradually (so it seems to us), the shadows of illusion will begin to lift from our minds. The form of "life beyond" the death we see will begin to take on definition and shape in our minds, and the illusion will become more and more shadowy. Our belief in death's many forms will weaken, and our belief in life will strengthen. The events of the illusion will have less and less effect on us, and we will experience the second phrase of this lesson's title: "The Son of God is free." We will know that we are eternally alive, and always have been, and there is nothing to fear.

Lesson 164—June 13

"Now are we one with Him Who is our Source."

PRACTICE SUMMARY

Generic Instructions: Morning and evening times, hourly remembrance, and response to temptation. See Lesson 153 (page 78) or the Practice Card, and also Robert's practice comments on pages 48–49.
Morning/Evening Quiet Time:

Let go all the things you think you want. Put away your trifling treasures and clear an open space in your mind. Let Christ come into this space and give you His treasure: salvation. Spend some quiet time with Him beyond the world, and you will remember the ancient peace, silence and holiness that you carry in your heart, the place in you the world of sin can never touch.

Remarks: At times the business of the world will allow you only a minute or less, or no time at all. At other times you will forget. Yet whenever you can, do your hourly remembrance.

COMMENTARY

To anyone who has done the Workbook lessons to this point, it is clear that the recent lessons are reaching for some new kind of level. There is a consistent emphasis on what the Course calls the holy instant, although many of the lessons do not use the term. But when a lesson, as this one, speaks of "this instant, now" as the time in which we come "to look upon what is forever there" (1:3), or of the time we give to spend in quiet "with Him, beyond the world" (3:2), it is clearly indicating times in which we enter the holy instant, a moment of eternity within time.

The practice being asked of us (since Lesson 153), day after day, is to set aside times of no less than five minutes, and as much as a half hour or more, morning and evening, to exercise our spiritual sight and hearing. We are being asked to listen to "the song of Heaven" (1:6) that is continually sounding beyond all the sounds of this world. This "melody from far beyond the world" (2:3) is the song of love, the call of our hearts to Him, and of His to ours.

These times are periods in which we forget all our sins and sorrows (3:3), and remember the gifts of God to us (3:4). We practice setting aside the sights and sounds of the world that constantly witness to us of the ego's message of fear, and we listen to the song of Heaven. We quiet ourselves, still our minds, and try to get in touch with the "silence into which the world can not intrude" (4:1), the "ancient peace you carry in your heart and have not lost" (4:2), and the "sense of holiness in you the thought of sin has never touched" (4:3). All of this, as the first paragraph said, "is forever there; not in our sight, but in the eyes of Christ" (1:3). We are not creating it; we are not making it happen; we are brushing away everything within our minds that veils it from our sight. "Now is what is really there made visible, while all the shadows which appeared to hide it merely sink away" (5:2).

Such practicing puts our minds in a state in which we feel pure joy. Joy is the word that comes to my mind to describe what a holy instant "feels like." There is a sense of contentment, an assurance that, despite all evidence to the contrary, all is well. There is a peaceful relaxation into the mind of God. Our minds naturally reach out in love to all the world from within this holy place, blessing rather than judging.

It may be difficult for us at this juncture to fully understand how such quiet practice, something that takes place completely within our own minds, can "save the world" (6:3). The lesson states in no uncertain terms that, by means of this practice, "We can change the world" (9:2). How can that be? It is so because all minds are joined, and while we may understand the concept, our sense of its reality may be very weak. That is normal; the effect on the world proceeds whether we are aware of it or not. We can, for the time being, focus on the personal benefit: "But this you can surely want; you can exchange all suffering for joy this very day" (9:4).

If you are like me, the reality and importance of this practice grows slowly. There are many days we let "slip by" without taking the time to do the work on our minds the Workbook calls for. The details of life, the press of business, the daily crises shriek for our attention, drawing us away, as they are meant to do. It takes some determination to put this "quiet time" with God first, above all else. But when we do so, an amazing thing happens. As Lesson 286 puts it: "Father, how still today! How quietly do all things fall in place!" I recall, long ago, reading how Martin Luther once wrote, "I have so many things to do today, I must spend three hours in prayer to prepare myself." There was a man who understood, within his own context, that preparing his mind with God was the most important thing, and that the more pressing the world seemed, the more he needed that quiet time in God's presence.

Lesson 165—June 14

"Let not my mind deny the Thought of God."

PRACTICE SUMMARY

Generic Instructions: Morning and evening times, hourly remembrance, and response to temptation. See Lesson 153 (page 78) or the Practice Card, and also Robert's practice comments on pages 48–49.
Purpose: To stop denying that the Thought of God, which created you, is your Source, your safety, your joy, your resting place. To experience it and then abandon all else as worthless in comparison.
Morning/Evening Quiet Time: Ask with desire for Heaven. Deny it no longer. Practice this asking in the manner that God's Word directs.
Comments: You need not be certain that this is the only thing you want. But when you receive it, you will be sure. Conviction lies in the experience. It will take you past all your doubts to God's certainty.

Practice in hope, for hope is justified. Your doubts mean nothing in the face of God's certainty.

COMMENTARY

Today's lesson, tomorrow's, and those just before and after, are a strong encouragement to move forward. The Course, in these days, is trying to draw us past the point of hesitation and into a firm commitment.

> What makes this world seem real except your own denial of the truth that lies beyond?...What could keep from you what you already have except your choice to see it not, denying it is there? (1:1–4)

Ken Wilber, the author of many books on transpersonal psychology and spiritual growth, points out that, viewed as evolution, spiritual growth proceeds to the degree we are willing to die to the lower level of life in order to transcend it and remember (or re-member) the higher level. The fact that our experience is on an ego level is not because the higher is not already here, it is because we have chosen the lower as a substitute for the higher, and we do so in every instant. It is not until the lower level is lived out, tried to the fullest, in a sense, and found lacking, that motivation exists to move us higher.

We need to become disillusioned with the ego to the point that we begin to see through its illusions. The degree to which the ego seems real to us is the measure of our denial of "the truth that lies beyond" (1:1). We can't see the real world because *we don't want to*. We are actively denying it. The reality of the real world, if perceived and accepted, will mean the end of reality as we now know it. Heaven appears to us as a threat to our imagined comfort on the ego level.

Jesus appeals to us,

> Deny not Heaven. It is yours today, but for the asking. Nor need you perceive how great the gift, how changed your mind will be before it comes to you. Ask to receive, and it is given you. Conviction lies within it. Till you welcome it as yours, uncertainty remains. Yet God is fair. Sureness is not required to receive what only your acceptance can bestow (4:1–8).

You don't have to be sure before asking for Heaven. You don't have to be certain. "Sureness is not required" (4:8). In fact, you cannot be sure or certain before asking because "Conviction lies within it" (4:5); that is, you don't find the conviction, the sureness, the certainty until you have Heaven, and you can't know you have it until you ask.

As we live thinking we are egos, considering moving forward, considering leaving the ego behind, the ego fights for its own existence. "You don't know what you are getting into here," it tells us. "How can you be sure you'd like it? You'd better make sure before you make a move."

Certainty, sureness and conviction come from experience. When you have experienced the real world, even a glimpse, you will know you want it, you will know it is what you want and what you have mistakenly been seeking in the shadow world of the ego's illusions. So ask for Heaven.

Another comfort is that we don't have to understand all that Heaven, or the real world, is, before we experience it. You don't have to have a clear idea of what you're asking for, of "how changed your mind will be" (4:3). That change of mind does not precede the decision to ask, it follows it. It is the desire that allows it to come.

You don't even need to be sure that Heaven is the only thing you want!

> You need not be sure that you request the only thing you want. But when you have received, you will be sure you have the treasure you have always sought (5:2–3).

It's all right to go into this with reservations, such as, "Maybe I can have the real world and still hold onto my special relationships. Or maybe I can have inner peace and still enjoy my little pleasures." Those reservations will vanish once you taste the real thing. A very poor analogy, but one that makes the point: "How can you keep them down on the farm after they've seen Paris?" Once you taste "the treasure you have always sought" why would you go back to lesser things?

We already have the certainty within ourselves, in reality. That's part of what we've covered over with ego illusions. When we find the Self, we find it complete with certainty. The process of the Course, of "removing blocks to the awareness of Love's presence," is restated here in terms of that inner certainty: "This course removes all doubts which you have interposed between Him and your certainty of Him" (7:6).

The process consists of becoming aware of our doubts, owning them, acknowledging them, and then not taking them seriously. This is exactly the same process we go through with other such blocks, like anger and sadness and pain. See them clearly so you can see that the doubts, too, are part of the illusion. They are "meaningless, for God is certain" (7:3). "His sureness lies beyond our every doubt" (8:3).

Certainty is not something we can generate for ourselves. "We count on God, and not upon ourselves, to give us certainty" (8:1). But for that to happen, we must be willing to move forward, to be willing to "die" to the level of life we know now and to ask for something more, a different way of seeing, a different kind of vision. We need to be willing to ask that "the Thought of God" enter our minds and displace the distorted thinking we have been doing. We need to "follow the instructions," so to speak, given in the Course; if we do, certainty is sure to come to us.

Lesson 166—June 15

"I am entrusted with the gifts of God."

PRACTICE SUMMARY

Generic Instructions: Morning and evening times, hourly remembrance, and response to temptation. See Lesson 153 (page 78) or the Practice Card, and also Robert's practice comments on pages 48–49.
Purpose: To give the gifts of God to those who still walk the lonely road you have escaped. To demonstrate through your happiness what it is to receive the gifts of God.
Response To Temptation: (Suggestion) Whenever you are tempted to be sorrowful, tearful, sick or fearful, repeat the idea. For these feelings will betray your trust, your mission. Whenever you are afraid, let Christ reply with: "It is not so." When you feel poor, let Him point out His gifts to you. When you feel lonely, let Him speak of His Companionship.

COMMENTARY

This lesson carries on the general tone of the previous one, attempting to persuade us to keep moving forward, past the illusion of ourselves we have been content to live with. It opens with the idea that God trusts us so much He has given everything to us. Everything. He knows His Son, and just because He knows us, He gives us everything without exception. His trust in us is limitless. We doubt our own certainty, but God's we can depend on.

I trust God's trust in me.

What we fear is that trust in God is "treachery" to ourselves (3:2). We are attached to this world we made.

To admit it is not real is to betray myself. If I have progressed beyond the point of believing that I can create like God, that I can make a world that is perfect somehow; at least I want to cling to the notion that I can unmake what God made, that I can destroy the world and shatter its perfection. To be told my actions, my sins, my denials, my doubts, and all their like are without effect is demeaning to my ego self. So I contradict the truth of Heaven to preserve what I have made.

There is a part of each of us that wants to be "a tragic figure," like some hero or heroine in an opera (6:1 and following). We want to be able to say, "Behold how nobly I withstand the slings and arrows of outrageous fortune." We think, all unconsciously, that without the "outrageous fortune" our nobility would be lost.

When I listen to my ego, this is how I want to see myself. Such a tragic figure! Poor thing, so weary and worn. Look at his threadbare clothing! How he must have been deprived! And his feet—Oh! Poor thing! They are bleeding.

We can all identify with this figure. "Everyone who comes here [to this world] has pursued the path he follows, and has felt defeat and hopelessness as he is feeling them" (6:2). You know what this is talking about. You've been there, maybe you are there now. You know what "defeat and hopelessness" means, you've felt it too.

> Yet is he really tragic, when you see that he is following the way he chose, and need but realize Who walks with him and open up his treasures to be free? (6:3)

Is "he," the tragic hero [who is you and me], really tragic? Or is he just foolish? Is he just making a silly mistake? When you see that he is *choosing* his path and could choose otherwise, can you consider his suffering tragic?

"This is your chosen self, the one you made as a replacement for reality" (7:1). This, folks, is the ego self we have chosen to be. It's how we've seen ourselves. This is the self we are defending. This is the person we have become, and we resist all the evidence and witnesses that prove that this is not us.

Jesus calls on us to drop the victim act and recognize, "I am not the victim of the world I see" (W-pI.31), that:

> I am responsible for what I see, I choose the feelings I experience, and I decide upon the goal I would achieve. And everything that seems to happen to me, I ask for and receive as I have asked (T-21.II.2:3–4).

You see yourself as this tragic figure, but Jesus' response is: "He would make you laugh at this perception of yourself" (8:3).

I'd like to meditate on that a while. Jesus wants to make me laugh! Jesus is a frustrated comedian. Well, maybe not frustrated; look at what he accomplishes through Marianne Williamson. He wants us to laugh at our egos! He wants me to see the humor of my position, pleading tragedy when I've deliberately chosen to be what I am.

> Where is self-pity then? And what becomes of all the tragedy you sought to make for him whom God intended only joy? (8:4–5)

The self-pity and the tragedy just disappear, that's what happens. When you laugh at the "sorry figure" of the ego, the tragedy vanishes.

The next paragraph describes very well where some of us are right now, just starting to realize that we are not the ego. This lesson is written on many levels, addressing first, as we've seen, the person hiding in the ego illusion of tragedy; then, in these next sentences, the person who has begun to realize that the miserable ego is not his true Identity; and finally, in paragraph 11 on, the person who has clearly seen and accepted that "you are not what you pretend to be" (11:2).

In paragraph 9 we see the person in the middle—feeling torn, afraid, almost under attack by God, Whom he has habitually avoided all his life. Let's listen in to our responses as Jesus tries to make us laugh, and see alongside it the humorous truth.

First, we sense the presence of God, Whom we have been hiding from: "Your ancient fear has come upon you now, and justice has caught up with you at last" (9:1).

Our reaction: *Oh, rats! It's God! Now I'm going to get it.*

Jesus: It's silly to be afraid of God, silly to think He is your Enemy and wants to hurt you. What a laughable idea, to be afraid of God!

The lesson: "Christ's hand has touched your shoulder..." (9:2)

Our reaction: *What was that really weird feeling? Oh, Christ—was it Christ? Is that His Voice in my mind? I must be losing it.*

Jesus: It is your brother, and he wants to bring you home. How foolish to fear him!

The lesson: "...and you feel that you are not alone" (9:2).

Our reaction: *And I'm not sure I like the idea of someone always with me, looking over my shoulder.*

Jesus: What a funny reaction! I am your Comforter and Teacher, not your judge. It's silly to think you prefer being alone.

The lesson: "You even think the miserable self you thought was you may not be your Identity. Perhaps God's Word is truer than your own" (9:3–4).

Our reaction: *I can't believe I've started to doubt these things I've believed all my life! I must be insane!*

Jesus: On the other hand, who has more chance of being right: you, or God? Be real!

The lesson: "Perhaps His gifts to you are real" (9:5).

Our reaction: *Yeah, and maybe it's just my imagination.*

Jesus: But what if they really are real, these gifts? Isn't it foolish not to find out?

The lesson: "Perhaps He has not wholly been outwitted by your plan to keep His Son in deep oblivion, and go the way you chose without your Self" (9:6).

Our reaction: *Yeah, and maybe He has. Maybe I've screwed it up so bad that even God can't fix it.*

Jesus: Now that's truly funny! You, outwitting God? Right, sure, that's really brilliant thinking. God decides He wants something and you are going to keep it from happening?

Our reaction: *But if I didn't outwit Him, then I must still be what He made me to be. I'm not sure I want to give up believing in what I've always thought I am. I feel threatened.*

Jesus: So, okay. Hold on to the picture of yourself you've always had; I'm sure you've really enjoyed being you, that way. Right? God isn't fighting it.

The lesson: "God's Will does not oppose. It merely is" (10:1–2).

You're not fighting with God, and He is not fighting with you. He doesn't fight, He doesn't oppose. He merely is. What you are fighting (and this is fall-down, bust-a-gut funny) is reality itself. Thinking you are separate from God is about as smart as a drop of water deciding it's not in the ocean any more. It's like a lion deciding it wants to be a mouse.

You're trying to be what you are not; that's what causes all the strain, when it should cause nothing but laughter. The fight is all on your side against an imagined enemy. You are the Answer to all your own questions. There is nothing to be afraid of here. The truth about yourself is wonderful, not frightening.

In the remainder of the lesson, Jesus talks of three things we need to know. First, all the gifts that God has given us, that is, the real Self that we are, whole, healed and abundant. Second, His Presence with us, our Companion on the journey. And third, that the gifts we have are made for giving away; we have a purpose here, to give these gifts to "all who chose the lonely road you have escaped" (13:1).

In a sense those are the three main thrusts of *A Course In Miracles*. First, learning the true nature of Self, the holiness and joy of our own being. Second, and equally important until we leave this world, is the sure knowledge of His Companionship on the way, the help we need to make it through. And finally, that the nature we have realized is that of Giver and Lover; to know we have the gift, we must give it. We must teach the world by showing it "the happiness that comes to those who feel the touch of Christ" (13:5).

Our mission is just that: to be happy. "Your change of mind becomes the proof that who accepts God's gifts can never suffer anything" (14:5). We are here to:

> ...become the living proof of what Christ's touch can offer everyone...Be witness in your happiness to how transformed the mind becomes which chooses to accept His gifts, and feel the touch of Christ. Such is your mission now" (15:2–5).

Recognize His gifts. Feel His touch. And share them with the world through our happiness (not through beating them over the head with it). Those are the three stages of moving forward.

Another way to put it: Drop the victim act and take responsibility as the source of your life. Choose Heaven instead of hell, ask your Companion for His help. And be the proof of Heaven's reality by your radiant joy and refusal to suffer anything.

Lesson 167—June 16

"There is one life, and that I share with God."

PRACTICE SUMMARY

Generic Instructions: Morning and evening times, hourly remembrance, and response to temptation. See Lesson 153 (page 78) or the Practice Card, and also Robert's practice comments on pages 48–49.
Purpose: To be children of God and accept that the life He gave us has no opposite, cannot change, cannot die and cannot sleep. To strive to keep His holy home as He created it, to let Him be Lord of our thoughts today.
Response To Temptation: (Suggestion). Whenever you feel tempted to ask for death in any form—as sorrow, anxiety, weariness, discomfort, etc.—repeat the idea.

COMMENTARY

There is a repetition here, or perhaps a statement that I anticipated when, in writing about Lesson 163, I said that, "Belief in death is just another form of the 'tiny, mad idea' at which 'the Son of God remembered not [i.e. forgot] to laugh.'" This lesson says that "death…is but an idea, irrelevant to what is seen as physical" (3:1–2). Later it says, "Death is the thought that you are separate from your Creator" (4:1). That is the essence of the idea of death: separation from Life.

This is why we can say, "There is no death." It is simply impossible. God is Life, and what He creates must be living. To cease living would be to separate from God, to become His opposite. Since God has no opposite, there is no death.

> There is no death because what God created shares His Life. There is no death because an opposite to God does not exist. There is no death because the Father and the Son are one (1:5–7).

"Ideas leave not their source" (3:6). That idea is central to the Course. Ideas exist only in the mind that thinks them. Ideas do not exude out from mind, take on an independent existence, become self-sustaining, and become capable of opposition to the mind that created them. They simply don't do that.

I am an idea in God's Mind. I am the thought of "me." I cannot depart from God's Mind, live independently of Him, dependent only on myself, capable of a will that opposes God's. I simply cannot do it. I can only imagine I am doing it.

> [Death] is the fixed belief ideas can leave their source, and take on qualities the source does not contain, becoming different from their own origin, apart from it in kind as well as distance, time and form (4:3).

I cannot do that; I cannot leave my Source and take on qualities not contained in that Source. Therefore, I cannot die.

We need to see that, as Lesson 163 (paragraph 1) said, death takes many forms. The "attraction of death" spoken of in the Obstacles to Peace section (T-19.IV) reflects all those forms. This lesson lists a few more:

> Yet we have learned that the idea of death takes many forms. It is the one idea which underlies all feelings that are not supremely happy. It is the alarm to which you give response of any kind that is not perfect joy. All sorrow, loss, anxiety and suffering and pain, even a little sigh of weariness, a slight discomfort or the merest frown, acknowledge death. And thus deny you live (2:3–7).

What is death? Any feeling that is not supremely happy. Any response to anything in our life that is not perfect joy. Can we see how anything less than supreme happiness and perfect joy is a denial of life and an affirmation of death? To be less than perfectly joyful is to assert there is something other than God, other than Life, other than Love; something "other" that dilutes the radiant Being of God.

I am not advocating becoming a bliss idiot, walking around in total denial of the pain and suffering of our lives and of those around us, frantically asserting, "Everything is perfect. None of this is real. It's all illusion, ignore it. Only God exists."

Rather, I am encouraging the exact opposite. I am suggesting that we need to start noticing just how much the idea of death influences us. We need to notice those little sighs of weariness, those twinges of anxiety, and recognize that the idea of death underlies them all, the idea that separation from God is real, that something other than God exists, opposing and nullifying His radiance. We need to notice how we believe we are that "something other," or at least part of it. Notice, and say to God, "I'm believing in death again. I'm feeling separated from You. And I know, therefore, this feeling doesn't mean anything, because there is one Life, and I share it with You."

It is only when you recognize that you are responsible for those death thoughts that you can truly understand they have no reality except in your own mind. To affirm they have no reality without first taking responsibility for them is unhealthy denial. It leaves them without a source, and they must have a source. So your mind supplies an imagined source in God or somewhere outside yourself, and you are back to the separation thought again, because there is nothing outside God nor outside you. By screaming "It's all illusion!" without truly knowing that you are the illusionist, you make the idea of death into something real, something to be fought against and repressed.

To recognize death thoughts as illusion does not require that you do violence to your mind. Seeing beyond illusion is the most natural thing in the world when it happens naturally, as the result of taking responsibility for the illusion. To see the world as illusion does not require concerted and sustained effort. It is not something you can try to do. If you are trying, you're doing it backwards.

The same principle operates when people say "I'm trying to see the Christ in him." You can't try to see Christ in a person; you either do or you don't. When your eyes are open and nothing is in the way you don't have to try to see! You just see.

Spiritual vision is the same. Christ is there, in every person, and you are quite capable of seeing Him there. The problem is, you've erected many barriers, many screens, that block your sight. You're seeing the reflection of your own ideas instead of seeing who the person really is, which is Christ.

The way to spiritual sight, the way to see Christ in a brother, therefore, is to become aware of all the screens you are throwing up, all the illusions you are projecting from your own mind, blocking true vision. Parodoxically, you don't see Christ in a brother by looking at him, squinting and trying to pretend he is a loving being; you see Christ in him by looking at your own mind, your own thoughts, which are the barrier to vision.

Perhaps you are afraid of the person in some way. He appears to you as a threat of some sort, perhaps prone to attack you physically, or to take your money. Instead of trying to see through that picture of him as a bad person, a threat to yourself, look at that picture itself and ask where it came from. With the Holy Spirit's help, you will see that it originated entirely in your own mind. It is the sum of your own judgments solidified into an opinion. It is how you have taught yourself to see your brother. And that is all.

You know, or you should, that you are not capable of judgment. You cannot possibly have all the evidence. So you can turn to the Holy Spirit and say, "I recognize that my opinion of my brother is my own creation. It is based on the idea of death, of something separate from and other than God. As such, I know it is only a bad dream. It has no meaning. My brother is not what I think he is, and I am not a bad person for having this thought; I'm just making a mistake. I am willing to let go of it, and since I am its only source, I can let go of it."

You may go on feeling afraid. The key difference is not whether or not the fear disappears, as it sometimes will. The key difference is that, if the fear (or whatever feeling or judgment it may be) is present, you are aware that you are making it up and it isn't real. This opens the way for a different vision to dawn on you. If what you have been seeing is illusion, there must be something else, some other way of seeing, that is real.

The vision of Christ, which is what the Course calls this different way of seeing, may not burst on your sight after one application of this mental process. It probably won't. We've got lots and lots of barriers to that vision, and you may have recognized only one of many things preventing you from seeing Christ in your brother. That's OK. You've understood that this particular barrier is an illusion, and affirmed there is another way of seeing your brother. That's all you have to do. You don't have to try to find the other way! When you are ready, when the barriers are recognized as something you make up, the vision will just be there.

It will "just be there" because it is already there. The Christ in you already recognizes Himself in your brother. The process is similar to tuning out static in a radio with electronic filters. There is a signal you want to hear, but too much noise and static prevents its being heard. You identify the static, isolate it, electronically "instruct" your equipment to ignore it, and eventually, the clear signal comes through.

What you are doing in the process the Course recommends—looking at the ego and its thoughts of death, identifying them, and deciding to ignore them because they come from an undependable source—is tuning out the static. Keep doing that, and the clear signal of Christ's vision will come through. It is there, in you, right now. You just can't "hear" it for all the noise the ego is making.

Lesson 168—June 17

"Your grace is given me. I claim it now."

PRACTICE SUMMARY

Generic Instructions: Morning and evening times, hourly remembrance, and response to temptation. See Lesson 153 (page 78) or the Practice Card, and also Robert's practice comments on pages 48–49.
Purpose: To ask God to give us His grace, by which He takes His final step, giving us first the gift of vision, and then eternal knowledge. This step will lift us into Heaven, restore all forgotten memories and give us certainty of Love. This is a new and holy day.
Morning/Evening Quiet Time: To God we pray, using the words He gave us: "Your grace is given me. I claim it now. Father, I come to You. And You will come to me who ask. I am the Son You love."
Hourly Remembrance: Sit quietly and wait on God's grace.

COMMENTARY

What is grace?

This lesson answers, not in the impassive terms of a formal definition, but in the picture of a warm, personal conversation with God. "God speaks to us. Shall we not speak to Him?" (1:1–2) Grace is the concomitant of God's love, something that comes along with it as part of the package. He has always loved us (1:7–11). Grace is the effect or application of that love which guarantees His Love will be fully recognized and received. Grace is whatever it takes to bring us out of our sleep. It is the movement of love that woos us back to Him, the quiet whisper of His Voice in our minds that will not let us go, the careful planning of our curriculum to help us unlearn everything we have taught ourselves of fear, the activity of Spirit that works constantly to win back our trust, restore our joy, assuage our guilt. It is His answer to our despair. It is the means by which we recognize His Will (2:3–4).

His grace is given me. His grace is "a given," a certainty, part of what it means that God is Love. It is a gift, always available, always being given, awaiting only my acknowledgment (2:5). It is "the gift by which God leans to us and lifts us up" (3:2). And ultimately, grace is that aspect of His Love in which "finally He comes Himself, and takes us in His Arms and sweeps away the cobwebs of our sleep" (3:4).

Shall I not, then, today, sit down for a few minutes of quiet conversation with this God of Love? Can I not take the time even to ask Him to grant me this grace, which He has already granted? Can I not express my willingness to receive it, to allow this sorry world to disappear from my sight, replaced by true vision? Can I not tell Him that I long, at least in part of myself, to be swept into His Arms? I may feel as though I am making some kind of surrender or concession; I may believe I am giving something up, or losing something dear to me. Yet if this opening to grace is surrender at all, it is surrender only to love. It is a sigh of lost resistance to what I have always, always wanted. It is a loss of pretense, a falling back into what I have always been. It is surrender to my Self. It is capitulation to my Beloved; nothing more than that, and nothing less. It is the ultimate manifestation of "falling in Love."

Do I doubt my own capacity to love, and to respond adequately to God's immaculate, eternal Love? "Our faith lies in the Giver, not our own acceptance" (5:2). It is not the power of my choice or my faith that works the miracle, it is the power of Him Who gives it. His grace gives me the means to lay down all my errors (4:3), even when I doubt my own ability to do so. That is what grace is for. Grace supplies everything I think I lack. As God once said to the Apostle Paul, "My grace is sufficient for thee" (II Cor. 12:9). What is grace? Everything we need to bring us home to God, whatever form that might take.

Lesson 169—June 18

"By grace I live. By grace I am released."

PRACTICE SUMMARY

Generic Instructions: Morning and evening times, hourly remembrance, and response to temptation. See Lesson 153 (page 78) or the Practice Card, and also Robert's practice comments on pages 48–49.
Purpose: To ask for grace, and the temporary experience of Heaven that comes from grace. And then to return and bring to others the gifts that you received from grace.
Morning/Evening Quiet Time: Use this prayer: "By grace I live. By grace I am released. By grace I give. By grace I will release."

COMMENTARY

Grace, Jesus tells us, "...is an aspect of the Love of God which is most like the state prevailing in the unity of truth" (1:1).

I suppose one might say that to live by grace means to live with full, conscious awareness of Love's Presence while in the world. In that sense, it is equivalent to living in the real world.

This fits in with the rest of the first paragraph. The state of grace, or living by grace and constantly receiving grace, is something beyond learning. Learning only prepares us for it, for learning is purely in this world. Really, what we are doing is un-learning all our denial of the truth about our Self.

"It is...the goal of learning, for grace cannot come until the mind prepares itself for true acceptance" (1:3). Learning prepares us to accept grace. It does not give us grace, but it prepares us to receive it, to accept it, which implies that grace is already available but we are not able to accept it.

"Grace becomes inevitable instantly in those who have prepared [a place in themselves where it can be] willingly received" (1:4). Grace is simply there, instantly, whenever we are ready to receive it. Learning is necessary to produce the state of willingness; then the grace just pours in. We don't have to do anything to bring it, but we do have to progress through (un)learning to remove our unwillingness to receive.

There then follows what is perhaps the best definition of grace in the lesson: "Grace is acceptance of the Love of God within a world of seeming hate and fear" (2:1).

Grace means seeing through the illusion. I am still in this world of "seeming hate and fear" and yet, somehow, I accept the Love of God. I accept that He is wholly love, not angry and vengeful, not something to be feared because of my sin, not someone to be blamed for the seeming ills of the world: God is Love. Instead of seeing the world as solid and real, and wondering how God can be loving when all this is going on, "...those whose minds are lighted by the gift of grace can not believe the world of fear is real" (2:2). Those who know grace know that God is real, love is real, and it is the world of fear that is the illusion.

> Grace is not learned. The final step must go beyond all learning (3:1–2).

This is not something you learn. It cannot be learned. It must come from outside the context in which learning occurs, which is purely the ego context. The Course often says there is no learning in Heaven, or in God. How could there be learning where everything is known?

> Grace is not the goal this course aspires to attain. Yet we prepare for grace in that an open mind can hear the Call to waken. It is not shut tight against God's Voice. It has become aware that there are things it does not know, and thus is ready to accept a state completely different from experience with which it is familiarly at home (3:3–6).

So, since learning is the goal of the Course, grace is not; it is beyond what the Course teaches because it cannot be taught. But the learning of the Course, which is really unlearning, prepares us for grace by loosening the tight grip of the ego on our minds. The goal of the Course, as seen in this paragraph, is an open mind and an awareness that there are things we don't know.

We do not realize the extent to which our minds have been closed, "shut tight against God's Voice." That is what we must learn. What we learn is all the ways we shut God out. When we learn that completely, there is nothing left to shut Him out and He is simply there, as He has always been.

The lesson then goes on to talk of the state of Heaven or oneness. I don't have time to comment on it here; the lesson speaks for itself when it says, "We cannot speak nor write nor even think of this at all" (6:1).

> Yet forgiveness, taught and learned, brings with it the experiences which bear witness that the time the mind itself determined to abandon all but this is now at hand (7:2).

In other words, forgiveness is what we now teach and learn, not grace. Forgiveness is the learning process, the preparation for grace, and it gives us witness experiences, foretastes of what it is like to live in grace.

> Now we have work to do, for those in time can speak of things beyond, and listen to words which explain what is to come is past already. Yet what meaning can the words convey to those who count the hours still, and rise and work and go to sleep by them? (10:3–4)

We are still in time. Let's be real and practical here. Talking about "things beyond" and trying to understand how "what is to come" (enlightenment or awakening which is in our future, as we perceive it) "is past already" (that is, the journey is already over, we're already enlightened, and oneness is a constant state which is here now, forever as it always was)—talking about these things can be fascinating, a little encouraging perhaps, but how on earth can we understand it? We can't! The words convey very little meaning to us while we live and order our lives by time, by counting the hours.

It is good to think of these things a little, but to do so is not our main task. In fact, it can be a waste of time if it distracts us from the fact that "we have work to do" here, now. Forgiveness work. Sitting around discussing what it means to live constantly by grace, in the Real World, or what follows in the experience of Heaven, is meaningless without that very real and practical work of forgiveness going on in our lives.

We won't understand Heaven until we get there. Grace foreshadows Heaven, and we can't even understand that yet, not fully. We can have tastes of it, though, in the holy instants in which we connect with God and with Love in our minds. So,

> ...now we ask for grace...Experience that grace provides will end in time...[it does] not replace the thought of time but for a little while (12:2–3).

The experiences of grace come, and they go. We experience being outside of time "but for a little while." These experiences, which come in moments of true forgiveness, are all we need for now. "The interval suffices" (13:1). The holy instants, the "little while" of each forgiveness experience, is enough. It is all we need.

"It is here that miracles are laid..." (13:2). In other words, the holy instant opens us to miracles. It is the way that miracles flow into our lives, "...to be returned by you from holy instants you receive, through grace in your experience, to all who see the light that lingers in your face" (13:2). When you "come back" from the holy instant, there is a light that lingers in your face. Other people see it, and to them, you bring the miracles you received in that moment.

> What is the face of Christ but his who went a moment into timelessness... (13:3)

This is talking about you and me. The face of Christ is your face, my face, when we have received a holy instant and "return" to the world of time; our faces glow with the light of Heaven.

> ...and brought a clear reflection of the unity he felt an instant back to bless the world? (13:3)

That is our function here in the world: to bring a clear reflection of Heaven's unity back to bless the world. To ask for grace, to open our mind to receiving grace from God, to choose, as often as we can, to "go" into that holy instant in which we feel the unity of Heaven, and then to return with a reflection of that to bless the world. Notice that the unity is "felt" and not just intellectually accepted and understood. It is felt. That is what happens in a holy instant.

We hear about living the in the Real World, or what it must be like to live in a constant state of oneness (Heaven), and we want it. We want it now. We get frustrated because the holy instants come and go, they last "but for a little while" and we find that disappointing. Jesus is explaining here that the learning stage is absolutely necessary, and we should not feel frustrated, we should not think we are failing in our work if the holy instants don't last.

> How could you finally attain to it forever, while a part of you remains outside, unknowing, unawakened, and in need of you as witness to the truth? (13:4)

Your brothers around you in the world, "unknowing, unawakened," are your own thoughts in form. They are "a part of you" which "remains outside." You have a mission here, a purpose to fulfill. Awakening must be communicated. You want a steady state of "holy instant-ness," but Jesus asks, "How could you attain that if part of you is outside that state of oneness, unknowing, unawakened, unaware?" Your oneness must include them.

Jesus says we should actually be grateful to "come back" from these holy instants, back to the world of time. Listen:

> Be grateful to return, as you were glad to go an instant, and accept the gifts that grace provided you. You carry them back to yourself (14:1–2).

If the holy instant is a moment in which you are aware of oneness, in a sense you have to come back. You have to come back because you are aware of your oneness with those who haven't seen yet. They are part of you, and so you have to "go back" to bring the gifts of grace to that part of yourself that is still not awake, as you see that reflected in your brothers.

Jesus tells us clearly to be content with this, to "not ask for the unaskable" (14:7). To want Heaven for myself while leaving my brothers behind is to fly in the face of what Heaven is: the awareness of oneness. A private salvation is unaskable. We go together or we go not at all.

Some might react to this as though the mass of humanity is holding us back and preventing our full enlightenment. Such a thought is still based on a consciousness of separation and so is totally alien to grace and Heaven. The world you see is not a force separate from you, restraining you. It is a reflection of your own self-restraint, your own resistance which has yet to be overcome or unlearned. The world is not outside your mind, but in it. You are the world, that is what you are learning.

You become what you always have been by accepting your role as savior to the world. Your salvation is the world's salvation. They are not two things, they are the same.

We "come back" to save the world. That doesn't mean that we have our little moment of bliss and then come back to preach to the world about it and tell them how enlightened we are, and why don't they get with it? If your salvation is the world's salvation, the reverse is true: the world's salvation is your own. You save the world by working on yourself. "The sole responsibility of the miracle worker is to accept the Atonement for himself." (T-2.V.5:1) You save the world by changing your own mind, because that is where the world is, in your mind. There is only one mind, only one of us here.

When you are at a movie, if there is a problem on the screen you don't run to the screen to fix it; you find the projector and fix that. Those "unenlightened people" you see out there are parts of your own mind that you haven't recognized as part of you; you don't bring them with you by trying to work to fix the screen (those separate people out there), you do it by working with the projector, the cause (your own mind).

Be glad to go an instant, and be grateful also to return, to bring the light of God to the world. You bring it to yourself. It is in seeing that fact that you will be saved. The returning is not a step back into time. No, it is a step forward in your own awakening, the means by which you bring all the world with you into timelessness, there to be the Oneness you have touched and known.

Lesson 170—June 19

"There is no cruelty in God and none in me."

PRACTICE SUMMARY

Generic Instructions: Morning and evening times, hourly remembrance, and response to temptation. See Lesson 153 (page 78) or the Practice Card, and also Robert's practice comments on pages 48–49.
Purpose: To look dispassionately upon the god of cruelty and choose to call it god no longer, and so to give your eyes to Christ and your voice to God.

COMMENTARY

The basic thought today's lesson contains is that our attempts at defending ourselves are what make external attack seem real to us.

We fear because we believe, somewhere deep in our hearts, that we have attacked, and deserve punishment for our attack. We sense within ourselves a belief that "to hurt another brings [us] freedom" (1:4). This belief lies behind every attack we attribute to self-defense. No matter how hard we try to justify our attacks, something in us knows that our intent is to hurt the other person because we believe that hurting them will somehow free us from something. In a nutshell, we believe that we are inherently cruel.

We project our belief in attack onto something external; we see the attack as coming from outside of our own mind. In reality, there is nothing outside of our mind; we are the ones who attack ourselves by our guilt, but we believe we see the attack external to ourselves, justifying further attack on our part. Thus fear and defense become the means of preserving ourselves. And, "Love is endowed with the attributes of fear" (5:3); that is, because love would counsel us to lay down our defenses, it becomes something to fear. Love becomes dangerous.

From this perspective, fear and cruelty become a "god," an idol, something to be preserved at all costs. To let go of fear becomes the ultimate danger. We fear being without fear more than anything else; we cling to our fear, believing that it protects us.

Taken to the extreme, this "worship" of fear and cruelty ends up being projected onto God Himself; we see Him as a vengeful God, breathing fire, threatening us with hell, ready to dupe us with His talk of love, laughing with savage glee as we go down to defeat. In fact, it is our fear of God, buried as well as we can, disguised in many forms when it leaks out of our unconscious, but ever present, that is "the basic premise which enthrones the thought of fear as God" (9:4). Ultimately, all our defenses are defenses against God. Buried deep in our psyche is our conviction that the universe is out to get us. Most of our lives, if we look at them with honesty, are spent in buttressing our fortifications against "things" that seem to threaten us.

The Course calls on us to lay down our defenses as the only way of discovering that the threat is unreal (2:6–7). God is not angry. The universe is not out to get us. If God appears to us to be separate from us, only the walls we have erected make it seem so. We are the victims only of our own defenses.

We have no reason to fear. We are not cruel; we cannot be, for God Who created us has no cruelty in Him. There is no punishment hanging over our heads. We are the innocent Son of God, the Son He loves. Without that primal fear, there is nothing to project upon others; when we cease to project our fear, there is no perception of attack from without; when no attack is perceived without, there is no need for defense.

If we assess our "god" of fear and defense honestly we have to see that it is made of stone. It has no life; it cannot save us. Fear begets fear; attack begets attack. The wars of the world testify to this endlessly. Hurting others *never* makes us safe; it only adds to the cycle of fear and attack.

To realize that our trusted method of securing safety is worthless, that our champion warrior is a traitor, can be a terrifying moment. The missile silos in which we have placed all our trust are pointed at our own hearts! "This moment can be terrible. But it can also be the time of your release from abject slavery" (8:1–2). To think of giving up defense entirely can momentarily paralyze us with fear. But it can be the moment in which we are free to recognize that what we fear does not exist, and the "enemy" we have striven to keep out is allowed to enter, bringing His peace with Him.

COMMENTS ON PRACTICE LESSONS 171-200

The practice with these lessons is still the same practice we were given in Lesson 153:

- Morning and evening quiet times, which should last as long as possible—at least five minutes and ideally more than thirty.
- Hourly remembrances, which ideally last a couple minutes, but which can be reduced according to circumstances.
- Additionally, as always, we should be on the lookout for our upsets and ego-based thoughts and respond to them with the lesson for the day (response to temptation).

Still preparing for Part II

Review V tells us that we are continuing to prepare for Part II of the Workbook. This preparation takes the form of various special emphases contained in these thirty lessons. We will explore these themes below.

More motivation, certainty, commitment and unified purpose

Review V and Lesson 185 both tell us that we have been lukewarm and ambivalent in our practice, and that this has "made us walk uncertainly and slowly on the road this course sets forth" (Review V). Therefore, Lessons 171–200 focus on finding "a greater certainty, a firmer purpose and a surer goal" (Review V). The introduction to Lessons 181–200 puts it this way: "Our next few lessons make a special point of firming up your willingness to make your weak commitment strong; your scattered goals blend into one intent."

More time and effort

As one way of firming up our sense of purpose and commitment, we are asked to devote more time and effort to our practice. In Lesson 153 we were told to give as much time morning and evening as we could. Now we are told to give even more. Review V says, "This time we are ready to give more effort and more time to what we undertake." Lesson 193 says, "Morning and night, devote what time you can to serve its [time's] proper aim, and do not let the time be less than meets your deepest need. Give all you can, and give a little more." Lesson 194 says that if we will see the lesson for what it really is, "You will not hesitate to give as much consistent effort as you can."

Going beyond special blocks

As another part of strengthening our commitment, Lessons 181–200 are devoted to briefly going beyond "the special blocks that keep your vision narrow, and too limited to let you see the value of your goal" (IN(181–200).2:1). What are these blocks? They are not always made clear, but we can take educated guesses based on what the lessons focus on. Here are my guesses:

- Mistrust in our brothers and involvement with past and future goals (181)
- The belief that our home lies here in this world or in our childhood home (182)
- Valuing other gods, idols of the world (183)
- What the world's inheritance gives us, a collection of separate things with separate names (184)
- The dreams you still want, in place of the peace of God (185)
- Our self-made roles, which stand in the way of our true function (186)
- The idea that giving is a sacrifice (187)
- Our wandering thoughts, which are fixed on the outer world (188)
- Our hatred and our judgmental thoughts, which cause our perception of a fearful world (189)
- The idea that the world causes us pain (190)
- The idea that we are weak, frail, at the mercy of a fearful world (191)
- Anger, unforgiveness (192, 193)
- Fixation on and fear of the future (194)
- Ingratitude (195)
- The belief in an enemy without (196)
- Requiring visible gratitude from others (197)
- Condemnation (198)
- Identification with the body (199)
- Seeking peace from idols (200)

Experience

The reason for trying to go past our special blocks is that the Workbook wants us to have experiences, however brief, of what lies beyond them. The purpose of these experiences, these holy instants, is clear: They will make us certain of what we want. They will strengthen our commitment and unify our purpose. This emphasis on experiencing holy instants began in Lesson 157 ("Into His Presence would I enter now"), picks up speed here and continues for the rest of the Workbook.

Going beyond words

With the focus on experience, and the focus on preparing for Part II, the reliance on words is beginning to diminish in the Workbook. In other words, we no longer want mere symbols. We want the reality to which the symbols point. We no longer want to rely on words to reveal what lies behind them. We want the thing itself. This theme of going beyond words begins in the introduction to Review V, is picked up in the introduction to Lessons 181–200, and is referred to in Lessons 182, 183 and 186.

Overall theme

The overall focus here, then, is to spend more time and effort in going past our special blocks, so that we can go beyond words into experience. Through this we will strengthen our commitment and unify our goals, so that we can sufficiently prepare for the summit of the Workbook: Part II.

Review V—June 20–29

"God is but Love, and therefore so am I."

PRACTICE SUMMARY

REVIEW V

Purpose: To prepare for Part II of the Workbook. To give more time and effort to practicing, that you may hasten your slow, wavering and uncertain footsteps, and go on with more faith, certainty and sincerity. Make this review a gift to Jesus and a time in which you share with him a new yet ancient experience.

Central Thought: "God is but Love, and therefore so am I."

This thought should start and end each day, start and end each practice period, and be repeated before and after each thought to be reviewed. Each of these thoughts, in turn, should be used to support this central thought, keep it clear in mind, and make it more meaningful, personal and true.

Morning/Evening Quiet Time: Five minutes, at least; ten, better; fifteen, even better; thirty or more, best.

- Repeat the central thought (**"God is but Love, and therefore so am I."**). Then repeat the first review thought, followed by the central thought. Then repeat the second review thought, followed again by the central thought.
- Let go of the words, which are only aids. Try to go beyond their sound to their meaning. Wait for experience, place your faith in it, not the means to it. If your mind wanders, repeat the central thought.
- Close with the central thought.

Hourly Remembrance: As the hour strikes, for more than one minute (reduce if circumstances do not permit).

(Suggestion) Do a brief form of the morning and evening practice: Repeat the review thoughts, surrounding them with the central thought. Then try to go beyond the words into experience. Close with the central thought.

A copy of these generic practice instructions for Review V can be found on the tear-out Practice Card which is bound into the book.

Lesson 171—June 20

Review V: "God is but Love, and therefore so am I."
(151) "All things are echoes of the Voice for God."
(152) "The power of decision is my own."

PRACTICE SUMMARY

See the Review V instructions on page 129, or the tear-out Practice Card.

COMMENTARY

Another review! As you read through the Introduction to the Review, you will notice that there are no detailed practice instructions. The summary, given in paragraph 11, is the only reference to the actual practice we are meant to follow. A morning time, an evening time, and keeping the idea in our remembrance throughout the day—that's all the instruction we are given. Actually, the full instructions were given in Lesson 153, paragraphs 15–18. There, the instructions were said to be "a form we will maintain for quite a while." That "while" is still continuing. The daily practice is well summarized by Robert on page 129, and on the tear-out Practice Card that comes with this volume.

In the ten days of review, I will be commenting mainly on the Review Introduction, rather than the daily ideas being reviewed. Today I'll cover the first three paragraphs, and then one paragraph a day for the remaining nine review lessons. The theme idea for the review is: "God is but Love, and therefore so am I." We are told (4:2) that each of the twenty thoughts we are reviewing clarifies some aspect of the theme thought; I will also attempt to point out some ways the theme is connected to each day's two thoughts.

The Introduction to our review opens with a powerful appeal to us to take our practicing seriously, to "give more effort and more time to what we undertake" (1:2). Once again, as in Review IV, we are reminded that this series of lessons is meant to help us in "preparing for another phase of understanding" (1:3). Review IV made it clear that this is a reference to the second part of the Workbook: "...this time...we are preparing for the second part of learning how the truth can be applied" (W-rIV.In.1:1). The realization that we are preparing for something more, a shift into another phase, is meant to motivate our efforts so that we "take this step completely, that we may go on again more certain, more sincere, with faith upheld more surely" (1:4). One gets the sense that the effectiveness of the second half of the Workbook depends, in large measure, on how much time and effort we are willing to put into our practicing right now.

I remember the first few times I did the Workbook, I always felt the second half was a bust. Anticlimactic. I also remember that I made no serious effort to follow the practice instructions; I just read the lesson every morning. I am absolutely certain that there is a direct connection between those two facts: my feeble practice, and my sense of anticlimax.

The Workbook recognizes that we have been wavering, and that we have had doubts that caused us to be less than diligent in practicing. It does not berate us over this, but it does make clear that if we want the results, we have to follow the program. The reward will be "a greater certainty, a firmer purpose and a surer goal" (1:6).

The prayer in paragraphs two and three would be, in my opinion, a good one to use every day during this review. It needs no comment; the meaning of every line is quite clear. It is a prayer for diligence in practicing. It is an affirmation of faith that, even if we forget, stumble, or wander off, God will remember for us, raise us up, and call us back.

Today's two thoughts connect easily to the theme idea. If God is only Love, and I am also only love, then everything echoes His Voice. Everything is nothing but an aspect of Him. The decision I face, today and every day, is whether or not to accept this fact. Will I live today as an expression of the Love of God, or will I choose to attempt what must be impossible: to be something else?

Lesson 172 (Review V)—June 21

Review V: "God is but Love, and therefore so am I."
(153) "In my defenselessness my safety lies."
(154) "I am among the ministers of God."

PRACTICE SUMMARY

See the Review V instructions on page 129, or the tear-out Practice Card.

COMMENTARY

Paragraph 4 of the Review Introduction:

"This is the thought..." (W-rV.In.4:1). The words refer to sentence 3 of the paragraph, the theme thought for the review. As we review, we are to dwell on this thought first, every day, every morning and evening, and often through the day. Each additional thought from the previous lessons "clarifies some aspect of this thought, or helps it be more meaningful, more personal and true, and more descriptive of the holy Self we share and now prepare to know again" (4:2). It would be good, in our reviewing, to meditate on how this central thought relates to the other two ideas. The focus is on the theme thought; the additional thoughts are meant to clarify it or expand on it.

Notice the word "prepare" used again in sentence 2. The new "phase of understanding" that we are preparing for will have something to do with once again coming to know our true Self. The first half of the Workbook has concentrated on undoing our old thought system; the second half will move us on into reclaiming the knowledge of the Self we thought we had lost.

The holy Self we are is simply an extension of God. He is Love; so are we. We are what He is, extended. That is what we are preparing to remember; more than simply to remember, to *know*. That one word implies worlds. I can write the words, I can agree with them, but do I *know* what I am saying? Knowing that I am an extension of God's Love will change everything about my life, banish all fear, and give me a sense of holy purpose unparalleled by anything I have every before experienced.

What is this Self, which I am, like? It is "perfectly consistent in Its thoughts; knows Its Creator, understands Itself, is perfect in Its knowledge and Its love, and never changes from Its constant state of union with Its Father and Itself" (4:5). This is a description of me and you as God created us. This is what our practicing is preparing us to "know again."

Isn't this a goal worth "more effort and more time"? (1:2) Try to imagine what it will be like (not "would be" but "will be") to be perfectly consistent in all your thoughts. Try to get a sense of what it will be like to know God and yourself perfectly. Try to imagine living in a constant state of union with the Father, and with your Self, without variation or change in that state of union.

Today's two review ideas help us to see the way to our goal, negatively and positively. If I am Love, how can I be defensive? To be what I am in truth, I must lay down my defensiveness. And if I am Love, what can I be but a minister of God? What can my purpose here be but to extend His Love, to reach out and touch my brothers with the touch of Christ?

Lesson 173 (Review V)—June 22

Review V: "God is but Love, and therefore so am I."
(155) "I will step back and let Him lead the way."
(156) "I walk with God in perfect holiness."

PRACTICE SUMMARY

See the Review V instructions on page 129, or the tear-out Practice Card.

COMMENTARY

Paragraph 5 of the Review Introduction:

The Self that is only Love, perfectly consistent in Its thoughts, is What "waits to meet us at the journey's ending" (5:1). I often need to remind myself of what it is I am "going for" in this spiritual walk. Sometimes it seems like such a long journey—"countless situations...through time that seems to have no end" (T-24.VI.7:2). Keeping the goal in view, in the forefront of my mind, is a necessity for me. "This," with a capital "T," "is promised us" (5:4). I am on a journey to find my Self, and at the end of the journey, it is promised, I will find It. A Self in constant union with God. A Self at perfect peace within Itself. This is worth "going for."

The journey seems long, but every step brings me a little nearer (5:2). Each time I pause for a minute to remember brings me nearer. Each time I open my heart in love to a brother brings me nearer. Each morning or evening I take the time to practice, sitting in silence, listening, brings me nearer. The path offered by the Course is not a flashy one. It is not, sometimes, a very exciting one. But it works. It is so clear to me that this work *must* be done somehow; the twisted thoughts of my ego must be undone and replaced with something else. The multitude of fear's disguises must be unmasked and replaced with love. Sometimes I wish it could happen overnight. Sometimes I wonder why it seems to take so long and proceed so slowly. And then I catch my own thoughts, turning me away, delaying me, and I know why. Occasionally I even feel gratitude that God does not force anything on me against my will, because, when at last I end the journey, there will be not one shred of uncertainty that it is my will, as well as His. And I return to the steady work the Course sets forth, knowing that—for me, at least—this is the only way I have found that works.

"This review"—done as we are asked to do it, of course—"will shorten time immeasurably" (5:3). So if I feel impatient, here is the means to shorten the time it takes. The means are being given to me, handed to me on a silver platter, put before my eyes day after day. Will I take them? Will I use the means given me to shorten time? I say so often that I want the journey to proceed more quickly. Yet if, given the means to shorten the time, I do not use them, what does that say about my wanting? My regularity in practice is the measure of my true desire.

If I practice with the goal in mind, if I remember why I am doing it, the benefit will be maximal. If, however, I trudge through the practice as if it were some kind of duty being imposed on me, a tedious chore, I will benefit less.

Today let me raise my heart from dust to life as I remember (5:4). Let me lift up my eyes and recall the glorious goal, the completeness of my Self that awaits my remembering. Let the inner hunger that never leaves me have its way and draw me onward.

Today's two review ideas dovetail nicely with the ideas in the paragraph from the review introduction. I "step back and let Him lead the way," willingly following His direction. And I am encouraged on my journey in knowing that as I go, "I walk with God in perfect holiness."

> ...this course was sent to open up the path of light to us, and teach us, step by step, how to return to the eternal Self we thought we lost (5:5).

Thank You, Father, for this course. Thank You for its step-by-step instructions. Thank You for this time of review, for the times I can spend with You, quietly, listening, waiting, knowing that every minute draws me nearer to my goal, every minute saves immeasurable time. Thank You for opening up the path of light.

Lesson 174 (Review V)—June 23

Review V: "God is but Love, and therefore so am I."
(157) "Into His Presence would I enter now."
(158) "Today I learn to give as I receive."

PRACTICE SUMMARY

See the Review V instructions on page 129, or the tear-out Practice Card.

COMMENTARY

Paragraph 6 of the Review Introduction:

In this paragraph, Jesus speaks in the first person: "I take the journey with you" (6:1). One aspect of the Course that seems to get less attention than many others is the personal presence of the author in our lives. No doubt many of us, feeling we have "escaped" from what we perceived as restrictive Christian backgrounds, many of which emphasized a "personal Savior" and the actual worship of Jesus as God's only Son, find ourselves uncomfortable with the notion of having Jesus by our side as we make this journey. It is too much like what we left behind.

In the Clarification of Terms section in the Manual for Teachers, we are reminded that, "Some bitter idols have been made of him who would be only brother to the world" (C-5.5:7). One relationship that may need healing is our relationship with him; we may carry with us many "shadow figures" from the past that distort our perceptions of him. We are asked, here in the Manual, to, "Forgive him your illusions, and behold how dear a brother he would be to you" (C-5.5:8). Yet the Course takes this issue, as all such issues, gently. "It is possible to read his words and benefit from them without accepting him into your life. Yet he would help you yet a little more if you will share your pains and joys with him" (C-5.6:6–7). So if you find this idea of relating with him a little unsettling or even distasteful, be at peace; it's okay.

Jesus offers to share our doubts and fears in order to make himself accessible to us. We can know he understands what we go through because he has been this way before. Even though he has reached a place where uncertainty and pain have no meaning, he understands them when we experience them. We don't have to feel that we are approaching some remote figure, high and mighty, who will dismiss our uncertainty as irrelevant with a wave of his hand. He sees what we see. He is aware of all the illusions that terrify us, and the reality they seem to have to us. But he holds in his mind "the way that led him out, and now will lead you out with him" (6:5). He is like an elder brother who has finished the journey, but has come back now to lead us home with him. He knows that the Sonship is not complete until we have walked the same way he walked. He is with us now, leading the way for us.

In my quiet time today, then, let me be aware of his presence. As I enter into God's Presence, let me be conscious of one who is at my side, perhaps holding my hand if I feel fearful. Let me be willing to bring my uncertainty and pain to him, so that he can help me overcome them. As I receive the grace from him enabling me to set aside my fears and doubts, let me learn to give as I receive. Let me come forth from this time with him to share what I have received with those around me. Let me act as God's representative in the world, to forgive the "sins" of those around me, ease their minds, and offer them the peace that has been given me.

Lesson 175 (Review V)—June 24

Review V: "God is but Love, and therefore so am I."
(159) "I give the miracles I have received."
(160) "I am at home. Fear is the stranger here."

PRACTICE SUMMARY

See the Review V instructions on page 129, or the tear-out Practice Card.

COMMENTARY

Paragraph 7 of the Review Introduction:

You know, from the way Jesus talks in the first sentence, it sounds like this is something he has experienced more than once! "My resurrection comes again each time I lead a brother safely to the place at which the journey ends and is forgot" (7:1). I'd certainly like to think that there have been more than just him; it would be disheartening if he were the only one so far. I think, today, that there have probably been far more than we realize who have reached the journey's end with him. Sometimes we wonder why there seem to be so few in this world who seem to have "made it," but if I think about it, it seems to me that "this world" is the last place we are likely to find such people! I'm just glad that Jesus, at least, has decided to hang around and be a "savior...with those he teaches" (6:5). (Actually the Course implies that there are others as well; see Chapter 26 of the Manual, "Can God be Reached Directly?", first two paragraphs.)

There is something uplifting about the idea that when I learn, in some circumstance, the way out of "misery and pain" (7:3), that Jesus is "renewed." Actually, of course, that is true of all of us; every one of us is renewed when a brother learns the way out of pain. Everyone we touch with a miracle enriches us when they receive it. When anyone shares an account of a miracle in their life, everyone who hears is renewed; that is what makes the sharing so refreshing. My own walk with God is strengthened every time I realize that something I have said helped someone. The Course often says that those we help help us, that our brothers see in us more than we can see in ourselves; that is how we learn to remember what we are.

Let me remember, today, that every time I turn my mind to the light within myself, and look for Him, Christ is reborn. This is how the Second Coming happens (see W-pII.9.3:2, in "What is the Second Coming?"). When we all have given our minds wholly to Christ the Second Coming will be complete. Each time I turn to the light within, I bring it nearer. Each time today that I remember, "God is but Love, and therefore so am I," I hasten that day. Each time I choose to give the miracles I have received, each time I remember that my Self, and not fear, is at home in me, Christ is reborn in the world.

No one has been forgotten. I love Marianne Williamson's line, "God hasn't lost your file." I like to imagine the hustle and bustle in the "heavenly office," with all sorts of entities working on my behalf, all unknown to me. Planting little clues where I'll find them. Arranging for me to meet the right people, stumble over the right books, and go through the experiences I need to go through.

But all of this needs my cooperation. The last sentence is almost paradoxical, stating that Jesus needs *my help* to lead me back to where the journey was begun. But it makes sense, for as the Course says all along, the one essential is my willingness. He *leads* me, he doesn't force me. My help consists in being willing to follow, stopping now and then to listen for directions. And in doing the practice he gives me to do.

I notice that he is leading me backwards (!) to where the journey began, in order that I can make "another choice." All of his work with me is to take me back to that moment when I made the wrong choice, so that I can make it differently. Nothing, then, is irrevocable. Even the pivotal choice that began the nightmare can be undone, and will be undone, and *has been* undone. He is leading us up the ladder that separation led us down (T-28.III.1:2). Each mistaken choice that I allow him to undo today is another step back up the ladder to the memory of my original state, to the memory of the fact that, "God is but Love, and therefore so am I."

We give the miracles we have received, and as we do, we remember we are at home, and it is fear that is the stranger.

Lesson 176 (Review V)—June 25

Review V: "God is but Love, and therefore so am I."
(161) "Give me your blessing, holy Son of God."
(162) "I am as God created me."

PRACTICE SUMMARY

See the Review V instructions on page 129, or the tear-out Practice Card.

COMMENTARY

Paragraph 8 of the Review Introduction:

Our practicing somehow releases Christ to the world. Opening our minds to the Holy Spirit makes us available as channels to those around us. The Holy Spirit, of course, is "Him Who sees your bitter need, and knows the answer God has given Him" (8:1). One of the things that makes the Course so unique, I think, is the way in which it both acknowledges our "bitter need" and yet affirms that in reality we have no needs. It is as if He is saying to us, "I know that the world of pain and loss is only an illusion and nothing to be disturbed about, but I also know that, to you, it is very, very real, and I am ready to work with you on that basis."

Quite clearly, we are being encouraged to develop a relationship with Jesus and the Holy Spirit. We review "together." We devote our time and effort to them "together." We are not simply individuals practicing some kind of mind manipulation; we are engaging in a relationship, a collaborative venture.

> Healing does not come from anyone else. You must accept guidance from within. The guidance must be what you want, or it will be meaningless to you. That is why healing is a collaborative venture. I can tell you what to do, but you must collaborate by believing that I know what you should do (T-8.IV.4:5–9).

So we are reviewing these thoughts *with him*. We are not just mulling them over by ourselves, but listening to that guidance from within as we do so.

"And together we will teach them to our brothers" (8:4). Have you noticed how nearly every time the Course talks about the process we are going through, it ends up with some aspect of sharing or extension, some kind of giving what we have received to our brothers? The Course is not a personal path of salvation. Indeed it teaches there *is* no such thing as individual salvation, because "individual" is an illusion. We are not alone. We are not separate individuals who can be individually saved. We are part of a Whole, and when we begin to receive what the Holy Spirit has to teach, we *must* share it, because sharing is what He is teaching. We teach "by actions or thoughts; in words or soundlessly; in any language or in no language; in any place or time or manner" (M-1.3:6).

We share precisely because the Whole is not Whole until everyone is included. As Jesus is incomplete without us, we are incomplete without our brothers. We, like Jesus, may recognize the wholeness in ourselves and in so doing, recognize it in our brothers. The wholeness is already there, but unacknowledged and unrecognized: "I am as God created me," as one of our thoughts for review reminds us. Our "ancient home" is being "kept unchanged by time, immaculate and safe" (8:8). We cannot lose it, but we *have* lost awareness of it, and that awareness is what we share with each other.

As we begin to accept our own wholeness we become reminders to the world of the wholeness that is also theirs, and that we share with them. There is no "preaching" quality, no spiritual elite telling the rest of the world "how it is." It is the happy communication that, "You are whole, as I am. I am as God created me, and you are as God created you." We come to our brothers, not as superiors, but asking their blessing on us, acknowledging them as the holy Son of God, along with us: "Give me your blessing, holy Son of God."

> Your holiness is the salvation of the world. It lets you teach the world that it is one with you, not by preaching to it, not by telling it anything, but merely by your quiet recognition that in your holiness are all things blessed along with you (W-pI.37.3).

Lesson 177 (Review V)—June 26

Review V: "God is but Love, and therefore so am I."
(163) "There is no death. The Son of God is free."
(164) "Now are we one with Him Who is our Source."

PRACTICE SUMMARY

See the Review V instructions on page 129, or the tear-out Practice Card.

COMMENTARY

Paragraph 9 of the Review Introduction:

Four more days of this review; four more days of our "gift" to him. Of course, every moment we connect with our right mind, every moment we taste the one holy instant, is a gift as well. This paragraph has a wonderful flavor to it: our hearing his words; us giving them to the world; Christ working through us to save the world; walking together to God with him; taking the hand of our brother as we go. A wonderful connective energy, all part of a magnificent Whole which is our Self, sourced from God. The energy flows to us and through us, from us to our brothers and from them to us, weaving us all together in the divine fabric. We are one with Him Who is our Source.

"For this alone I need; that you will hear the words I speak, and give them to the world. You are my voice, my eyes, my feet, my hands through which I save the world" (9:2). This is the real purpose of my existence and my experience here in the world. I may feel confusion, day to day, about my purpose and the form it is taking. I may have my doubts about those with whom my life is now interacting, wondering how in Heaven's name they could ever be part of any divine plan. I may wonder the same about myself. But Jesus speaks in these words from the Course saying, in effect, "My only need is you. I need your physical presence to reach through you to the others who are lost in the illusion of bodies."

How can this be? How, in the mess I find myself in, can this happen? I don't know. But I believe that the Holy Spirit knows. All I can do is to make myself available, to be willing for it to happen. Let me remember that these thoughts of anxiety, doubt, lack of trust and sadness are all just forms of the belief in death, and let them go, placing them in His hands. Let me place myself in His hands as well, remembering that I am one with Him Who is my Source; I am Love as God is, I am the extension of His Being, as are we all. If I can believe this I am free.

Donna Cary has written a wonderful song, one of many based on her experience with the Course. The chorus of it repeats over and over, "He's asking me to give myself to Him, Calling me to give myself to Him." The song speaks of the fear that arises when we hear this call.

Can I say, today, "He needs me. He wants my hands, my feet, my eyes and my voice. Father, I am frightened, but here I am. Use me"? Let me be the instrument of His peace. Or, in the words of a Christian poet of the last century, Amy Carmichael:

Love through me, Love of God.
Make me like Thy clear air,
Through which, unhindered, colors pass
As though it were not there.

God is nothing but Love, and "therefore, so am I." Let that Love flow through me, unhindered by anything. Let me be clear and clean. Remind me, God, that I am free today; there is no death, there is no opposite to Love, or to life. Let my life be an expression of that truth.

Lesson 178 (Review V)—June 27

Review V: "God is but Love, and therefore so am I."
(165) "Let not my mind deny the Thought of God."
(166) "I am entrusted with the gifts of God."

PRACTICE SUMMARY

See the Review V instructions on page 129, or the tear-out Practice Card.

COMMENTARY

Paragraph 10 of the Review Introduction:

The practice of the Workbook is meant to induce, not just new thoughts and new permutations of thoughts, but an experience: "a new experience for you, yet one as old as time and older still" (10:1). How can an experience be older than time? How but in being part of eternity? "The holy instant reaches to eternity, and to the Mind of God" (T-15.V.11:5). "The holy instant is a miniature of eternity" (T-17.IV.11:4). These times spent in quiet with God are occasions when we step out of time and into timelessness; what we experience here is older than time, incredibly ancient and yet immediately present, always present.

We are experiencing our Self. "Hallowed your name. Your glory undefiled forever" (10:2–3). These are words that sound to us (if our background is Christian, at any rate) as if they should be spoken of God. Yet here they are spoken of *you* and of me. What is it like to experience such a thing? What is it like to know yourself as One of whom these words can be spoken, one who is entrusted with the gifts of God? I do not think words can convey it, although many have attempted to do so. What is required is an experience; then, words become unnecessary and even unwanted.

"There is a kind of experience so different from anything the ego can offer that you will never want to cover or hide it again" (T-4.III.5:1). That is what we are seeking in these quiet times. Not desperately or anxiously, not with concern or fear that it will not come to us, but peacefully, quietly, trustingly. We cannot force it to happen, we can only "let" it happen. We do not seek to add anything to ourselves, we simply seek to stop *denying* the Thought of God, which is the whole truth about us.

In this moment we can experience our "wholeness now complete, as God established it" (10:4). Once you have known your own wholeness, why would you ever again want to cover or hide it? Only the lie that what you are is something you do not want to know could have ever persuaded you to hide it. Outside the holy instant our Self is surrounded by a ring of fear; we shy away from approaching the Self because we have been tricked into believing that what we will find is fearful.

The time it seems to take to find the holy instant is not because it is mysterious and inaccessible; the time is only the measure of our fear of our Self. It takes this time to gently still our fears, until we are ready to find the Self that lies outside of time, older than time itself, whole and complete as God created It. This Self is the Thought of God. Our unawareness of it is only our denial of this Thought. Our experience of it is only the ending of our denial. The Self does not change, nor come and go. It ***is***.

In this Self we are "completing His extension in your own" (10:5). The creative extension of God is made complete as we, in turn, extend ourselves. The Love that made us flows through us to enliven others. We are practicing what we have always known; we knew it before the ancient truth seemed to disappear into illusion, and we will know it again. In the holy instant we know it now. And what we know is this: We are entrusted with the gifts of God. Our giving of them completes His giving. "We remind the world that it is free of all illusions every time we say: *God is but Love, and therefore so am I*" (10:7–8).

Lesson 179 (Review V)—June 28

Review V: "God is but Love, and therefore so am I."
(167) "There is one life, and that I share with God."
(168) "Your grace is given me. I claim it now."

PRACTICE SUMMARY

See the Review V instructions on page 129, or the tear-out Practice Card.

COMMENTARY

Paragraph 11 of the Review Introduction:

The paragraph is once again about specifics of Workbook practice. I don't mean to belabor this point, but since I am simply following the content of this Introduction, the emphasis is really not mine but that of the Course itself.

The Workbook places a great emphasis on repetition of the ideas it presents. Repetition is one of the primary techniques for mind training that it encourages. If we are doing it as directed—and I am the first to admit that I am still far short of doing so—we will be meditating on this theme thought for a minimum of five minutes in the morning and evening, with up to half an hour each time being even better. We will be recalling it every hour, and using the theme idea, "God is but Love, and therefore so am I," to frame the two additional thoughts we are reviewing for the day.

This is not a radical or strange idea. Repetition of spiritual thoughts is common in many religions. I even ran into it in fundamentalist Christianity. A teacher at an evening class I once attended at Moody Bible Institute in Chicago, in 1959, taught his students what he called Bible meditation. The general idea was to memorize verses from the Bible so as to have them handy in one's mind, and to meditate on them all during the day—upon arising, as you walked from place to place, whenever you sat waiting for anything, riding the bus or the train, and again at night just before sleeping. He defined meditation as, "Sharing with the Lord His own Word, prayerfully, and with personal application." This teacher claimed that such meditation had revolutionized his life.

It revolutionized my life as well. In time I memorized more than a thousand Bible verses. I knew entire chapters by heart, word for word. I'm sure that the practice is a good part of what took me, eventually, beyond the confines of fundamentalism.

I still remember one of the first times that I set aside time right before sleeping to meditate. I sat up for five or ten minutes, ruminating on the verses for that day, turning them into prayer, communing with God over them, applying them to my life. Then I fell asleep with the words still going through my mind.

The next morning, I woke up and lay in that half-awake state just before you open your eyes. And there in my mind, like a mantra, the words were still being repeated. I believed then, and do now, that they had been playing over and over like a tape loop in my mind all during the night. I woke that morning with a joyful burst of faith, realizing that I was truly feeding my mind with nourishing thoughts.

It is a wonderful thing to find the words of the Course springing into your mind spontaneously during the day, or as you wake up. But that doesn't happen without a lot of repetition. Without practice of these thoughts, the tape loops running in our minds are something very different, because we have already trained our minds very well, but with the wrong thoughts. It takes a conscious effort, repeated choices to remember the thoughts for the day and to repeat them, to meditate on them, and to apply them to our lives. This is a course in mind training, and "training" means "training."

When we enter wholeheartedly into the training, there will be results. "We will have recognized the words we speak are true" (11:5). So let us remember today, and often, that, "There is one life, and that I share with God." Let us affirm to ourselves, constantly, every time we can, "Your grace is given me. I claim it now."

Don't be discouraged if you forget. I still forget often. But I remember more often than I used to. If you have done nothing more before today than read over the lesson in the morning, then if today you remember just one time during the day, or take a few minutes before sleeping, thank God. Try to remember today just one more time than yesterday. If, yesterday, you forgot entirely, then resolve today to remember at least once. Every time you remember is a great step forward.

The paragraph we will cover tomorrow reminds us that the words are only aids, and the practice is just a means to produce an experience. Don't make a ritual out of the practice; the experience is what counts.

Lesson 180 (Review V)—June 29

Review V: "God is but Love, and therefore so am I."
(169) "By grace I live. By grace I am released."
(170) "There is no cruelty in God and none in me."

PRACTICE SUMMARY

See the Review V instructions on page 129, or the tear-out Practice Card.

COMMENTARY

Paragraph 12 of the Review Introduction:

Yesterday we thought again about the means of practice that we are being taught, the frequent repetition of the thoughts for the day. Today's paragraph reminds us that the words are only aids. Their purpose is simply to "recall the mind, as needed, to its purpose" (12:1). The purpose is in the experience, the communion with God experienced during the holy instants we spend. "We place faith in the experience that comes from practice, not the means we use" (12:2).

What is the mind's purpose to which we are being recalled? It is remembering Who we are, and sharing that with the world, reminding them of their true Self, shared with us. The repetition of words only brings us back to this memory of a Self that is in constant union with Its Father and Itself, His natural extension. The goal of our practice is to experience that state of right-mindedness, even if only for a brief moment. We are remembering that what we are is only Love, because that is all that God is. If that is so, there can be no cruelty in God, nor any cruelty in us.

The experience of the Self is what brings conviction (12:3). The words, "God is but Love, and therefore so am I," or, "By grace I live," cannot bring conviction or certainty. The experience of it not only *can* bring conviction, it *does* bring conviction. The goal of practice is to go beyond the words to the experience, to their meaning, "which is far beyond their sound" (12:4).

How does that happen? I can't tell you; no one can. But I can tell you that it does happen. It won't happen without practice. Practice does not make it happen, but it prepares the mind. It opens the door. It washes the mind clean with crystal pure thoughts, and readies it for the experience that is always there, always waiting. And in that experience, we find our rest.

Introduction to Lessons 181 to 200
June 30 to July 19

You'll recall that we have twice been told we're now in preparation for the second part of the Workbook. This Introduction is telling us a little more specifically how the next twenty lessons are meant to prepare us.

First of all, the overall goal is to strengthen our commitment and unify our goals into one intent.

The immediate goal of our practicing these lessons is *experience* of the peace, liberation and freedom that unified commitment can bring; holy instants when we have a foretaste of right-mindedness.

The method of making such experience available is a focus on the remaining blocks to it, with the intent of, even if just briefly, lifting those blocks.

If the *overall goal* is to firm up our willingness to commit ourselves more strongly to the Course's path, then obviously the Workbook is recognizing that at this point, about halfway through the Workbook, our willingness is probably still a bit irresolute, and our commitment less than complete. "You are not asked for total dedication all the time as yet" (1:2). There are probably a few of us that are quite relieved to hear that. I think it is likely that, if the Course is not yet asking for total, continual dedication at this stage, it would be unwise and counter-productive to be asking it of ourselves. We have to bear in mind those two little words, "as yet," indicating that "total dedication all the time" lies somewhere in our future; it is where we are being led. But we should not berate ourselves for not having that total dedication *now*.

What *is* being asked of us is to practice. The experience of the holy instant at this point in our spiritual growth is not expected anything more than "intermittently" (1:3). Notice how that idea is repeated several times in these three paragraphs. We are lifting the blocks "however briefly" (2:2). We aim to go past our defenses "for a little while each day" (3:4). We are practicing, each day, to bypass one major block to the awareness of love's presence, just for a short time. We aren't supposed to be worrying about making this our permanent mental state—not yet. It is the cumulative experience of these holy instants that will provide the motivation to make that total dedication; we aren't sufficiently motivated without that.

> It is experiencing this that makes it sure that you will give your total willingness to following the way the course sets forth (1:4).

> Your motivation will be so intensified that words become of little consequence. You will be sure of what you want, and what is valueless (2:5–6).

> No more than this [little while each day] is asked, because no more than this is needed. It will be enough to guarantee the rest will come (3:5–6).

In Chapter 13 of the Text we are admonished: "Be you content with healing" (T-13.VIII.7:1). And as we progress through the Workbook we need to be content with practicing—same thing. Our experience of grace at this stage may still be intermittent, just a little while each day; that's okay, and we can be at peace with its being so. Just that little while each day will be enough to *guarantee* the rest will come, so there need be no panic nor discouragement. Just do the practice and full enlightenment will surely follow; that is the promise being made here.

Lesson 181—June 30

"I trust my brothers, who are one with me."

PRACTICE SUMMARY

Generic Instructions: Morning and evening times, hourly remembrance, and response to temptation. See Lesson 153 (page 78) or the Practice Card, and also Robert's practice comments on pages 48–49.
Purpose: To go past the special blocks of mistrust in your brothers and involvement with past and future goals. This will intensify your motivation and strengthen your commitment.
Morning/Evening Quiet Time:

- Let go your focus on the sins of others. Let go your focus on your past and future goals and beliefs.
- Have only one intent: to look upon your own sinlessness. Trust in this experience for which you ask.
- If you think of a brother's sin, causing anger to block your way, say: *"It is not this I would look upon. I trust my brothers, who are one with me."*

Response To Temptation: If a brother's sins occur to you, say: *"It is not this I would look upon. I trust my brothers, who are one with me."*

COMMENTARY

This lesson is not encouraging naive blindness to people's flaws. It isn't saying that you should unlock your house and car and leave your money lying in the street, trusting no one will steal it. It is talking about looking *beyond* others' errors and mistakes (their egos) to see their sinlessness. It is speaking of being aware of a person's mistakes (and taking them into practical account), while at the same time looking past them to their perfect innocence. Not seeing the mistakes as *sins* to be condemned and punished. As my friend Lynne once said of a man who had previously been abusive to her, "I may love a rattlesnake, but that doesn't mean I sleep with it."

The "block" this lesson is helping us to lift (however briefly) is our focus on the sins of our brothers and sisters. The lesson is telling us not to look for what is wrong in people, but what is right. The point behind this is that, by focusing on the sins of others, we block their true Self from our sight, and thereby block the Self within us from our sight as well. If I cannot overlook the mistakes of my brothers, I cannot overlook my own. "Perception has a focus" (2:1). We need to change our focus. "Remove your focus on your brother's sins, and you experience the peace that comes from faith in sinlessness" (2:5). Remember the aim of these twenty lessons: to remove a block and thus *experience* something different; in this case, "faith in sinlessness."

As the Introduction said, we are not trying to do this for all time! (Not yet anyhow.) Not even for all day; just for a brief period. Do you have someone you feel you cannot forgive? How about trying to "practice" forgiving them, just for five minutes? Just for a brief period, be willing to let go of your judgments about them, to forget the past and to forget the future, and to look for the innocence in them, to see them as a holy child of God, deserving of His Love. How about trying, even for five minutes, just to be *willing* for this kind of experience? Don't worry about the fact that for the last month, or year, or however long, you've wanted to kill them; don't worry about the fact that ten minutes from now you will be fantasizing about how they will get what is coming to them. Maybe so. "How could this matter?" (5:1) The concerns we have about the past or the future "are but defenses against present change of focus in perception" (5:3). If we can let ourselves experience, even for a brief moment, what it feels like to see past their sins to innocence, that experience will be enough to motivate us to go all the way.

I encourage us all to bear these instructions in mind, not just for today's lesson, but for all the rest of the Workbook. When you sit down for a quiet time, put aside how you felt just before, and don't worry about how you will feel afterwards. "We do not seek for long-range goals" (7:2). All we are looking for is the experience of an instant of release, because that is all that is needed. At any moment during the day we can stop and say, "This instant is our willing one with His" (9:7). That instant is all we need.

Somehow, we seem to think that we can shift from total egoity to immediate spirituality. We think that if we spend five minutes with God in the morning, the rest of the day ought to be totally transformed, immediately. Our resistance is simply too great for that to happen; we have *overlearned* the ego's lessons, and unlearning them will take some effort. The ego tells us that, "It isn't working," because we "forgave" our brother in those five minutes in the morning and spent half the rest of the day dreaming up ways to make him, or her, suffer. But something is happening; the ego is trying to make us guilty because it *knows* something is happening. Those five minutes when we lay our judgment aside bring us an experience of inner peace that we have never known before, and we know a good thing when we see it. Our motivation to forgive will grow, and grow, and grow. The experience of "surcease an instant from the misery the focus upon sin will bring" (7:3) will be such a relief that we will seek it again and again, until it grows to encompass our entire mind, all the time. All it takes is the willingness to practice.

Lesson 182——July 1

"I will be still an instant and go home."

PRACTICE SUMMARY

Generic Instructions: Morning and evening times, hourly remembrance, and response to temptation. See Lesson 153 (page 78) or the Practice Card, and also Robert's practice comments on pages 48–49.
Purpose: To go past your belief that your home lies here in this world or in your childhood home. To go home for an instant with the Child Who is your Self. This experience will intensify your motivation and strengthen your commitment.
Morning/Evening Quiet Time: Be still. Let the world recede from you. Let valueless ideas no longer have value in your mind. Let the Child Who is your Self take you home. Stay with Him there, beyond all words, in perfect, silent peace, certain you are at home.
Hourly Remembrance: (Suggestion) Be still an instant and go home with the Christ Child.
Response To Temptation: (Suggestion) When tempted to take up your shield and sword to defend yourself, remember that this Child is your defenselessness and strength.

COMMENTARY

Another lesson about the holy instant. Notice how the thread about "instants," "moments," and "intervals" of stillness, quiet, and withdrawal from the world, begun in the Introduction to this series of lessons and in Lesson 181, carries through nearly every lesson up to Lesson 200, the end of this series. It wasn't until my third or fourth time through these lessons that I realized they were all instructions in consciously setting aside short periods every day and attempting to enter the holy instant. The themes seem to differ, but all the difference lies in which block to our awareness of love's presence is being considered. The aim is always the same: a short suspension of that block, and the experience of a new awareness that comes when the block is momentarily removed.

The block being considered today is simply the temptation to find satisfaction, or to feel at home, in this world. We spend most of our lives in an attempt to adjust to the world, or to adjust the world to ourselves. It seems quite natural to us to try to be comfortable here, and we expend a great deal of effort trying to do so. This lesson appeals to us to set that effort aside, just for a brief while, and to recognize the childlike voice within us that is crying to go home—home to Heaven. We need to acknowledge that, "This world you seem to live in is not home to you" (1:1). And, recognizing this is so, to take time each day to allow this Child within us to "rest a while" (5:3) and, for "just a few instants of respite...[to] return to breathe again the holy air that fills His Father's house" (5:4).

This lesson is perhaps the most poetically beautiful lesson in the entire Workbook. Some of you have heard, perhaps, the poignant reading of most of this lesson by Beverly Hutchinson on the tape, "The Forgotten Song." It is hard for me to listen without tears, and I don't bother trying. Tears are fine, but not enough; we need to hear the appeal and to act upon it: "Rest with Him frequently today" (9:1). "Go home with Him from time to time today" (10:3). "Be still an instant and go home with Him, and be at peace a while" (12:9).

The thought of this lesson has had a powerful effect in my life. Sometimes when I am feeling my lowest—dry, dull, and discouraged—just quietly closing my eyes and saying, "I want to go home," is enough to break the spell and allow the peace of God into my mind.

Another passage, towards the end of the lesson, has had an equally powerful effect on me:

> You have not lost your innocence. It is for this you yearn. This is your heart's desire. This is the voice you hear, and this the call which cannot be denied (12:1–4).

When I remember these words, I seem to be always surprised at the soothing effect they have. I had not realized, until I repeated them, how deeply I was feeling that I *had* lost my innocence, how much the source of my depression was a hidden belief in my own loss of innocence. I suddenly realize that, yes, this *is* what I am yearning for; this *is* my heart's desire.

If you can, right now as you read this, stop, and be still and instant, and go home with me. It is so easy to do. Why delay an instant longer?

Lesson 183—July 2

"I call upon God's Name and on my own."

PRACTICE SUMMARY

Generic Instructions: Morning and evening times, hourly remembrance, and response to temptation. See Lesson 153 (page 78) or the Practice Card, and also Robert's practice comments on pages 48–49.
Purpose: To go past your special defense of valuing other gods, of valuing the idols of the world, and so experience the gift of grace. This will intensify your motivation and strengthen your commitment.
Morning/Evening Quiet Time:
- Repeat idea.
- Then sit silently and repeat God's Name slowly, over and over again. Let His Name become the all-encompassing idea that occupies your mind completely. Let it become your only thought, your only word, the only Name of anything you want. Call to God, realizing that He is all you want to call upon and all there is to call upon.
- If any other thoughts enter your mind, respond with God's Name. Realize that your distracting thoughts call upon other names, other gods. Realize, however, that there is only one Name. Call on it, and see it replace the thousand names you gave your thoughts.

Response To Temptation: (Suggestion) When tempted to value the little gods of this world, when tempted to cherish an idol, repeat God's Name, and watch the idol become a nameless and unwanted thing.

COMMENTARY

God's Name, as the term is used in this lesson and the next, symbolizes His Identity and our identity with Him. God's name is not Jehovah, or Krishna, or Allah. Yet any of those symbols could be used to represent Him. When this lesson urges us to "repeat God's Name," what, then, do we say? The actual word we use does not matter; it is the concept of His Identity that is to be foremost in our minds. We might say the word "God" over and over, or "Father," or "Divine Mother," or whatever word best symbolizes for us the Identity of God.

The general practice outlined in this lesson is very similar to practices in Eastern religions of repeating the Name of God over and over, and the intent is very much the same. In the Eastern spiritual practices, this often takes the form of chanting. The Hare Krishna religion, for instance, gains its name from the practice of repeatedly and seemingly endlessly chanting, "Hare Krishna, Hare Rama," which (I think) basically means "Praise Krishna. Praise Rama," with Krishna and Rama being names of God. A Christian group I once belonged to had a major emphasis on the practice of repeating the words, "O Lord Jesus," for extended periods of time, with exactly the same kind of intent, and with often remarkable results. Although this kind of practice is not a major emphasis of the Course, clearly it is one means offered by the Course for helping us find the holy instant. The one difference I see here is that (in 5:4) the repetitions are meant to be *silent* and done "within your quiet mind," rather than aloud.

By focusing on God's Identity, we loosen the hold that all lesser names have on our minds. We counter the illusion of separation in recognizing the one Name that represents everything there is: "There is one Name for all there is, and all that there will be" (8:5).

Many results are attributed in this lesson to repeating the Name of God: it reminds us of our identity with Him (1:5); it invites the angels to surround us and keep us safe, recognizing the holiness we share with God (2:2); it prompts the world to lay down all illusions (3:1); it causes all idols to fall (4:1,3–4); it calls upon our Self, the extension of God that we are (5:1); it acknowledges God as sole Creator of reality (8:1).

We are encouraged, almost as an aside, to do this practice with someone else, sitting together in silence and repeating God's Name in our minds; this seems to have particular merit, for by it we establish "an altar which reaches to God Himself and to His Son" (5:4). This is the only place I am aware of in the Course in which meditation with another person is even mentioned, but it is a very favorable mention, and indicates there is some added value in joining with others in meditation.

The primary idea of the practice seems to be that the thought of God replaces every other idea in our minds, and if other ideas enter, we can respond to them with God's Name (8:3–5). Instead of praying for any specific thing, or any specific persons (all of which have names that distinguish them from everything else), we repeat the Name of God which includes them all. "No prayer but this is necessary, for it holds them all within it" (10:2). As we repeat God's Name we can alter our mental state to experience the gift of grace (9:1); eventually we come to a place where, "The universe consists of nothing but the Son of God, who calls upon His Father" (11:4).

Lesson 184—July 3

"The Name of God is my inheritance."

PRACTICE SUMMARY

Generic Instructions: Morning and evening times, hourly remembrance, and response to temptation. See Lesson 153 (page 78) or the Practice Card, and also Robert's practice comments on pages 48–49.
Purpose: To go past the inheritance you gave yourself, a collection of separate things with separate names, and so experience the Name that God gave as your true inheritance. This experience will intensify your motivation and strengthen your commitment. You cannot fail today.
Morning/Evening Quiet Time:

- Repeat idea.
- Let your mind accept the Name God gave you. This is the answer to the pitiful inheritance you made for yourself. Use only this one Name in your practicing. If other names enter your mind, respond with this Name. Realize that all other names refer to nothing.

Remarks: You need this interval in which you leave the dark prison house of the world and go into the sunlight. Here you understand the name which God gave you, the one Identity that all things share. And then step back into darkness, to proclaim its unreality using names that have meaning in the world of darkness.
Response To Temptation: (Suggestion) When tempted to think someone's name defines them as a separate identity, silently apply God's Name to them.

COMMENTARY

There is a lot we could think about in this lesson. The way names, which are symbols, are based on separation and distancing of things. The way that perception is built up by these names and distinctions. How all of this forces us to view wholeness as an enemy. The way that the learning of the world consists primarily in learning all these names and ways of classifying things.

All of this is in contrast to the reality that is represented by the Name of God. The Name of God stands for wholeness, oneness, "the one Identity Which all things share" (10:2). Our perception has taught us an illusion, based on thousands of names for discreet parts we see as separate things; reality, however, is Wholeness, undifferentiated, unseparated. The picture of parts we have manufactured hides the reality of the Wholeness from us.

So, then, are we to attempt to completely set aside our perception of parts with separate names, and to live, somehow, seeing only the Oneness? Is it somehow "wrong" for us to use the names and symbols of the world, to act as though Marilyn is different from Bob? Are we to treat a bluebird like our own baby? No. The lesson affirms the absolute truth, but it does not insist we attempt to make this world fit into that picture.

First, it says quite clearly that learning all the little names and symbols of separation "is a phase of learning everyone who comes must go through" (7:2). As some teachers of transpersonal psychology (the branch of psychology that teaches that ultimate wholeness transcends individual ego development) have said, you cannot transcend the ego until you have developed a healthy ego. Ego development seems to be a necessary step in our overall growth. Children have to become healthy, adult egos before they can successfully go beyond the ego. If an adult is still wrestling with problems of personality development that, in "normal" growth, should have been handled in childhood or adolescence, those problems probably need to be addressed, on their own level, before the person seeks to transcend their ego entirely.

I am extrapolating on the lesson a good deal here, and expressing what have to be classed as opinions, not necessarily something taught by the Course. But I do think this section comes pretty close to implying this; *everyone* has to pass through the "teaching of the world" stage before they can begin to question its premises. We do not want to "stop short" at the teaching of the world (7:4), but it does seem we have to pass through it. "In its proper place, it serves but as a starting point from which another kind of learning can begin" (7:5).

Not only do we all need to pass through the world's kind of learning as a starting point, but after we have begun to "go beyond all symbols of the world," there is still reason for us to continue to use them: we have a teaching function (9:1). We still continue, for instance, to call people by name, to treat them as individuals with individual needs, but we are "not deceived" (9:3) by these apparent differences. The names and symbols of the world are necessary for purposes of communication, but, "They become but means by which you can communicate in ways the world can understand, but which you recognize is not the unity where true communication can be found" (9:5). We are using the symbols of the world to communicate the fact of Wholeness; we are using symbols to undo the symbols.

This is a tricky game. It is easy, remaining in the world and playing by the rules of separation, so to speak, to forget the reality these symbols of separation are hiding. That is exactly why the practice of holy instants is so important!

> Thus what you need are intervals each day in which the learning of the world becomes a transitory phase; a prison house from which you go into the sunlight and forget the darkness. Here you understand the Word, the Name which God has given you; the one Identity which all things share; the one acknowledgment of what is true. And then step back to darkness, not because you think it real, but only to

> proclaim its unreality in terms which still have meaning in the world that darkness rules (para. 10).

Practicing with the Name of God enables us to let go of "all foolish separations...which kept us blind" (14:3). In our quiet times we remember the Wholeness and forget the differences. We may still see differences, but what we see has not changed the truth (13:3). All things still have One Name. In our practicing we renew this awareness, and then we "step back to darkness"; we return to the world of symbols and dreams in order to proclaim to it the reality we have experienced in the holy instant.

> Father, our Name is Yours. In It we are united with all living things, and You Who are their one Creator (15:1–2).

Lesson 185—July 4

"I want the peace of God."

PRACTICE SUMMARY

Generic Instructions: Morning and evening times, hourly remembrance, and response to temptation. See Lesson 153 (page 78) or the Practice Card, and also Robert's practice comments on pages 48–49.
Purpose: To go past the dreams you still cherish and recognize that you really want the peace of God. Experiencing His peace will intensify your motivation and strengthen your commitment. You cannot fail today.
Morning/Evening Quiet Time:

- Search your mind carefully to find the dreams you still cherish. Forget the words; what does your heart really ask for? What do you think will comfort you and make you happy? Do not hide some dreams; bring them all to light.
- Ask of every dream you thus uncover: *"Is this what I would have, in place of Heaven and the peace of God?"*
- After this, practice recognizing that you really mean the words of today's idea.

Response To Temptation: (Suggestion) When tempted to want something besides the peace of God, say: *"Is this what I would have, in place of Heaven and the peace of God?"* Then try to recognize that what you really want is the peace of God.
Overall Remarks: You have often been weak, uncertain of your purpose and desire, unsure where to turn for help. Today have one intent. Make the request for God's peace, realizing that in so doing you join your mind with the call of every mind. Through this joining, you cannot fail to find the Help you need.

COMMENTARY

Kind of interesting that a lesson about the peace of God falls on the day that celebrates a revolution (Independence Day in the USA). Our local Unity minister suggested that instead of "Independence Day" we should celebrate "Inner-dependence Day," which I thought was a nice play on words and quite appropriate.

This lesson teaches two seemingly opposing things. First, it teaches us that we do not yet really mean it when we say, "I want the peace of God." For if we meant it, we would have it. "No one can mean these words and not be healed" (2:1).

> Many have said these words. But few indeed have meant them. You have but to look upon the world you see around you to be sure how very few they are (2:6–8).

Indeed, all you need to do is watch the evening news. Or spend one day at your job.

Second, it teaches us that, in spite of our obvious dedication to things other than peace, at heart we *really do* want the peace of God. All of us do. "We want the peace of God. This is no idle wish" (7:2–3). "You want the peace of God. And so do all who seem to seek for dreams" (10:1–2).

The task the Course sets before us is uncovering and fully accepting *both* of these facts. To accept them fully, they must be accepted as true of everyone, not just of ourselves. Underneath all the seeking for illusions, everyone wants peace. This is something that is universally true, a fact that can be totally depended upon. It is true, as the line I quoted in the last paragraph asserts, even of those who seem to be seeking for something else. They may not be *aware* that the peace of God is what they really want, but it is true, nevertheless (10:4). Our job in interacting with others is to remember this universal longing of every heart, and to join ourselves with it in the other person, even when they are totally unaware of it themselves.

Yet before we can firmly believe that we, and everyone, want the peace of God above all else, we have to face the fact that we have foolishly believed we wanted something else more than peace. For if we wanted only peace, we would have only peace; that is how the power of our minds works. So there must be something, or some things, that we have valued more than peace. Our first job, then, is uncovering these competing desires, assessing them honestly, recognizing that they are only idle wishes, and letting them go in favor of peace.

We want the most amazingly trivial things instead of peace. I watch a young child burst into tears and throw a tantrum because he cannot have his favorite breakfast, and I think, "The only difference between him and me is that I have developed sophisticated ways of camouflaging my tantrums." I share a house with Robert Perry and his family and another single man, and we often have guests. I have found myself losing my peace over empty ice cube trays and vanishing rolls of toilet paper. I have given away my peace in concern about who last emptied the garbage.

Perhaps, today, we can all stop ourselves when these "little" moments of separation occur and ask ourselves, "Is this what I would have, in place of Heaven and the peace of God?" (8:8) Do I really value a roll of toilet paper more than God's peace?

Let me point out one more interesting observation of this lesson: you cannot have peace alone. "The mind which means that all it wants is peace must join with other minds, for that is how peace is obtained" (6:1). To have peace we have to be willing to let the other person into our hearts. We have to recognize their desire for peace equally with our own.

The temptation is always to think, "I want peace; the problem is with the other person." Always remember, though: if you want peace, you will have it. No one else can take it from you. If you cannot be at peace when the other person seems to want something besides peace, what you are teaching that person is that your peace depends on their changing. This just reinforces the same belief in the other person, and they continue to believe that their peace depends on them changing you.

Our job is to see past the competing desires in that other person to the universal reality that lies underneath. However we respond to them, if we are to teach peace, our actions must affirm to that person that peace already lies within them, ready for them as soon as they are willing to receive it. We join our own intent with what they seek above all things (10:4). By our faith in that intent, however hidden it may appear, we draw it out of them; we give them the opportunity to recognize it within themselves and align their mind with it.

> It is this one intent we seek today, uniting our desires with the need of every heart, the call of every mind, the hope that lies beyond despair, the love attack would hide, the brotherhood that hate has sought to sever, but which still remains as God created it (14:1).

Lesson 186—July 5

"Salvation of the world depends on me."

PRACTICE SUMMARY

Generic Instructions: Morning and evening times, hourly remembrance, and response to temptation. See Lesson 153 (page 78) or the Practice Card, and also Robert's practice comments on pages 48–49.
Purpose: To go past your self-made roles, which stand in the way of your true function, and hear the Voice for God tell you of your part in the salvation of the world. To go beyond words and images to experience. This will intensify your motivation and strengthen your commitment.
Morning/Evening Quiet Time: Relinquish the roles and functions you gave yourself and listen to the Voice for God telling you your part in His plan. Do not doubt your adequacy to His plan, do not think what He says is impossible. Such false humility is arrogance. Trust that He knows you better than you do; your strengths, your wisdom and holiness. Do not cling to words and self-made images, but be willing to go beyond them to experience. Experience the Holy Spirit telling you that salvation needs your part and that you have the strength to fulfill it, that you are not weak, ignorant, helpless or sinful, but are God's Own Son.

COMMENTARY

Our individual salvation and our happiness depends on our accepting what this lesson teaches: the salvation of the world depends on us. Our function is to save the world, to bring the light and joy and peace of God to every mind within our reach—which is a far greater number than we imagine.

The lesson is not simply saying that it would be a good idea for us to accept this thought. It is saying that acceptance is imperative to our own personal freedom:

> There is one way, and only one, to be released from the imprisonment your plan to prove the false is true has brought to you. Accept the plan you did not make instead (5:1–2).

The Course is often so uncompromising: "one way, and only one." If we want to experience our own wholeness, if we want to find our Self, we *must* accept that salvation of the world depends on us. Why? Because the nature of Who we are demands it. If I am an extension of God, and if Love, which created me, is what I am, then how can I possibly accept that fact and *not* accept that my function is to give myself to the world? Giving is what Love does!

To take our place among the saviors of the world is not arrogance, if we are as God created us. It is merely accepting what has been given to us by our Creator: "We did not establish [our function]. It is not our idea" (2:2–3). In fact it is arrogant *not* to acknowledge this as our function. The self-image we make in arrogance pictures us as weak, ignorant and helpless (6:3–4). It seems humble, but it is mountainous arrogance masquerading as humility. This self-image thumbs its nose at the Creator and says, "I am what I make of myself, and not what You created me to be."

The last week or so I have frequently been finding myself feeling at loose ends. I seem to drift from one task to another, and to have a great deal of difficulty concentrating on anything. The description in 10:4 seems to describe me exactly: "The functions which the world esteems are so uncertain that they change ten times an hour at their most secure." And as I read this lesson I recognize that I have been trying to define my function for myself, instead of simply accepting the one God gave me. I have been fighting my function. Yet when it is accepted, it is so unambiguous that life simply straightens out, and all the confusion is gone: "In lovely contrast, certain as the sun's return each morning to dispel the night, your truly given function stands out clear and wholly unambiguous" (11:1).

So then, let me today stop resisting my function. Let me stop listening to my self-made image, which trembles as God speaks to me of my true function, sensing that the basis of its existence is being cut away (7:1–2). Let me simply let go of my plans for myself and surrender to the plan I did not make, trusting that everything I need to fulfill it has been given me; trusting that I am worthy to be counted among the saviors of the world; trusting that all my needs are answered by God, even though He does not see them, in whatever form is most useful at the moment (13:4–5).

> Salvation of the world depends on you who can forgive.
> Such is your function here (14:5–6).

Lesson 187—July 6

"I bless the world because I bless myself."

PRACTICE SUMMARY

Generic Instructions: Morning and evening times, hourly remembrance, and response to temptation. See Lesson 153 (page 78) or the Practice Card, and also Robert's practice comments on pages 48–49.
Purpose: To go past your belief that giving is a sacrifice and so experience the abundance that lies at the altar within. This will intensify your motivation and strengthen your commitment.
Morning/Evening Quiet Time: Be willing to look on the altar within, the altar to the one God. There you will see the lilies your brother offers you and those you offer him, in all their lovely holiness. There you are joined with all your brothers and with God. There you stand in blessedness and give as you receive. As you look within, repeat the Name of God.
Remarks: By receiving this blessing, you can bless the world. Offer this blessing to everything you see today.

COMMENTARY

We find it easy to understand that in order to give a thing, you first must have it. That's obvious. We find it more difficult to believe that giving actually increases what you have.

The key to understanding this, says the lesson, lies in the fact that, "Things but represent the thoughts that make them" (2:3). To understand how giving away what we have increases it, we have to begin to recognize that "things" are not real; what is real are the thoughts behind them. This is not necessarily saying that if I give $100 to a brother in need I will immediately receive $200 in return from some other source. However, it is saying that when I give $100 away knowing that money is just an idea I will be increasing the thought that brought money to me in the first place. Therefore, that will eventually result in more money, or more "wealth and abundance" in some form. The form may be identical or it may not.

> Perhaps the form in which the thought seems to appear is changed in giving. Yet it must return to him who gives. Nor can the form it takes be less acceptable. It must be more (2:5–8).

In other words, what is returned is always greater than what is given.

I have begun to learn this by giving away ideas directly, in my study group and in my writing. I have indeed found it true that as I give away these ideas, they increase in me. I get at least as much, if not more, benefit than anyone who is "receiving" from me. I am quite aware that I am blessing the world because I am blessing myself; I am doing this for my own benefit.

It is harder when it comes to material things. It is not so easy to make the connection that money is just an idea, or a tape is just an idea, a book is just an idea, a car is just an idea. I learn in little ways. I give away newsletters that cost me money, believing that it will return to me eventually. I give hours of my time to the study group, believing that the return will come. I still *feel* that as basically giving it away. The return has only just begun.

I think when I learn this lesson fully it will be no big deal to give up the idea of ownership entirely and to share everything I possess with anyone who needs it. But I am a long way from that as yet.

The next paragraph is very important:

> Ideas must first belong to you, before you give them. If you are to save the world, you first accept salvation for yourself. But you will not believe that this is done until you see the miracles it brings to everyone you look upon. Herein is the idea of giving clarified and given meaning. Now you can perceive that by your giving is your store increased (3:1–5).

To give salvation I must first accept it for myself. But to know I have it, I have to give it away. That must mean that I have to start giving before I know I have it! The gift that giving brings is knowing that I have the gift I give.

The lesson advises us to protect what we have by giving it away. It warns, "Yet value not its form" (4:3). In other words, you may not get it back in the exact form you give it. If I give $100 cash, I may receive a gift in a different form: a tape player, computer software, a burst of physical energy, or whatever. If I give away a particular book, I may not ever receive that particular form again, and I have to learn not to value the form, but the thought behind the form. It is foolish to value forms. "No form endures" (4:5). Remember,

> What [the giver] seems to lose is always something he will value less than what will surely be returned to him (5:8).

Every gift I give is always a gift to myself. I never lose! I gain, and so does the recipient of my gift, especially if he or she learns from me to give again. "Who understands what giving means must laugh at the idea of sacrifice" (6:2). Laugh, because there is no such thing as sacrifice. What I give is given to myself; I never lose; I always gain. How can that be called sacrifice!

The lesson clearly applies this to all forms of "giving" and all forms of "sacrifice," including pain and loss, sickness, grief, poverty, starvation and death. When I "give up" a relationship in the form I thought I wanted, according to this lesson I receive something I will value far more. Perhaps I may learn to accept the gift of self-sufficiency, for instance.

I'm sure the same will be true as I make other "sacrifices." Mistakenly I fear the "loss" I will feel with these things absent from my life. There will be no loss, no sacrifice. What I gain will far exceed the apparent loss. And in reality I lose nothing except a false identification.

For instance, I think I get a certain satisfaction and comfort from eating a nice meal. The pleasure of the taste; the pleasure of being full. I falsely identify these feelings with the object, the food. But pleasure, satisfaction and comfort are just the ideas behind the food. If I were to dissociate food from those ideas, I would not be giving up those ideas; I would be affirming them. I retain them, and they grow. There will be pleasure, satisfaction and comfort in other forms, more lasting and more generalized. I have gained the general form by giving up the specific identification of those ideas with "food."

In general, we will go through many iterations of apparent giving up, apparent sacrifice, until we learn that the thing is not the idea, that no particular form can be identified with the idea behind it. We will learn, eventually, to hold on to no form, but to always value, not the form, but the thought behind it.

Ultimately we go beyond the idea of many different thoughts to see only one Thought—the innocent Son of God, the Christ. We see that Thought within ourselves, and, "What we have looked upon we would extend, for we would see it everywhere" (11:2). "To ensure this holy sight is ours, we offer it to everything we see" (11:5).

Lesson 188—July 7

"The peace of God is shining in me now."

PRACTICE SUMMARY

Generic Instructions: Morning and evening times, hourly remembrance, and response to temptation. See Lesson 153 (page 78) or the Practice Card, and also Robert's practice comments on pages 48–49.
Purpose: To go past your wandering thoughts, which are fixed on the outer world, and so experience the peace of God shining in you now. This will intensify your motivation and strengthen your commitment.
Morning/Evening Quiet Time:

- Say: *"The peace of God is shining in me now. Let all things shine upon me in that peace. And let me bless them with the light in me."*
- Sit quietly, close your eyes. You have let your thoughts wander, stray. You have thrown them outside of you where they have become tainted by the world. Now gently bring them back. Exclude the outer world and let your attention be washed clean of insane wishes and desires. Allow your now honest and untainted thoughts to fly to the peace within. Let the light in your mind draw them home. There, they become God's holy messengers. There, they fall in line with your real thoughts, the ones you share with God. There, they become your real thoughts, having been restored to their holy inheritance. These thoughts recognize their home and point the way there. They lead you back to peace. They urge you to listen to God's Voice when you do not; to accept His Word instead of fantasies and shadows.

Remarks: As you let your thoughts go to the peace within, the peace of God in you extends from your heart around the world, blessing each living thing, restoring them to the memory of God.

COMMENTARY

I always seem to hear the emphasis in this sentence on the last word, "now." It speaks to me of the holy instant. It tells me that, whatever storms seem to be raging in my mind, whatever chaotic circumstances I find myself in, that there is within me a constant beacon of peace, forever shining, uninterrupted and uninterruptable. It calls me to stop for a moment, withdraw my attention from all the turmoil that makes up my "life" in this world, and re-connect to that peace. Somewhere within me, there is a place that is always at perfect peace, like the eye of a hurricane. And I can find that place any time I choose to do so, truly desiring to find it.

The Course is consistent in its vision. Nothing separates us from the love of God. Complete salvation, perfect peace, pure joy, and full forgiveness are always available right now. "Enlightenment is but a recognition, not a change at all" (1:4). What we call enlightenment is simply recognizing the presence of the light, which has never left us. It is realizing that the only reason we cannot see the light is that we have our hands over our eyes. That is why we "need do nothing." We don't have to *do*, we simply *un*do. We stop blocking the light, which is always there.

The particular block being addressed in this lesson (You'll recall that this series of lessons was billed as directly addressing certain specific blocks, W-pI.Int(181–200).2:1) is simply the tendency to see enlightenment as a future thing. The opening words sound the keynote: "Why wait for Heaven?" "Why wait to find it in the future, or believe it has been lost already, or was never there?" (2:2) All that we need do to discover its reality is to look for it within ourselves, where it has always been.

But the peace of God is not only *within* me, it is *shining in* me. "The peace of God is shining in you now, and from your heart extends around the world" (3:1). I may feel as bottled up as Custer at the Last Stand; I may feel as fertile as the Sahara. But from within my being, nevertheless, the peace of God is being broadcast like a universal beacon to the entire world. My right mind is extending itself in global beneficence to all creation, pausing "to caress each living thing" (3:2) (What a beautiful image that brings to my mind!), and leaving an everlasting blessing with whatever it touches. That is part of what I am bringing to my awareness; that is part of the picture of my Self that I am learning to recognize each time I stop, become quiet, and look within. When the Course tells me that I am among the saviors of the world, it isn't telling me about something I have to *achieve*, it is telling me what I already am.

Within me there is, even now, and even in my darkest moments, a living flow of thoughts of light. There is a heavenly current constantly surging through me to extend love and blessing to the world, and to myself. That flow of thoughts is something I can, in the holy instant, become aware of and tune in to.

"Accept His Word for what you are" (8:2); that is what this lesson is calling on us to do. We read of the Christ, we read of the Buddha and his heart of compassion. The Buddha is you. And that is Jesus' message to us, that we are as he is. "He that saith he abideth in him ought himself also so to walk, even as he walked" (1 John 2:6). We are the Christ; that is what we are; that is what we need to accept. It seems too high, too far beyond our concept of ourselves. But in the holy instant, in the quiet, when we withdraw from the world and "let [our] thoughts fly to the peace within" (6:4), we can know ourselves in this way. We can sense the depth of love that wants to express itself through us.

Oh, we may not do such a great job, just yet, at letting that love out. We may get in the way more often than not. But the love that would embrace the world, heal its wounds and dry its tears, is in us, and *is* us. We all know that is so, if we are willing to look at it. We can look upon the whole world today and everyone within it, and we can say:

We will forgive them all, absolving all the world from what we thought it did to us....Now we choose that it be innocent, devoid of sin and open to salvation. And we lay our saving blessing on it, as we say:

The peace of God is shining in me now. Let all things shine upon me in that peace, And let me bless them with the light in me. (10:2, 4–7).

Lesson 189—July 8

"I feel the Love of God within me now."

PRACTICE SUMMARY

Generic Instructions: Morning and evening times, hourly remembrance, and response to temptation. See Lesson 153 (page 78) or the Practice Card, and also Robert's practice comments on pages 48–49.
Purpose: To go past all your hatred and your judgmental thoughts, which cause your perception of a fearful world, and so experience the Love of God within you now. This will intensify your motivation and strengthen your commitment.
Morning/Evening Quiet Time: Be still and empty your mind of all images of yourself, all concepts of the world, all beliefs in what God is, everything you think is true, false, good, bad, your "worthy" thoughts and "shameful" thoughts, all thoughts you learned from the past. Forget even this course. And come with empty hands, quiet heart and open mind unto your God.
Remarks: Do not point out the road by which God must come to you. Merely let Him be. Open a door to Him and His Love will blaze a pathway to you, shining outward from its home within.

COMMENTARY

By this point in the Workbook, any time we see the word "now" we should be seeing it as a probable reference to the holy instant. The word "feel" also has significance, directing our attention to the realm of experience, as opposed to conceptual understanding. Given these two points we can realize that this lesson is about entering a holy instant in which we have an experience of God's Love within us.

"There is a light in you the world can not perceive" (1:1). The lesson begins by referring, as did yesterday's lesson, to the light that is within us, inherent in our creation. It is not something visible to the body's sense organs (1:2), but quite visible to a different kind of sight. To see this light and to feel the Love of God are synonymous (1:7). We are being directed to experience this other kind of seeing.

We can see "through darkened eyes of malice and of fear" (3:2), or with a mind permeated with the experience of Love's Presence within the mind. What we see within determines how we see the world. Based on our state of mind, we see either a world poised to attack us, or a world that reaches out to bless us. Either picture of the world makes the other picture inconceivable to us (3:5, 4:1).

If I am seeing "a world of hatred rising from attack" (3:5), the description of the world given in paragraph 2 seems to be no more than wishful thinking. People encountering the teaching of the Course for the first time often raise this objection. For instance, I once heard a man who had listened to a lecture on forgiveness say, "You people must be crazy! All you have to do is walk down the street in New York and you can't possibly maintain that love is all there is." He was seeing a world of hatred rising from attack; there was no room left in his mind to see anything else.

If I am seeing the world of hatred, how can I possibly see a world of love? No logical argument will ever change my mind. What is required is something that will change what my mind is seeing within itself, because the world I see is nothing more than a reflection of that, the outside picture of an inward condition (T-21.Int.1:5). If I am seeing a world of attack it is because within myself I am seeing an attacking mind. "What they have felt in them they look upon, and see its sure reflection everywhere" (4:3). The holy instant can, and does, change that self-perception. "I feel the Love of God within me now." That experience will literally transform the way I see the world. "If you feel the Love of God within you, you will look out on a world of mercy and of love" (5:5).

This is why we are asked to "lay aside all thoughts of what [we] are" (7:1), to be still, and to allow something else to enter our minds. We are being asked to set aside every conclusion we have ever made about anything, to allow—for a moment at least—that all of it may be misinformed and misguided, and to "come with wholly empty hands unto your God" (7:5). In asking us to forget even "this course" the lesson is not saying that intellectual comprehension of the course is not useful, but it is saying that only something that transcends the intellect can truly turn the tide of our wrong perception. Even our understanding of the Course is bound to be distorted when it is based on a mind firmly rooted in fear and in the concept of self we have built up. We may mistakenly use that imperfect understanding to dictate to God the way He should come to us. So we are asked to set even this aside, and to allow God to come to us in whatever way He wants to come.

To forget the Course is not a permanent principle, but a temporary expedient to be practiced in our moments of stillness, designed to allow a new kind of experience. It is merely part of removing the barriers to the experience of ourselves as Love, for even our ego-based "understanding" of the Course can interfere with the experience of its true meaning. So we are being told, when seeking the holy instant, to lay aside any assumption that we understand anything at all. Let everything be open to change. If we are willing to do this, "His Love will blaze its pathway of itself" (9:4).

We cannot force ourselves to see the world differently. But if we can, just for an instant, see *ourselves* differently, and feel the Love of God within ourselves, the way we see the world will change of itself, because the way we see the world *is* the way we see ourselves.

Lesson 190—July 9

"I choose the joy of God instead of pain."

PRACTICE SUMMARY

Generic Instructions: Morning and evening times, hourly remembrance, and response to temptation. See Lesson 153 (page 78) or the Practice Card, and also Robert's practice comments on pages 48–49.
Purpose: To go past your idea that the world causes you pain and experience the joy that lies beyond it. This will intensify your motivation and strengthen your commitment.
Morning/Evening Quiet Time: Lay down all thoughts of attack, judgment, danger and fear and come into the quiet place of Heaven's peace. Here you will understand that instead of pain, the joy of God belongs to you.
Response To Temptation: (Suggestion) When tempted to think that the world causes your pain, or to believe in any form of danger and attack, choose the joy of God instead of pain.

COMMENTARY

This is a tough lesson. It confronts us with another of those blocks we've been talking about: the apparent reality of pain. As the lesson very clearly states, pain seems to bear witness to "a nightmare of abandonment by an Eternal Love" (2:5). "It witnesses to God the Father's hatred of His Son…" (1:7).

Anyone who has experienced serious pain knows what this is talking about. Anyone who has had a loved one endure deep, constant pain, knows the questions it raises in the mind. "How could God allow this to happen, if He is love?" Even the milder forms of pain tell the same story, raise the same questions.

I am not going to pretend that I have entirely succeeded in removing this block from my mind. I find it hard to write about this lesson because I recognize that a very present part of me still sees pain as real, rather than illusion. Yet, I do believe that what the lesson says is true. I choose to believe it, and I want to believe it. So I do not see myself as being in conflict over this issue. I am learning, more and more, to look my fears straight in the face, and to recognize that I still do believe, in large measure, that pain is real. And if this lesson is true, this must mean that part of me believes there is no God (3:3–4), that the impossible has happened, and Eternal Love has abandoned me. If I have been reading the Text with any discernment, this is not news to me.

What then? Do I need to wallow in guilt because my mind has not yet been entirely renewed? Of course not.

> The time has come to laugh at such insane ideas. There is no need to think of them as savage crimes, or secret sins with weighty consequences (4:2–3).

If the way to remember the Love of God is to look without judgment on my denial of Him, then seeing these "insane ideas" in my mind is a necessary part of the process, and an indication of progress, not regression. And the cure is not guilt, but laughter!

Basically, we have two choices in regard to pain. Either it is caused by something outside of us, which means ultimately that we are innocents suffering at the hands of an angry God (or that there is no God and we are subject to blind fate), or it is caused by myself, my own thoughts. If the former is true I have no hope of escape. If the latter is true, I *can* escape by changing my thoughts. I prefer to believe the latter! Even if I am wrong, what have I got to lose?

The Course's position is crystal clear:

> It is your thoughts alone that cause you pain. Nothing external to your mind can hurt or injure you in any way.... No one but yourself affects you" (5:1–2, 4).

It takes some practice to learn to use these thoughts without any guilt. We are responsible, but not guilty; the Course is very clear on that as well. It also takes practice, perhaps even more, to use these thoughts when interacting with someone else who is in pain. May God forbid that we should ever use this line of reasoning to make someone guilty for their pain! The Course is equally clear that, if we are unable as yet to fully accept this, if our level of fear is still too high to rely solely upon the mind to relieve pain, a compromise approach is necessary. To attempt to forgo medication, for instance, when to do so increases our fear, is counterproductive (see T-2.IV.3–5 and T-2.V.2). Healing is the release from fear; what increases fear cannot be healing.

Let me, then, learn to increasingly apply this lesson in ways that my level of fear can tolerate. Let me realize, for instance, that the person who cuts me off in traffic has not hurt me; only my thoughts about it hurt me. Let me realize that the person who seems to reject my love has not brought me any pain; only my thoughts about it cause me pain. Let me practice with physical pain as well as I can; if I have a headache, upset stomach or cold, let me realize that my thoughts are the source, not anything outside of my mind. Let me realize that if I take medication I am masking the symptom, not curing the problem, and let me give equal attention to the healing of my mind. If I experience more severe or chronic pain, let me deny what it seems to witness to (God's anger or non-existence), laugh at the idea that God is angry, and realize that the pain is only showing me that my mind is mistaken in what I think I am (2:3). Let me not focus on making the pain go away, but on healing the thinking that causes it. Using "magic" (physical means) to alleviate the pain while I devote myself to retraining my mind simply makes sense, and frees my mind to do what it needs to do.

And let me take frequent holy instants, to "come without defense into the quiet place where Heaven's peace holds all things still at last"

(9:1). Let me feel the Love of God within me, and set aside my unmerciful self-judgment (9:4), even if I can do so only momentarily. I can testify to having experienced this, at least; I have seen pain disappear during the holy instant, both in myself and in a friend who was in chronic pain. These holy instants can train us to experience deeper and more lasting release from all pain, and liberate the joy that has been smothered by our pain.

> Pain is illusion; joy, reality. Pain is but sleep; joy is awakening. Pain is deception; joy alone is truth (10:4–6).

Lesson 191—July 10

"I am the holy Son of God Himself."

PRACTICE SUMMARY

Generic Instructions: Morning and evening times, hourly remembrance, and response to temptation. See Lesson 153 (page 78) or the Practice Card, and also Robert's practice comments on pages 48–49.
Purpose: To go past your self-perception as weak, frail and at the mercy of a fearful world and remember that you are the holy Son of God Himself. This will intensify your motivation and strengthen your commitment. And it will save the world from suffering.
Morning/Evening Quiet Time:

- (Suggestion) Begin by saying: "I am the holy Son of God Himself. I cannot suffer, cannot be in pain; I cannot suffer loss, nor fail to do all that salvation asks."
- Then seek to go past your images of yourself as weak, frail, helpless and attacked and remember that you are God's holy Son, with all power in earth and Heaven.

COMMENTARY

Once again the Course sounds its keynote: You are as God created you. Anything God creates is like Himself—holy, sinless, guiltless, an endless spring of Love, and immortal. To put a different twist on a familiar saying, we are not human beings seeking a spiritual experience; we are spiritual beings who *think* we are having a human experience. We did not suddenly spring into existence at birth, and we do not pass out of existence when the body stops functioning. We are aspects of an immortal being, existing entirely outside of time. "I am the holy Son of God Himself."

How we see ourselves determines how we see the world. It may not be obvious at first, but if we see ourselves as other than the holy Son of God, we are "giving to the world the role of jailer to the Son of God" (1:3). If we see ourselves as separate, isolated beings, we are inevitably cast in the role of victim. We become a mote of dust in a hurricane, whirled about by the universe without any consideration for our well-being (3:2).

The world then takes on an appearance that reflects this mistaken identity we have assumed. The whole world witnesses to our frailty; all our experience here seems to testify that death is certain, and loss inevitable (2:5–6). That is what projection does. The world becomes our jailer, our victimizer. If we deny our Identity as the holy Son of God, as God created us, we make the world into a place of chaos, evil, sin and death. We then resent the world for it, although we have laid this role on the world! As I look at the world today, let me ask myself, "What have I done that this should be my world?" And let me answer myself, "I have denied my Identity as God's Son." Thus, to accept my Identity is to forgive the world for what it did not do to me.

Rectify that single mistake, and we have changed the world we see. The world cannot truly be as we see it, because Identity cannot truly be denied. Our imagined identity as *not-the-Son-of-God* is no more than a silly game, with no real effects and no real consequences. If we can begin to accept our Identity, all illusions that derive from this error disappear (4:1–6).

Again we are asked to "practice" recognizing our Identity in the holy instant. For a brief time, we "let today's idea find a place among [our] thoughts" (5:1). In that holy instant we rise far above the world (5:1) into a place of safety, where we recognize the impossibility of the world's victimizing us, because we see our own eternal, invulnerable nature. And from that place of safety we *return* to the world and set it free (5:2). Notice the similarity of this description to the earlier one in Lesson 184 (paragraph 10). In the holy instant we accept Atonement for ourselves, we recognize our true Identity. And then we return to bring the message of this shared Identity to all the world, that it may be free with us.

The realization of our Identity is enough to free us from every problem forever, and to free the world with us. To cling to our little, individual identity is to perpetuate "a devastating image of yourself walking the world in terror, with the world twisting in agony because your fears have laid the mark of death upon its heart" (7:5). Do I really want to go on playing this silly, tragic game? Do I want to continue to hold the world to task because it has not met my needs, but has denied me what is my right? Or will I recognize today that I have done this, I have denied my Self and blamed the world for it?

In the latter part of this lesson it speaks in glowing terms of "the Son of God" Who "has come in glory to redeem the lost" (8:3). Who is this "Son of God"? It is not speaking of Jesus. It is speaking of *you and me*. It appeals to us to realize that our glory is the light that saves the world, and asks us not to withhold it (10:5–6). It asks us to see the suffering in the world (not to brush over it, saying, "It's only an illusion!"), and to find it in our hearts to respond to it (10:7–8).

How can we release our brothers from suffering? By accepting our own release, by finding our own Identity (11:1–5).

> You are the holy Son of God Himself. Remember this, and all the world is free. Remember this, and earth and Heaven are one (11:6–8).

Lesson 192—July 11

"I have a function God would have me fill."

PRACTICE SUMMARY

Generic Instructions: Morning and evening times, hourly remembrance, and response to temptation. See Lesson 153 (page 78) or the Practice Card, and also Robert's practice comments on pages 48–49.

Purpose: To go past anger, to fulfill your function by forgiving your brother his sins and so experiencing that you are what he is: the Son of God. This will intensify your motivation and strengthen your commitment. And it will save the world.

Response To Temptation: Whenever someone tempts you to anger, realize you hold a sword over your head which will fall or be averted by your choice. Realize that you owe this brother thanks, for he has given you a chance to free yourself and is thus your savior.

COMMENTARY

In Heaven we have a high and holy function: it is creation. The first paragraph describes it as well as it can be put into words, although when it comes down to it we on earth cannot even truly conceive of what it is (3:1). Creation is to complete God, to extend Love in His Name. What does that mean? We cannot fully know until we are there again, experiencing its meaning directly.

On earth, therefore, we have "a function in the world in its own terms" (2:1), something we can grasp and understand in the context in which we find ourselves. "Forgiveness represents your function here" (2:3). "Forgiveness is the closest it [creation] can come to earth" (3:3). Creation is formless; forgiveness is creation translated into form, a kindly dream so close to Heaven that, when we fully enter into it, our eyes are "already opening to behold the joyful sights" the happy dreams are offering us (3:4–6).

Forgiveness as presented in the Course is far more than just letting go of specific grievances we hold against those we feel have wronged us. It is a radical shift in our perception of the entire world. The basic stance of the ego is to see the world as the cause of our unhappiness. There seems to be ample reason for such a view. How can we ever be content when nothing lasts, when pain and suffering seem to be everywhere, when things and persons dear to us are snatched away by fate, and when, no matter what we do, death awaits us at the end? Forgiveness means that we set aside such a view of the world, and allow the Holy Spirit to replace it all with a new perception. It includes even a reassessment of our own bodies, in which we disidentify with them and no longer see ourselves as bound to them. We come to see the body as "a simple teaching aid, to be laid by when learning is complete, but hardly changing him who learns at all" (4:3). We realize that we are, in reality, a "mind without a body" (5:1). "Only forgiveness can relieve the mind of thinking that the body is its home" (5:5).

That is the goal to which the Course is leading us. Yet although forgiveness is far more than letting go of specific grievances, it begins there. Through working with the specifics we learn the principles, and gradually learn to generalize them and apply them to the entire world, including our physical cages.

It may seem we are being asked to give up a lot. Indeed, we are being asked, eventually, to give up the entire world, including our bodies; this entire "life" in which we think we live. Yet, when it has been achieved, when our anger at the world is gone, we

> ...will perceive that, for Christ's vision and the gift of sight, no sacrifice was asked, and only pain was lifted from a sick and tortured mind. Is this unwelcome? Is it to be feared? (6:1–3)

If we can come to forgive the world we will see it as the illusion it has always been, and let it go gladly, aware that it was never more than a nightmare of pain and death. Paradoxically, if we have not forgiven it, we end up "worshipping what is not there" (7:4). We value it precisely because it punishes us, because in our insanity of guilt we secretly believe we deserve it.

Our anger at the world imprisons us. We become the jailer, vigilant to hold the world at fault, and in so doing condemning ourselves to prison with the prisoners we are watching. Unless the "jailer" forgives "everyone he sees or thinks of or imagines" (8:1), he has to live in the jail keeping watch on the criminals. This is the very thing that holds us to this world; not its beauty, not its potential, but our anger at it for not being what we think it should be. Our anger is holding a sword above our own heads (9:4).

Therefore, the way out of prison is to release all the prisoners. We can learn this by recognizing that every time we are tempted to be angry, which can be anything from intense fury to a mild twinge of annoyance (W-pI.21.2:5), we are being offered an opportunity to release ourselves. We can be merciful instead of wrathful. We can forgive. We can even be grateful for the opportunity (9:7). This is our only true function here (10:6). This is *the* lesson all of life is teaching us. This is *A Course in Miracles*.

Lesson 193—July 12

"All things are lessons God would have me learn."

PRACTICE SUMMARY

Generic Instructions: Morning and evening times, hourly remembrance, and response to temptation. See Lesson 153 (page 78) or the Practice Card, and also Robert's practice comments on pages 48–49.
Purpose: To go past your unforgiveness and so experience the freedom and peace that lie beyond it. This will intensify your motivation and strengthen your commitment. And it will save the world.
Morning/Evening Quiet Time: As you practice, think about all the things you kept to yourself to solve alone. Then give them all to the Holy Spirit. He will show you how to see them through the eyes of forgiveness, so that they may disappear.
Remarks: Give all the time you can today, and give a little more. This is what time was made for. For now you would go in haste to your Father's home, from which you have been away too long. Do not hold mercy off another day, minute or second.
Hourly Remembrance: Apply the lesson, *"I will forgive, and this will disappear,"* to the happenings of the previous hour. Do not let it cast its shadow on the hour to come. Thus you unloose the chains of time and remain unbound while still in time.
Response To Temptation: Whenever pain seems real in your perception, hold these words in full awareness: *"I will forgive, and this will disappear."* To every apprehension and care, to all that speaks of terror, and whenever you are tempted to choose death, say: *"I will forgive, and this will disappear."*
Remarks: These words give you power over the events that seemed to have you at their mercy. They release your mind and every mind from bondage. They end all pain, temptation, tribulation and guilt. They give you the key to Heaven's gate.

COMMENTARY

The central thought of this lesson sounds similar to things said in many spiritual teachings: There is a lesson in everything, if we are open to see it and to learn. But the meaning here is quite different. Many people believe that every event, even every adversity, carries some meaning for us. "What is the lesson in this for me?" is the natural question when something seems to go wrong. If we follow this line of thinking, we can spend a great deal of our time trying to figure out the answer to that question, over and over, and we can become quite puzzled at times when we cannot seem to find what "the lesson" is.

But this Workbook Lesson is quite forthright in telling us, flat out, that the lesson is always the same in content, no matter what the form.

We do not need to waste our efforts trying to figure out what the lesson is. There is only one lesson. It is always the same.

> Each lesson has a central thought, the same in all of them. The form alone is changed, with different circumstances and events; with different characters and different themes, apparent but not real. They are the same in fundamental content. It is this:
>
> *Forgive, and you will see this differently* (2:3–7).

Lest we miss the point, it is stated again in slightly different words towards the end of the Lesson:

> This is the lesson God would have you learn: There is a way to look on everything that lets it be to you another step to Him, and to salvation of the world. To all that speaks of terror, answer thus:
>
> *I will forgive, and this will disappear* (13:1–3).

Forgiveness is the central theme of the Course. It entails, as we saw yesterday, a radical shift in our perception, one that allows the light of Heaven to shine upon everything we see. Forgiveness is the one lesson that everything, literally everything, is teaching us. Everything can teach us this lesson because, in our madness, we have a grievance against the universe. What the Course is teaching us is a different way of looking on everything, a way that allows us to see it, not as a threat, not as some kind of loss, not as an attack that deprives us of our happiness, but as a step to God, and to the salvation of the world.

When the Course tells us, as it did in earlier lessons, that forgiveness offers everything we want, that forgiveness is the key to happiness, we cannot at first understand. We are confused by the message because we do not see unforgiveness as a major problem in our lives. The lesson recognizes this:

> Certain it is that all distress does not appear to be but unforgiveness. Yet that is the content underneath the form (4:1–2).

The consistent direction of the Course's instruction is towards helping us to recognize, in all the wide variety of forms of distress in our lives, this same underlying content. Gradually, as we study the Course and apply it to our daily lives, we begin to recognize the one, unique problem that besets us, whatever form it may appear to take: unforgiveness. Forgiveness is the answer to every problem, the "hidden" lesson in every distressing event of our lives.

I am not saying that you had a flat tire because you got angry at the grocery clerk, nor that you suffer lack of success in your relationships because you haven't forgiven your mother or father. Although sometimes such things may be true, the lesson God is trying to teach us is more far-reaching than that. What ultimately must be corrected is our unforgiveness of everything and everyone in the world, everything that appears to be outside of our own minds. Our general attitude towards the world is at issue here.

When I first read this lesson, I thought it was saying that whenever something went wrong in my life I had to start searching my heart for what or whom I had not forgiven. Often that search was just as frustrating as trying to figure out, "What is the lesson in this?" I went through a period in which, one by one, I dug up every imaginable grievance I had against anyone, and tried to let it go. That can be a useful exercise, but it is only scratching the surface of what real forgiveness means. Forgiveness is aimed at transforming my perception of everything I see.

What does the Course mean by unforgiveness, or misperception? Hear this very clear definition, and let it sink into your awareness:

> How can you tell when you are seeing wrong, or someone else is failing to perceive the lesson he should learn? Does pain seem real in the perception? If it does, be sure the lesson is not learned. And there remains an unforgiveness hiding in the mind that sees the pain through eyes the mind directs (7:1–4).

"Does pain seem real in the perception?" That is the sure indicator of unforgiveness, as the Course understands it. Remember that difficult Workbook lesson about choosing the joy of God instead of pain (Lesson 190)? Forgiveness is the answer. What is forgiven no longer hurts. In response to the question, "How can you tell when you have really forgiven someone?" someone once said, "You know you have forgiven someone when you feel comfortable in their presence." That is saying the same thing; when you have forgiven, there is no more pain. Another way of picturing it is that you are free to laugh with the person. God's Will is that laughter should replace all tears (9:4–5).

Forgiveness is what time was made for (10:4). This is where our attention is best focused. This is what speeds us on the way to Heaven. In our quiet practice times, we can "think about all things we saved to settle by ourselves, and kept apart from healing" (11:4). We do not know how to look on them so that they disappear, but the Holy Spirit knows; give them to Him. We are even advised to stop every hour, review the hour that has passed, and bring each little grievance to Him for healing, so that it does not carry over into the hour that follows. "Let no one hour cast its shadow on the one that follows" (12:4). This is the way we learn to "remain unbound, in peace eternal in the world of time" (12:5).

Lesson 194—July 13

"I place the future in the Hands of God."

PRACTICE SUMMARY

Generic Instructions: Morning and evening times, hourly remembrance, and response to temptation. See Lesson 153 (page 78) or the Practice Card, and also Robert's practice comments on pages 48–49.
Purpose: Another giant stride. To go past your fixation on and fear of the future and so experience a holy instant, free of the bondage of time. This will intensify your motivation and strengthen your commitment. And it will save the world.
Morning/Evening Quiet Time: Let the future go. Place it in God's Hands. And then rest there yourself, untroubled, certain only good can come to you. Thus you call His memory to come to you and replace all your insane thoughts with the truth.
Hourly Remembrance: Use the lesson, "I place the future in the Hands of God," to forgive the happenings of the previous hour. Do not let it cast its shadow on the hour to come. Thus you unloose the chains of time and remain unbound while still in time.
Frequent Reminder: Give as much consistent effort as you can to the idea today, to make it part of you.
Response To Temptation: If you are tempted to engage in resentment or attack, repeat the idea, and you appeal to the Holy Spirit to choose for you and leave temptation behind.
Remarks: Make today's idea a rule of thought, a habit in your repertoire of response to temptation. (Notice that we are presumed to be building a repertoire of ways to respond to temptation!) Be sure that if your perception is faulty, it will be corrected. If you forget, you will be reminded.

COMMENTARY

The block to remembering our Self that is dealt with in today's lesson is the "fear of future pain" (7:6). Again, the holy instant is a major part of the remedy. All the references to "in no one instant" and "the instant in which time escapes the bondage of illusions," are indirect references to the holy instant, which is directly referred to in 5:3: "Then is each instant which was slave to time transformed into a holy instant."

The idea is a simple one: placing the future into God's Hands. Yet it is referred to as another "giant stride" toward quick salvation. (The other "giant strides" were in lessons 61, 66, 94 and 135.) This giant stride is said to take us all the way to the lawns that welcome us to Heaven's gate. It is the remedy for anxiety, pits of hell, depression, thoughts of sin, and guilt. How can this simple idea be so powerful?

Think, for a moment, how your life and your mental attitude would change if you deeply and fully knew—not just *believed* but *knew*—that your future was wholly in the hands of a loving God. Isn't it fairly easy to see how this would remove anxiety, fears of hell, depression, temptation and even guilt? Simple as it is, this is an extremely powerful idea, and a powerful one to practice.

Once again we are not expected to suddenly shift from a state of near-constant anxiety (Ernest Becker, in his book, *The Denial of Death*, refers to man's so-called normal state as one in which there is "the rumble of panic underneath everything") to one of blissful trust in God. We are being asked to practice having *instants* of such trust, free of panic. For a moment, just for a moment, "let the future go, and place it in God's Hands" (4:5). In so doing, we will understand that by doing this we have given past and present to God as well. In that holy instant we will be free of grief and misery, pain and loss. The light within us will be free to shine and bless the world.

In any particular instant, when we take that instant for itself, without past or future, we cannot feel depression, experience pain, or perceive loss; nor can we experience sorrow, or even die (3:1–3). Every such experience depends on our awareness of the past or future to sustain it and give it the illusion of reality, but none of them exist in the present moment.

Take grief, for instance. Grief is so clearly based on the past that it hardly requires explanation to say that if the past were momentarily put out of our minds, grief would vanish. The mind is calling up memories of our loved one, and then insisting that the absence of that loved one now demands emotional pain. Yet when the loved one was part of our life, there were thousands of moments in which they were not physically present with us, and we were still happy; why, then, cannot we be happy now? Grief is really nothing more than a cruel mental trick we are playing on ourselves. The future enters into grief because we envision an endless string of moments that lack the beloved. But those moments are not now; again, it is a mental trick. Grief does not exist when we are wholly in the present moment, in the holy instant.

As we learn to give the future into God's Hands, one instant after another, we are released. "And so each instant given unto God in passing, with the next one given Him already, is a time of your release from sadness, pain, and even death itself" (3:4). Note the similarity to yesterday's practice of applying forgiveness at the end of each hour to all that has passed in the hour, freeing the hour that follows. This kind of thing, says the lesson, needs to become "a thought that rules your mind, a habit in your problem-solving repertoire, a way of quick reaction to temptation" (6:2). That is what all this practice is about: developing new *habits* of spirituality that break the pattern of our deranged thinking, freeing us for a new experience. The more we experience, the more we will want it, until eventually it takes over our minds entirely.

Lesson 195—July 14

"Love is the way I walk in gratitude."

PRACTICE SUMMARY

Generic Instructions: Morning and evening times, hourly remembrance, and response to temptation. See Lesson 153 (page 78) or the Practice Card, and also Robert's practice comments on pages 48–49.
Purpose: To go past your ingratitude—your envy and false gratitude—and so experience the freedom and peace that lie beyond it. This will intensify your motivation and strengthen your commitment.
Morning/Evening Quiet Time: Thank your Father that you are separate from no living thing and are therefore one with Him. Rejoice that there are no exceptions to this oneness, for they would reduce your wholeness. Give thanks for every living thing, and so recognize God's gifts to you.
Hourly Remembrance: Use the lesson, "Love is the way I walk in gratitude," to forgive the happenings of the previous hour. Do not let it cast its shadow on the hour to come. Thus you unloose the chains of time and remain unbound while still in time.
Response To Temptation: When tempted to think of anger, malice or revenge, or to see yourself as mercilessly pushed about by the world, substitute these thoughts with the idea for the day.

COMMENTARY

Gratitude is viewed in this lesson both from a dark side and a light side. The lesson first considers how, so very often, when our thinking is aligned with our egos, our gratitude is really a kind of attack on others. Then, it goes on to consider sincere gratitude, which can only occur when joined with love (4:3).

The dark side of gratitude comes from an ego perspective. This is the "gratitude" that prays, "Thank God I am not as others; thank God I am better off." It is the kind of gratitude based firmly on comparisons. It is the thankfulness we feel when we have a bigger house than others, a better car, a more attractive spouse. It is a kind of thankfulness that depends on others who have less, who suffer more than we do. It comes from a view that sees our brother as the rival for our peace (3:1), and rejoices when he is in distress. This kind of "gratitude" is really nothing more than a form of vengeance. And if we examine ourselves honestly we will find ourselves indulging in this kind of false gratitude far more often than we realize.

True gratitude is something far different. "We thank our Father for one thing alone; that we are separate from no living thing, and therefore one with Him" (6:1). "We offer thanks to God our Father that in us all things will find their freedom. It will never be that some are loosed while others still are bound" (4:4–5). This gratitude gives "thanks for every living thing, for otherwise we offer thanks for nothing" (6:3).

Today I am joyful that the gifts I have received belong to everyone. I am grateful for every living thing, every person I meet. I rejoice that everyone goes with me, that no one is excluded. I am grateful that each of you who read this is a part of me, that none of you can ever lose your inheritance and so diminish me. I recognize that if anyone is diminished, I am diminished, and I thank God that "everything has earned the right to love by being loving," for all is part of my Self (8:6).

Today, if I feel badgered by the world, or pushed about without any thought or care for me, I will choose to replace such foolish thoughts with gratitude (9:1–4). "God has cared for us, and calls us Son. Can there be more than this?" (9:5)

Another word for gratitude is "appreciation." I offer you these thoughts about appreciation from the Course:

> Only one equal gift can be offered to the equal Sons of God, and that is full appreciation (T-6.V(A).4:7).

> Only honor is a fitting gift for those whom God Himself created worthy of honor, and whom He honors. Give them the appreciation God accords them always, because they are His beloved Sons in whom He is well pleased (T-7.VII.6:1–2).

> There are no idolaters in the Kingdom, but there is great appreciation for everything that God created, because of the calm knowledge that each one is part of Him (T-10.III.6:1).

> God knows His Son as wholly blameless as Himself, and He is approached through the appreciation of His Son (T-11.IV.7:2).

> Only appreciation is an appropriate response to your brother. Gratitude is due him for both his loving thoughts and his appeals for help, for both are capable of bringing love into your awareness if you perceive them truly (T-12.I.6:1–2).

> In the holy instant we share our faith in God's Son because we recognize, together, that he is wholly worthy of it, and in our appreciation of his worth we cannot doubt his holiness. And so we love him (T-15.VI.2:5–6).

Lesson 196—July 15

"It can be but myself I crucify."

PRACTICE SUMMARY

Generic Instructions: Morning and evening times, hourly remembrance, and response to temptation. See Lesson 153 (page 78) or the Practice Card, and also Robert's practice comments on pages 48–49.
Purpose: To take this one step in the way of salvation, that you may go ahead from here rapidly and easily. To go past the belief that there is an enemy without that you fear. This will free you of the fear of God so that you can welcome Him back into your holy mind.
Hourly Remembrance: Use the lesson, "It can be but myself I crucify," to forgive the happenings of the previous hour. Do not let it cast its shadow on the hour to come. Thus you unloose the chains of time and remain unbound while still in time.
Response To Temptation: Whenever tempted to believe that you can attack another and thereby escape attack yourself, repeat idea.

COMMENTARY

This is a restatement of one of the fundamental lessons of the Course, the first step of forgiveness in another form: taking the problem back from outside ourselves, withdrawing the projection, and seeing that "I am doing this to myself."

The ego likes to misuse this idea to punish us, or to make us think we inevitably punish ourselves. The ego makes us think we are inherently self-destructive. The truth is, we do self-destructive things but we have a choice in the matter. We don't have to do that, and at the core it is not our will to do so. We are not devils; we are the holy Son of God.

The block to awareness this lesson addresses is our belief that we have injured or "crucified" the world. It is the belief that we have made ourselves into monsters who cannot be trusted, ready to lash out without provocation to hurt and to kill.

The Course calls the acceptance of today's idea—that any way in which we crucify another is actually crucifying ourselves—"one step we take in leading us from bondage to the state of perfect freedom" (4:1). It urges us to take "every step in its appointed sequence" (4:2), that is, not to skip steps. Today's idea is a step that is differentiating self from the body and the ego:

> Thus do you also teach your mind that you are not an ego...You will not believe you are a body to be crucified (3:1–3).

Because we believe we made ourselves into egos, we think we are guilty. Because we believe in guilt, we made the body to suffer punishment. Recognizing that we are the ones inflicting punishment upon ourselves is the first step in freeing ourselves from the whole mess. To recognize that we are the ones inflicting punishment we have to step back from the ego and body, and become aware of a greater part of ourselves. We thus realize that the Self is something other than ego or body, something greater than both. This something greater also includes my brothers and sisters. We are all part of that Self. The "others" I thought I injured are really parts of my Self.

If I believe that I can "attack another and be free" myself (6:1), I am really reacting, says the lesson, from a hidden fear of God; from the belief that God is other, an enemy who waits to destroy me. My relationship to those around me always reflects the unconscious belief I have about my relationship to God, to the ultimate Unity and Whole. "The fear of God is real to anyone who thinks this thought [that I can attack another and be free myself] is true" (6:4). If I can attack another and still be free, so can God. Therefore, God is to be feared.

Paragraph 7 seems crucial to me. It is saying that the thought I can attack others and still be free has to be *changed in form* before I can even question the idea, at least to the point where I stop being afraid of retaliation and start to become responsible, start to realize that "it is but your thoughts that bring you fear, and your deliverance depends on you" (7:3). If I begin to realize that I am not attacking others, but attacking myself, I can stop being afraid of retaliation from these "others" I thought I was attacking. Before this thought changes, I am afraid of others; after it changes, I realize my fear is coming from my own thoughts. If that is true, I have the potential for changing those thoughts.

It seems to me from the lesson that the turning point, the point at which the fear begins to abate, is found in 9:2: "If it can but be you you crucify, you did not hurt the world, and need not fear its vengeance and pursuit." Freedom from fear of vengeance from the world is the start of freedom from fear of God, when "God…can be welcomed back within the holy mind He never left" (8:5).

I feared my own strength and freedom because I thought I was dangerous! I thought I was a threat to the world; I thought that I had injured it. No wonder I don't want to be strong and free. If I were, I might destroy the universe. I thought I might attack and damage things to the point where the universe would turn in anger and wipe me from the face of the earth. In fact I have secretly believed, all along, that this describes things exactly as they are, and that is why I have been afraid, both of the world and of God.

The Course seems to be saying here that our unconscious fear of ourselves, hidden by our projection of cause to outside factors, has to become conscious, at least for a brief, terrifying moment. "When you realize, once and for all, that it is you you fear, the mind perceives itself as split" (10:2). "Now, for an instant, is a murderer perceived within you, eager for your death, intent on plotting punishment for you until the time when it can kill at last" (11:1).

This seems like a terrible moment; why would we deliberately seek it? "Yet in this instant is the time as well in which salvation comes" (11:2). Now, seeing the enemy within instead of outside our mind, we no longer have reason to fear God. Recognition of our own terrible responsibility makes us realize that it has not been God Who was punishing us; it has been ourselves. We stop projecting our own dreams of vengeance onto God. "And you can call on Him to save you from illusions by His Love, calling Him Father and yourself His Son" (11:4).

Lesson 197—July 16

"It can be but my gratitude I earn."

PRACTICE SUMMARY

Generic Instructions: Morning and evening times, hourly remembrance, and response to temptation. See Lesson 153 (page 78) or the Practice Card, and also Robert's practice comments on pages 48–49.
Purpose: To go past the special block of requiring visible gratitude from others and so to experience what lies beyond this: your gratitude toward your Self and all its parts and God's gratitude toward you. This will intensify your motivation and strengthen your commitment.
Hourly Remembrance: Use the lesson, "It can be but my gratitude I earn," to forgive the happenings of the previous hour. Do not let it cast its shadow on the hour to come. Thus you unloose the chains of time and remain unbound while still in time.
Response To Temptation: (Suggestion) When tempted to withdraw a gift you have given, repeat idea.

COMMENTARY

This lesson identifies itself as "the second step" in freeing our minds from the belief in outside forces pitted against us. Yesterday's lesson was the first step (W-pI.196.2:1–2). It taught us that our attacks are always directed at ourselves, and that the attacks we thought were coming from outside of ourselves were really coming from our own minds. In other words, "It is impossible that you be hurt except by your own thoughts" (W-pI.196.8:3). Today's lesson takes the other side of the coin: gratitude. This is definitely a step beyond yesterday's lesson. We may understand that our attack is coming from ourselves, and yet not realize that any gratitude we receive is *also* coming from ourselves, and not from outside forces.

I remember attending a workshop of Ken Wapnick's with a friend, when Ken was talking about how to respond to criticism and even outright attack from people who were close to us. Ken's advice was to remember that such attacks are just the other person's ego reacting to its perception of our ego; "Don't take it personally," Ken advised. The next day my friend went to Ken with a personal issue. He'd begun to lead some groups in healing techniques, and he had received many glowing compliments. He was worried that all the praise (or gratitude) would go to his head. Ken's advice to him was quite memorable, coming on the heels of the earlier advice about criticism: "Don't take it personally!"

While some of us may have problems with *receiving* gratitude, we have a much greater problem with *not* receiving it. Every Course student goes through the experience of expressing love, kindness and forgiveness to someone, only to have it rejected or thrown back in their face. This lesson directly addresses the way we react to such a situation.

What we are being asked to do is to express that kindness and love, to "give our gifts," without any attachment to the response of the other person. All the gratitude we require, the lesson says, is *our own gratitude* for the opportunity of giving and forgiving! (3:3) Gratitude does not come from outside us any more than attack does.

If we fail to understand this, when someone fails to acknowledge our gifts, we will typically react by taking them back. "Well, I tried to forgive you and overlook your error, but if this is how you are going to treat me in response, then to hell with you!" And quite obviously, our attempts at kindness have turned into attack! (See 1:2–3.)

The lesson says it quite directly: "It does not matter if another thinks your gifts unworthy" (4:1). In other words, in our giving, let us be completely unconcerned with the response of the person we are giving to, and whether or not they express gratitude. Our giving to them is sufficient gift to ourselves, and our own gratitude for the gift we have given is all that we need. If we take back the gifts we give when they are not received with "external gratitude and lavish thanks" (1:3), then we will always suspect that God's gifts are equally undependable. If we take back our gifts, we are taking them away from ourselves. I am the one who needs to be grateful for the gift I have given, for I am the one who has received it! (3:5)

To help us understand why external gratitude isn't necessary, Jesus explains that there is a part of the other person's mind that *is* grateful, even when that isn't expressed outwardly (4:2). The other person's "right mind" is very grateful to you for the gift, and receives it with thanks. The gift will be held, waiting until the person is consciously ready to receive it. As the Manual puts it:

> No teacher of God should feel disappointed if he has offered healing and it does not appear to have been received. It is not up to him to judge when his gift should be accepted. Let him be certain it has been received, and trust that it will be accepted when it is recognized as a blessing and not a curse (M-6.2:7–9).

The Manual goes on in a way that very clearly echoes the thought we have been discussing:

> It is not the function of God's teachers to evaluate the outcome of their gifts. It is merely their function to give them (M-6.3:1–2).

This entire chapter in the Manual, and the one that follows, might be very interesting reading in light of today's lesson.

If we fail to learn this second step, that gratitude as well as attack comes only from within ourselves, we will forever be uncertain about the gifts of God (5:3).

Lesson 198—July 17

"Only my condemnation injures me."

PRACTICE SUMMARY

Generic Instructions: Morning and evening times, hourly remembrance, and response to temptation. See Lesson 153 (page 78) or the Practice Card, and also Robert's practice comments on pages 48–49.
Purpose: To use forgiveness to go past your condemnation and experience the freedom that lies beyond it. To come nearer to the end of all that blocks you from the final vision. To be glad, for today your deliverance has come.
Hourly Remembrance: Use the lesson to forgive the happenings of the previous hour. Do not let it cast its shadow on the hour to come. Thus you unloose the chains of time and remain unbound while still in time.
Frequent Reminder: Repeat: "Only my condemnation injures me. Only my own forgiveness sets me free."
Response To Temptation: When tempted to succumb to any form of suffering or injury, realize it hides a condemning thought and say, "Only my condemnation injures me. Only my own forgiveness sets me free."

COMMENTARY

When I condemn another, I am offering injury to myself. How is that so?

When I condemn anyone, I am wishing injury on them, some form of punishment for their "wrong." At the very least, my condemnation states that the person is less worthy of love. I am believing, therefore, that I can injure, even that I would be justified in offering injury or withholding love. The principle I have established by this belief, however, can be turned against me. I can be injured, too. If I measure my love to others according to my perception of them, I am affirming that this is how love works. Therefore, I am asserting that God measures His love to me based on my appearance or my current state of character development, for instance. Do I really want that?

In reality, "Injury is impossible" (1:1). Neither God, nor my true Self as His creation, can be injured in any way. Nor have they been. But "illusion makes illusion" (1:2), and the illusion of condemnation makes the illusion of injury. We will continue, therefore, to experience injury until we lay down condemnation as an undesirable tool, "unwanted and unreal" (1:4).

There is a principle that lies underneath the surface of this lesson that is really quite important in understanding the Course. Injury is impossible; so is condemnation (2:5). "What seems to be its influence and its effects have not occurred at all" (2:6). Thus, as the Course says in many places, the separation never happened; there is no sin; there is no death; sickness is illusion; and even our bodies and this world do not really exist. "There is no world!" (W-pI.132.6:2). We are not really here where we think we are; we are asleep in Heaven, dreaming of exile. The apparent problem has already been solved, and indeed, it never happened! This is the truth on the level of what the Course calls knowledge or Heaven.

And yet...what? For there is an "and yet" to the Course's teaching. It does not state the ultimate truth and stop; it has something to say about the apparent illusion. It affirms with meticulous care the unreality of the illusion, *and yet* it deals with it!

> What seems to be its influence and its effects have not occurred at all. Yet must we deal with them a while as if they had (2:6–7).

What are the influence and effects of condemnation? Every form of "injury" imaginable. The apparent effects of our self-judgment include the making of the world and of bodies as well. These are the things, then, that we must deal with *as if they had really occurred*—for a while. Time itself is an illusion, yet the Course talks a good deal about saving time, and urges us to use time wisely, particularly in the practice instructions that are part of these lessons. It knows time is illusory, and yet it deals with it as if it were something real, using the very illusion to lead us out of illusion; using time to bring us back to eternity.

We meet illusion with illusion; we meet the effects of condemnation with forgiveness. In reality there is nothing to forgive because nothing happened. But to undo the *illusion* of what happened and so become aware of the unchanging reality, we need the illusion of forgiveness.

The Course affirms that this world is illusion, and yet, for a time, it teaches us to deal with it as if it were not an illusion; as if it had really occurred. The only way to thus deal with it is to forgive it, to proclaim to it that "there is no condemnation in God's Son" (10:1). Forgiveness is the bridge that brings illusion to the truth, that provides the escape passage out of illusion entirely.

Lesson 199—July 18

"I am not a body. I am free."

PRACTICE SUMMARY:

Generic Instructions: Morning and evening times, hourly remembrance, and response to temptation. See Lesson 153 (page 78) or the Practice Card, and also Robert's practice comments on pages 48–49.
Purpose: To go past your identification with the body and so experience the freedom of not being tied to it. To free your mind and give it to the Holy Spirit's use, that you may carry freedom to those who think they are imprisoned in the body.
Hourly Remembrance: Use the lesson to forgive the happenings of the previous hour. Do not let it cast its shadow on the hour to come. Thus you unloose the chains of time and remain unbound while still in time.
Frequent Reminder: Repeat: "I am not a body. I am free. I hear the Voice that God has given me, and it is only This my mind obeys."
Response To Temptation: (Suggestion) When tempted to engage in any thoughts which reinforce a bodily identity, say: "I am not a body. I am free. I hear the Voice that God has given me, and it is only This my mind obeys."
Overall Comments: Practice well this thought, today and every day. Cherish it. Use it in every practice period.

COMMENTARY

To the ego, today's idea is "quite insane" (3:2). Yet it is one of the basic principles the Course uses to free us from our bondage. The lesson attaches a great deal of importance to it, more than to most ideas the Course presents. We are told to "cherish" it and "practice it today and every day" (5:1). And evidently Jesus expects us to integrate the idea that "I am not a body" into every practice period from now on! (5:2)

Let's face it: Before we encountered the Course, the body was something we took for granted. If we knew anything, we thought, we knew we were a body. Our bodies held a very different place in our lives from every other physical object. If someone stepped on a CD we owned, we might say, "Hey! You're breaking my CD." But if they stepped on our toe (part of our body), we would say, "Hey! You're stepping on *me*!" It is part of our consciousness. "I" am where my body is. We say, "I am eating. I was asleep. I am in my car. I am sick." And all of those "I's" refer to the body. Even if we have been Course students for ten or fifteen years, we are probably still saying those same things, and still, out of habit, thinking of the body as our self.

The ego has expended millennia of effort at mentally programming into the mind the identity of "me" and the body. It isn't something the mind will let go of easily; it is a habit of thought that will take a great deal of counter-programming to unlearn. That is why we are urged to make it a part of daily practice. The body-as-self identity will not be broken by a few simple repetitions. We all still believe in it. As Ken Wapnick has said, if you doubt that you still believe in the identity of body and self, just try holding your breath for ten minutes.

What are we to do with our awareness that we hold this false belief about ourselves? The lesson tells us, "Be not concerned" (3:2). Like a runner practicing to break the four-minute mile, we need not be concerned that we haven't done so yet. We just need to keep on practicing, doing what needs to be done to achieve that goal. Our goal is to realize we are a "mind...[that] no longer sees itself as in a body, firmly tied to it and sheltered by its presence" (1:4). That is the state of mind in which total freedom is found. When we have entered that state of mind, we will be right-minded, and in the real world. Our only concern now is to move in that direction.

The holy instant offers us foretastes of that state of mind. The body recedes from awareness in the holy instant, and what we are aware of is Oneness, something so vast no body or collection of bodies could ever contain it. As we experience this state more and more it will come to dominate our consciousness. We still have a body, but we realize we are not bound to it. It becomes simply:

> [a] useful form for what the mind must do. It becomes a vehicle which helps forgiveness be extended to the all-inclusive goal that it must reach, according to God's plan (4:4–5).

Ironically, the more we detach our mind from our body, the more perfect the body becomes. "It becomes perfect in the ability to serve an undivided goal" (6:4). If perfecting the body is the goal, we will never achieve it; the body will find wholeness only when our goal becomes unified with the Holy Spirit in seeking to extend forgiveness to everyone and everything, which places the body in its proper place. Trying to hold on to the body destroys it; letting it go brings it health.

The body is not the home of the mind; the Holy Spirit is (6:1). Our aim in practicing, in each holy instant we take, is to free our mind from its connection to the body, and to give our minds to the Holy Spirit for His purposes. Our energy then is not directed at acquiring food or clothing, or housing, or physical well-being, but at bringing forgiveness to the world. If we do this, the Holy Spirit promises that He will take care of all the rest. As Jesus put it in the Bible: "Seek ye first the kingdom of God, and his righteousness; and all these things shall be added unto you" (Matthew 6:33).

Or, as the Course puts it: "Once you accept His plan as the one function that you would fulfill, there will be nothing else the Holy Spirit will not arrange for you without your effort" (T-20.IV.8:4).

Lesson 200—July 19

"There is no peace except the peace of God."

PRACTICE SUMMARY

Generic Instructions: Morning and evening times, hourly remembrance, and response to temptation. See Lesson 153 (page 78) or the Practice Card, and also Robert's practice comments on pages 48–49.
Purpose: To no longer seek peace from idols, but only from God. To no longer lose our way but take the straight path to God.
Hourly Remembrance: Use the lesson, "There is no peace except the peace of God," to forgive the happenings of the previous hour. Do not let it cast its shadow on the hour to come. Thus you unloose the chains of time and remain unbound while still in time.
Frequent Reminder: Repeat: "There is no peace except the peace of God, and I am glad and thankful it is so."
Response To Temptation: (Suggestion) When tempted to seek peace from anything of this world, quickly repeat: "There is no peace except the peace of God, and I am glad and thankful it is so."

COMMENTARY

The basic message of this lesson is that every means we use to try to find peace *through or from the world* will fail; only the peace that comes from God, a peace that we already have as part of our created being, is real and eternal. (Some good sections to read in conjunction with today's lesson are Chapter 11 in the Manual, "How is peace possible in this world?" and the Text, Chapter 31, Section IV, "The Real Alternative.")

Everything in this world ends in death. This world is hell, because no matter what course we follow, no matter how hard we strive, we wind up losing everything in the end. What a depressing game it is, when the only outcome is losing! This is the source of "the agony of bitter disappointments, bleak despair, and sense of icy hopelessness and doubt" (1:3). If we are playing the game of the world, seeking for "happiness where there is none" (2:1), we can only be hurt. We are "asking for defeat" (2:3).

We may not be fully conscious of this despair, yet it underlies everything we do. Ernest Becker's book, "The Denial of Death," is all about the ways in which we anxiously and firmly push the awareness of death out of our minds, burying it in the trivia of daily life, struggling to find meaning in something to which we can attach ourselves and somehow achieve immortality. Becker reaches the same conclusion as the Course, in some respects: that we are all insane, all bound up in denial and projection. The only difference between us and those called "insane" is that our form of denial is a little more successful than theirs. Yet in some ways the "insane" are more honest than we are. They have admitted the emptiness of the world and have chosen to create their own fantasy world in its place, or have become suicidal in despair. The rest of us still stumble along in naive hope that the world will yet bring us satisfaction.

The Lesson asks us to give up the futile search for happiness through our bodies and the world, and to relax into the peace of God. If we can simply accept the fact that we will not find happiness or peace anywhere else, we can save ourselves all this misery. If I look at my own life, my most miserable moments have been those in which someone or something on which I had pinned my hopes for happiness failed me: a marriage, a church, a job, a noble purpose, a hope of romance. The lesson is saying these are not isolated events. They represent the whole. The search for peace apart from the peace of God is hopeless, and the sooner we realize it, the sooner will we find true happiness.

"This world is not where you belong. You are a stranger here" (4:3–4). So give it up. Let it go. Stop expecting it to make you happy; it never will. "But it is given you to find the means whereby the world no longer seems to be a prison house or jail for anyone" (4:5). *There is a way out*! "You must change your mind about the purpose of the world, if you would find escape" (5:2).

The Text tells us the same things:

> Until you see the healing of the Son as all you wish to be accomplished by the world, by time and all appearances, you will not know the Father nor yourself. For you will use the world for what is not its purpose, and will not escape its laws of violence and death (T-24.VI.4:3–4).
>
> To change all this, and open up a road of hope and of release in what appeared to be an endless circle of despair, you need but to decide you do not know the purpose of the world. You give it goals it does not have, and thus do you decide what it is for. You try to see in it a place of idols found outside yourself, with power to make complete what is within by splitting what you are between the two. You choose your dreams, for they are what you wish, perceived as if it had been given you. Your idols do what you would have them do, and have the power you ascribe to them. And you pursue them vainly in the dream, because you want their power as your own (T-29.VII.8).

If we can decide that we do not know the purpose of the world, we will be free to receive the purpose the Holy Spirit sees in it. Until we give up our imagined purposes, His purpose will seem dim and indecipherable. It is the letting go of what we think the world is for that allows its only true purpose to dawn upon us. That purpose, in a word, is forgiveness; or as the line in Chapter 24 put it, "the healing of the Son." Forgiveness is needed in hell, and this world, therefore, must be hell (6:4). Forgiveness offers, to me and to everyone, "the escape...from evil dreams he imagines, yet believes are true" (6:5). All the world is good for, we might say, is for us to "learn to look on it another way, and find the peace of God" (7:6).

If the world is such a terrible, depressing place, we might think that logically, the way to find peace is to leave the world. To die. To get out of this body. But that is not what the lesson says. "Peace," we are told, "begins within the world perceived as different" (8:2). Notice: peace begins *within the world.* It begins with a new perception of the world, not as a prison house, but as a classroom. Beginning here, the road of peace will lead us on "to the gate of Heaven and the way beyond" (8:2). But it must begin here.

In poignant images of a road "carpeted with leaves of false desires," we can see ourselves lifting our eyes away from the "trees of hopelessness" to the gate of Heaven (10:3). It is the peace of God we want, and nothing but the peace of God. In the holy instants we enjoy in today's practicing, we recognize the peace we have sought, and "feel its soft embrace surround your heart and mind with comfort and with love" (10:6).

The closing lines, given us for practice, sum up the whole lesson. Most of us, if confronted with the thought that there is no peace but the peace of God, do not yet respond with gladness and thanks. The message that, "There is no hope of answer in the world" (T-31.IV.4:3), seems a dour and bitter pill to swallow. Instead of joy, we feel sad, and a bit resentful. We wistfully cling to our vain hopes that the idols of this world will still, somehow, satisfy us. We want them to, so very much. Only when we have learned to release them gladly and thankfully will we be, finally, free of their hold upon us.

Let me, then, in today's practicing, seek to find that gladness and thanks within myself. The Christ in me wants to "come home" (4:1). There is a part of me that breathes a sigh of relief as I begin to realize the world can never satisfy me, and whispers to me, "At last! At last you are beginning to let go of the source of your pain. Thank you!" Let me connect with that part of my mind that is native to Heaven, and knows it does not belong here; it is the only part there is in reality. The more I connect with it, the sooner will I know the peace that is my natural inheritance.

COMMENTS ON PRACTICE
Review VI

This is the final review of the Workbook and the end of Part I. Like the previous two reviews, all practice is centered around a central thought, which in this case is a combination of Lesson 199 ("I am not a body. I am free.") and the "star" lesson of the Workbook, "I am as God created me" (W-pI.94, 110, and 162). Yet unlike every other review, this one reviews only one lesson per day and thus lasts twice as long—twenty days, instead of ten.

The beginning of full-blown Workbook practice

Now, after 200 lessons, as Part I comes to a close, the four-fold structure of the practice is finally put together. All that we have learned in Part I is assembled into a single four-tiered pyramid. This is what we will carry into Part II, in which our practice is meant to take off and soar. The instructions for Lessons 153–200 laid down the first two tiers of this pyramid. We spent those forty-eight lessons solidly putting into place the morning and evening quiet times and the hourly remembrances. This review adds on the third tier. This is clear in its opening lines: "Besides the time you give morning and evening, which should not be less than fifteen minutes, and the hourly remembrances you make throughout the day, use the idea as often as you can between them" (W-pI.rVI.In.1:2). This sentence says a great deal. It says that we should maintain the practice we have been doing since Lesson 153—the morning and evening times and the hourly remembrances—and then *add onto* this the frequent reminders in between the hour. Here, then, are three of the four kinds of practice. Since the final mode of practice—response to temptation—is present throughout the Workbook, and is also mentioned in this review, here we have all four kinds of practice in the Workbook put together.

The specific structure is further withdrawn

This review is the home stretch of Part I, the last bit of preparation for the crowning Part II. An essential part of this preparation is the withdrawal of the Workbook's specific instructions and structure. This is a process that began as early as Lesson 124 and has been gathering speed since then. Here, in Review VI, that process accelerates and takes several forms:

- We attempt to go beyond words.
- We attempt to go beyond special forms of practicing.
- Our only instructions for the longer periods are to empty our minds of clutter and forget all we thought we knew.

- We give our practice periods to the Holy Spirit, Who will teach us what to think, say and do, and Who will guide our practice periods.

There are two exceptions to this lack of structure:

- We are specifically told to let no idle (wandering) thoughts go unchallenged during our quiet time.
- We are given a few specific thoughts (a few lines) for each day's lesson to aid our practicing.

Review VI Introduction
July 20 to August 8

This is the final review of the Workbook, the end of Part I. Back in the Introduction to the Workbook we were told: "The workbook is divided into two main sections, the first dealing with the undoing of the way you see now, and the second with the acquisition of true perception" (W-Int.3:1). The last forty lessons or so have said they were preparing us for Part II of the Workbook. So now we are coming to the end of the first phase of our training. Presumably, if we have been doing the exercises as instructed (and that is the real key, of course), we are now ready to enter a new, higher phase of our practicing.

Two things are clearly different about the second part of the Workbook. First, the written lessons are much, much shorter; none is more than a half page, although we will be asked to read a one-page teaching section ten times, once each day along with the lesson. The emphasis in the second part, as we will see, is much less on learning new ideas (or unlearning old ones), and much more on having new experiences, and on reinforcing the habits we have formed during Part I.

The second major difference is that, from this review which ends Part I and the Introduction to Part II forward, the lessons contain *no more practice instructions*. It seems quite clear that the pattern of practice we are meant to follow has been established, and we are expected to know what it is, and to follow it for the remaining 145 lessons of Part II.

That pattern was begun in Lesson 153, which established the longer morning and evening quiet times, and the hourly remembrances. The remaining two elements—frequent reminders between the hours, and response to temptation as needed—remained somewhat optional for the rest of the lessons through 200. It is only here, in the Introduction to the final review, that they are added in as something definitely expected of us every day.

"Besides the time you give morning and evening, which should not be less than fifteen minutes, and the hourly remembrances you make throughout the day, use the idea as often as you can between them" (W-pI.rVI.1:2). The word "besides" makes it clear that these frequent reminders are now being given *in addition* to the morning and evening quiet times and the hourly remembrances. The response to temptation is clearly added as well, in paragraph 6:

> When you are tempted hasten to proclaim your freedom from temptation, as you say: This thought I do not want. I choose instead _____. And then repeat the idea for the day, and let it take the place of what you thought (6:1–4).

Those four elements of practice, firmly set in place in this final review, are meant to be the instructions we follow on a daily basis for the rest of the year:

1. Morning and evening quiet time of not less than fifteen minutes each.

2. Hourly remembrances of a few minutes, in which we recall the idea for the day and apply it to the hour past and the hour to come.

3. Frequent reminders in between the hours, when we simply call the idea to mind.

4. Response to temptation, in which we deliberately replace our ego thoughts with the thought for the day.

We are told that any one of the ideas we are given is "sufficient for salvation, if it were learned truly. Each would be enough to give release to you and to the world from every form of bondage, and invite the memory of God to come again" (1:3–4). This is true of the ideas to come, and also of the ideas in the last twenty lessons. Notice the conditional phrases that modify this statement, however: "...if understood, practiced, accepted, and applied to all the seeming happenings throughout the day" (2:2). Any one idea is enough...*if* we apply that idea without exception (2:4).

If any single idea is enough, why do we need 365 lessons? The answer is simple. The author knows perfectly well that we won't apply any single idea without exception to every happening throughout every day. "And so we need to use them all and let them blend as one, as each contributes to the whole we learn" (2:5).

In this final review, which lasts for twenty days, repeating each day one of the thoughts from the previous twenty days, we are asked to let our practicing center around a unifying theme:

> I am not a body. I am free. For I am still as God created me (3:3–5).

We are asked to repeat these three short sentences every morning and evening, every hour, and every time in between that we remember our true function here. We repeat it along with the review idea for the day. That simple repetition is the only specific instruction we are given. Beyond that, all that we are asked to do in our practice times is, in a short phrase, to clear our minds of any opposing thoughts (3:8). This is to be a "deep relinquishment," not simply a blanking of the mind; a letting go of every thought that stands in the way of sanity and truth.

> We merely close our eyes, and then forget all that we thought we knew and understood (4:3).

In this final half of the Workbook we are moving "beyond all words" (4:1). We are seeking to experience serenity and the peace of God.

The only exception is something we do when an "idle thought" intrudes itself into our quiet. Paragraph 5 gives us clear instructions about how to deal with these intrusive thoughts, which will surely occur. The main point is not to allow such a thought to simply pass by unchallenged. Rather, we instruct our minds, "This is not a thought I want," and replace it with the idea for the day. We follow the same practice all through the day, whenever we are tempted by our egos.

This is a rigorous kind of mind training. It asks a great deal of us. I believe it is what is meant by the phrase in the Text, "Be vigilant only for God and for His Kingdom" (T-6.V(C)). How can we expect our minds to become free of ego thinking if we let the ego's thoughts go unchallenged? Early in the Text, Jesus tells us we are much too tolerant of mind wandering (T-2.VI.4:6); this vigilant watchfulness, challenging the ego thoughts and replacing them with thoughts of God, is the Course's remedy.

Jesus, the author, says that he places our practice periods in the hands of the Holy Spirit (6:6 and 7:1–2). We are to listen to Him for specifics about what to "do and say and think, each time you turn to Him" (7:2). The primary emphasis seems to be on simple quiet (6:6). Yet the mention of what we do and say and think leaves us a great deal of latitude. Generally speaking, I think, we can use any of the techniques we have practiced earlier in the Workbook, such as forgiveness exercises, offering peace to the world, reviewing situations in our lives and applying the idea for the day, and so on. The major emphasis is on quietly listening to the Voice for God and allowing our minds to come to serenity and peace. The Workbook has ended its specific practice instructions, but now we are to learn to listen to the Holy Spirit instead:

"...allowing Him to teach us how to go, and trusting Him completely for the way each practice period can best become a loving gift of freedom to the world" (7:4).

Practice Instructions for Review VI

Purpose: To carefully review the last 20 lessons, each of which contains the whole curriculum and is therefore sufficient for salvation, if understood, practiced, accepted and applied without exception.

Morning/Evening Quiet Time: Fifteen minutes, at least.

- Repeat: "I am not a body. I am free. For I am still as God created me."
- Close your eyes and relinquish all that clutters the mind; forget all you thought you knew. Give the time to the Holy Spirit, your Teacher. If you notice an idle thought, immediately deny its hold, assuring your mind that you do not want it. Then let it be given up and replaced with today's idea. Say: "This thought I do not want. I choose instead (today's idea)."

Remarks: We are attempting to go beyond special forms of practice because we are attempting a quicker pace and shorter path to our goal.

Hourly Remembrance: Repeat: "I am not a body. I am free. For I am still as God created me."

Frequent Reminder: As often as possible, as often as you can.

Repeat: "I am not a body. I am free. For I am still as God created me."

Response To Temptation: Permit no idle thought to go unchallenged. If you are tempted by an idle thought, immediately deny its hold, assuring your mind that you do not want it. Then let it be given up and replaced with today's idea. Say: "This thought I do not want. I choose instead (today's idea)."

These instructions can also be found on the tear-out Practice Card.

Lesson 201—July 20

"I am not a body. I am free. For I am still as God created me."
(181) "I trust my brothers, who are one with me."
"I am not a body. I am free. For I am still as God created me."

PRACTICE SUMMARY

See the instructions on page 204 or the Practice Card at the end of the book.

COMMENTARY

Today, let us remember, as often as we can, that there is no one who is not our brother. Let us remember that we are all part of the one Self, and that our oneness with All-That-Is is a blessing we can never lose.

Together, we are a Whole. Apart, we are nothing.

There is only One of us.

Everyone is linked immutably to God and to each other. Everything that is, is a direct offshoot of the Creator, equally worthy, equally holy, equally loveable.

My brothers and sisters are my joy and my delight. Let me see each one today as the blessing that they are to me.

Lesson 202—July 21

"I am not a body. I am free. For I am still as God created me."
(182) "I will be still an instant and go home."
"I am not a body. I am free. For I am still as God created me."

PRACTICE SUMMARY

See the instructions on page 204 or the Practice Card at the end of the book.

COMMENTARY

Right now, this very instant, and every instant of this day, I have the opportunity simply to be still, to quiet my mind, and to go home to Heaven. Heaven is here. Heaven is now. There is no other time and no other place.

This world of turmoil is not my home; my home is in peace. This world of sorrow is not my home; my home is in joy. This world of hatred is not my home; my home is in love. This body is not my home; my home is in God.

The Voice of God is calling me constantly to come home, and I can do so any time I choose to. How thankful I am today for this inner calling! How grateful I am that, no matter where I go, no matter what I do, this Voice is always with me, always calling me home.

When I hear this Voice, why would I choose to stay an instant more where I am not at home? Every reason I might think to give dissolves into nothing when I become aware of the sweet and gentle calling of His Voice. I will remember right now, and at every opportunity during this day. "I will be still an instant and go home."

Lesson 203—July 22

"I am not a body. I am free. For I am still as God created me."
(183) "I call upon God's Name and on my own."
"I am not a body. I am free. For I am still as God created me."

PRACTICE SUMMARY

See the instructions on page 204 or the Practice Card at the end of the book.

COMMENTARY

To "call upon" the Name of God is not simply to repeat a word, but to reach out from within myself, affirming my connection to my Source. To call upon this Name means to remind myself of my union with God. "It is my own [name] as well as His" (1:2). In a sense, it is similar to the way soldiers in battle might cry out the name of their king, or the way a football crowd chants the name of a favorite player. It is a means of identification, an affirmation of a solidarity and unity.

Yet it is more than any such thing that we might compare it with in this world, because God's Name is my name in a much deeper sense than mere emotional identification. I am the extension of God. What He is, I am as well. I am created of the essence of Godhead. "I am still as God created me" (1:5). I affirm this every time I call upon His Name.

To call upon God's Name is to remind myself that the lesser name and the lesser self with which I commonly identify is not who I am. "I am not a body" (1:3). In the midst of the daily crunch of "busy-ness," when I call on this Name, I am delivered "from every thought of evil and of sin" (1:2). When I feel limited or confined, I can rediscover my freedom by calling on His Name. I remember that I am not this body; I am free.

As I sit in quiet today, let me open to the experience of God. Let me become aware of the vast Love without boundary or restriction. Let me sink into His limitless peace. Let me be transported in His joy. And as I do, let me remember that all that I experience of God, I AM. Let me call, too, on *my own name*. In remembering God, let me remember, "This is me."

Lesson 204—July 23

"I am not a body. I am free. For I am still as God created me."
(184) "The Name of God is my inheritance."
"I am not a body. I am free. For I am still as God created me."

PRACTICE SUMMARY

See the instructions on page 204 or the Practice Card at the end of the book.

COMMENTARY

If I bear the Name of God, I am His Son. I have the heritage of God's family—and what an inheritance that is! I am not the offspring of random molecules of DNA. I am not the product of survival of the fittest in a vicious battle for supremacy in life. I am not the product of my human family, my upbringing, my education, my failures, or my culture. What I am I have inherited from God Himself.

As the Son of God I am "not slave to time" (1:2). I am not limited to the short span of my body's "life" on earth. I do not require long years of development to attain my inheritance; it is mine now. Nor am I the product of my past. I do not need to fear the future. I am free of all limitations time might try to impose on me.

I am "unbound by laws which rule the world of sick illusions" (1:2). Laws of time, of space, of economics, of health and nutrition, or any laws we think are immutable and inevitable here, do not rule me. I am a child of God. I am spirit. I am free. I am "forever and forever one with Him" (1:2).

Lesson 205—July 24

"I am not a body. I am free. For I am still as God created me."
(185) "I want the peace of God."
"I am not a body. I am free. For I am still as God created me."

PRACTICE SUMMARY

See the instructions on page 204 or the Practice Card at the end of the book.

COMMENTARY

Review VI says that, "Each of these ideas alone would be sufficient for salvation, if it were learned truly" (W-rVI.Int.1:3). It adds, "Each contains the whole curriculum if understood, practiced, accepted, and applied to all the seeming happenings throughout the day" (W-rVI.In.2:2). I find that easy to believe about today's lesson. If you are into memorization (as I am), this lesson is an excellent one to add to your repertoire.

It's worth noticing the list of four verb forms that are identified as steps in making any of these ideas into "the whole curriculum":

Understood: No matter how strongly the Course advocates experience, and points out that a universal theology is impossible (C-Int.2:5), you cannot get around the fact that it makes understanding very important. How can we enter into the experience of an idea if we do not understand it? Understanding is here presented as the fundamental step. Before we can really utilize the idea, "I want the peace of God," we have to understand it. Implied in the idea (and clearly presented in Lesson 185) is the fact that there is a very strong thought in my mind, perhaps unacknowledged, that I do not want the peace of God, and this is demonstrated by the fact that I do not experience it. That contrary thought, however, is a mistaken one, to be dismissed whenever we become aware of it, and replaced with the truth: I *do* want the peace of God.

Practiced: That is what we are doing in these Workbook lessons. Practicing. Repeating frequently. Spending some extended time allowing the thought to soak in and penetrate the recesses of our minds.

Accepted: Notice that acceptance comes after practice. Our minds do not accept the idea at the start, even after we understand the idea. When we begin to practice, we do not truly accept that we want the peace of God. We think we want something else, something more, something besides peace. It takes a good deal of practice to retrain our minds, until we begin to realize that "the peace of God is everything I want."

Applied: Having accepted the idea, we can now begin to apply it to each different "seeming happening" during the day. When the car cuts us off in traffic: "I want the peace of God." When we find ourselves wistfully longing for a more fulfilling relationship, "The peace of God is everything I want." When we begin to feel driven to obtain some earthly goal at any cost, "The peace of God is my one goal." When we start to think we don't know what to do or where to go, "The peace of God is the aim of all my living here." And when we start to feel impelled to fulfill some need of our bodies, "I am not a body. The peace of God is everything I want. I am free."

Thank You, Father, for today's reminder of Your peace. There is nothing else I need, and nothing else I want. Oh, may today's lesson become the keynote of my life, so that I can say and truly mean, "The peace of God is my *one* goal."

Lesson 206—July 25

"I am not a body. I am free. For I am still as God created me."
(186) "Salvation of the world depends on me."
"I am not a body. I am free. For I am still as God created me."

PRACTICE SUMMARY

See the instructions on page 204 or the Practice Card at the end of the book.

COMMENTARY

I am not a body; I am the Son of God. I am spirit, endowed with the gifts of God. I am not what I appear to be, nor what I have thought I was for most of my life. I am a spiritual being having a human experience, and my mission here (if I will accept it) is to give the gifts of God wherever He asks me to give them. And that is to everyone.

The Course requires a radical revision of my self-concept. I have thought of myself as some sort of poor, lost soul, wandering, alone, afraid. I have thought of myself as needy and lacking. I have felt like an orphan; as though, no matter how hard I tried, no matter how many places I visited, I never quite fit in. I have seen myself at the bottom trying to get up.

Now, this book comes along, a message from God to me, and tells me that the salvation of the world depends on me. I am a key figure in the plan of the ages. Everything depends on me, and that seems frightening. And yet, I have the gifts to give the world that will save it. I can give it my love. I can give it my trust. I can give it my kindness and my mercy. I can give those around me my understanding and my faith in them. Through my forgiveness I can release them from guilt.

This is such a startling idea of what I am that at first it seems ludicrous. I think at first that to see myself this way would be the height of arrogance. And yet...and yet, if this is how God created me, if this is what He created me for, it is arrogant to refuse the task being given to me. He is not asking me to set myself above anyone else. On the contrary, He is asking me to demonstrate to everyone that they have the gifts of God as well, that they are all like me.

God is asking me, "Are you ready yet to help me save the world?" (C-2.9:1) All Heaven waits breathlessly to hear my decision. Will I say, "Yes"? Will I dare to say, with understanding, meaning every word: "Salvation of the world depends on me"?

Lesson 207—July 26

"I am not a body. I am free. For I am still as God created me."
(187) "I bless the world because I bless myself."
"I am not a body. I am free. For I am still as God created me."

PRACTICE SUMMARY

See the instructions on page 204 or the Practice Card at the end of the book.

COMMENTARY

All that I need is already within me. It is released for me when I release it to others, because in reality, there are no "others," there is only one. We get caught up in questions such as, "Do I forgive myself first, and thus release myself to forgive others? Or do I forgive my brother, and thus find forgiveness for myself?" and, "Must I love myself before I can love others, or vice versa?" When we ask such questions we are trying to figure out a unified reality on the basis of duality; we can't get a clear answer because the question is framed in the wrong terms.

To "accept His boundless Love for me" (1:3) and to accept that love for others is the same thing, because all of us are merely fragments of the one mind we all share. There is no such thing as loving myself to the exclusion of loving others; that is not love at all. Nor is it love to "love" someone else and sacrifice myself on their behalf.

"I bless the world because I bless myself." This doesn't mean that meeting the demands of my ego benefits everyone else. Many people, in the wake of what ACIM teachers Hugh and Gayle Prather call "separation psychology" (in their book, *I Will Never Leave You*), think that loving yourself means such things as looking out for your own happiness at the expense of marriage partners and children. This is not what the Course is teaching here. The pendulum has swung from sacrificing yourself for the family or your partner (in the 1940's and 1950's) to sacrificing the family and partner for yourself (in the 1980's and 1990's). Both are mistaken approaches based on dualism.

"I bless the world because I bless myself" could be reversed, with equal truth, to read, "I bless myself because I bless the world." Giving and receiving are the same thing; this is one of the major lessons of the Course, and, by its own admission, one of the hardest for us to learn.

"God's blessing shines upon me from within my heart, where He abides" (1:2). The radiant and all-embracing Love of God is within me. When I turn to It, It engulfs me and instantly spills over to embrace everyone through me. Discovering that is what the Course is all about. "I am still as God created me." I am still that Love. How can I know that I am Love without expressing it? Love, by Its nature, extends to others and includes them in Its heart. The marvelous discovery of my own nature as Love cannot be made without the extension of that Love to my brother. To bless myself and to bless the world is a single event. It is when I bless the world that I learn to love myself; and likewise, when I truly love myself, I become a blessing to the world around me. I need my brothers, not to give me what I do not have, but to be the recipients and sharers of What I am.

Lesson 208—July 27

"I am not a body. I am free. For I am still as God created me." (188) "The peace of God is shining in me now." "I am not a body. I am free. For I am still as God created me."

PRACTICE SUMMARY

See the instructions on page 204 or the Practice Card at the end of the book.

COMMENTARY

Over and over again, the Course urges us to "be still." It is remarkable how much benefit can be derived from simply pausing, even just for ten seconds, closing the eyes, and remembering the peace of God that is within me. Just the word "peace," repeated silently, can have a soothing, healing effect on the mind. This is not something that will come to us without conscious cooperation. Practice is necessary. "I *will* be still"; it is an act of the will, a choice, a decision. The frantic onflow of thoughts and concerns has to be interrupted, and the mind turned towards that "stillness" (1:3) that "is within my heart" (1:4).

Most of our waking hours (and probably most of our sleeping hours as well, although we aren't aware of it) are spent in various concerns that, when stripped down to their basics, are concerns about our bodies, in one way or another. The daily caretaking of bathing, grooming, dressing, feeding, and resting our bodies goes on and on. The time we spend "earning a living" is necessitated by the need for money to purchase food, clothing and shelter, and to entertain ourselves. But we are not bodies. We need frequent reminders of that fact. We need to pause and say, "Peace, be still" to ourselves. It seems easier not to make the effort, to just let the current of bodily concerns carry us onward from one moment to the next. Yet when we make the effort, when we step out of the flow for a minute to simply be still and find the peace of God, everything begins to go more smoothly. We find ourselves happier than we were before. As an old Christian hymn put it, "Things that once were wild alarms cannot now disturb my rest."

We have a wellspring of peace within our hearts. It waits for us to simply dip into it and drink from its refreshing pool. It is there now, shining within us. Right now, and often today, "I will be still." I will draw on that inner wealth, "which witnesses to God Himself" (1:4).

Lesson 209—July 28

"I am not a body. I am free. For I am still as God created me."
(189) "I feel the love of God within me now."
"I am not a body. I am free. For I am still as God created me."

PRACTICE SUMMARY

See the instructions on page 204 or the Practice Card at the end of the book.

COMMENTARY

I was created by the Love of God (1:2). Creating and loving are the same (T-7.I.3:3). Love, by its nature, extends outward and creates more of Itself, creates like Itself. "...God created you by extending Himself as you..." (T-7.I.5:2). "Think you that you can judge the Self of God? God has created It beyond judgment, out of His need to extend His Love" (T-15.V.11:1–2). Our Self was created out of the need of Love to extend Itself. We are the natural result of Love's extension.

Therefore, we are that Love, extended. What I am is Love; Love is what I am. It is everything I am. There is no part of me that is not Love. I am wholly Love. That in me which seems to be something else—which may seem this morning to feel fearful, or depressed, or dull, or lifeless, or angry, or spiteful—is only illusion, a figment of my imagination. It is not real. It is not me. I am only Love, and therefore I teach only Love.

I am Love's Son, by Love's own proclamation (1:4). I am made in the image and likeness of Love. I cannot be anything other than loving, nor have I ever been anything other than loving. When I have believed I was something else, I was only dreaming. I am not a body, obsessed with self-preservation. I am free to love, and free to love freely. "God will never cease to love His Son, and His Son will never cease to love Him" (T-10.V.10:6).

"The Love of God within me sets me free" (1:5). It is connecting with that Love within myself that liberates me from my self-imposed bondage. It is accepting this Love *as* myself that frees me from guilt. It is allowing that Love to flow through me that frees me from sorrow and fills me with joy. Love is my liberator.

Let me accept today that the Love of God is in me. Let me *feel* Its presence. Let me be glad that Love is what I am. All the little things that seem to trouble me, that seem to tell me I am less than Love, or that anyone is less than Love, fade into nothing as I open my heart to Love.

Lesson 210—July 29

"I am not a body. I am free. For I am still as God created me."
(190) "I choose the joy of God instead of pain."
"I am not a body. I am free. For I am still as God created me."

PRACTICE SUMMARY

See the instructions on page 204 or the Practice Card at the end of the book.

COMMENTARY

If we saw, clearly, that this was our choice—*joy* or *pain*—would there be any difficulty in making the choice?

Learning that this *is* the only choice is what takes so much time.

We are so confused about what brings us joy. We are quite convinced that our bodies can bring us joy. We are certain that a good, romantic relationship would bring us joy (Is that an oxymoron, "a good, romantic relationship"?). We are very sure that giving up certain things in this world would bring us a great deal of pain. It takes time, and sometimes the illusion of "giving up," to learn that we give up nothing. "It takes great learning both to realize and to accept the fact that the world has nothing to give" (M-13.2:1).

"Pain is my own idea" (1:2). What a stunning statement! Pain is an idea I thought up independently of God. In fact, pain *is* thinking independently of God. Pain is trying to find happiness *in this world.* I have taught myself that the greatest pleasure of all is total autonomy, complete independence, absolute self-sufficiency. I have chosen this, and in doing so, invented pain. Now, I am unlearning what I taught myself. Now, I am learning to choose God's Will instead of what I made, joy instead of pain. "I am teaching you to associate misery with the ego and joy with the spirit" (T-4.VI.5:6).

Let me realize today that in saying, "I am not a body," I am choosing joy instead of pain. In continuing to affirm, "I am a body," I am choosing pain instead of joy.

Lesson 211—July 30

"I am not a body. I am free. For I am still as God created me."
(191) "I am the holy Son of God Himself."
"I am not a body. I am free. For I am still as God created me."

PRACTICE SUMMARY

See the instructions on page 204 or the Practice Card at the end of the book.

COMMENTARY

To seek the glory of God in my Self—that sounds a little pretentious. Yet the lesson says we seek this glory "in true humility." Naturally, the Course is speaking of *the* Self, and not *my* self. "This does not refer, however, to the self of which the world speaks" (M-4.VII.2:2). When someone says, "The glory of God is in me," or "I am the Son of God Himself," it makes a very big difference what "me" is being spoken of. If it is the self that we believe exists separate from the billions of other selves in this world, we are not speaking the truth. We *are* being pretentious. If it refers to the Self that is shared by all those billions, the Self of which my little consciousness is just one fragment, it is the Truth that sets us free.

The glory of God does not reside in the little self, but it does reside in the Self. And beholding that glory "in the Son whom He created as my Self" does not lead to delusions of grandeur, but to true grandeur, a grandeur that is instantly perceived as shared with all living things. There can be no setting of myself above any others, for the glory in them is my own.

These final review lessons, before Part II of the Workbook, refer a lot to things like silence, and beholding the glory of God. In these times of practice, let us seek to open ourselves to that kind of experience, to a seeing that is not of the eyes, to an awareness of the reality of our Self, God's Son. Let my little thoughts be silent, and let me hear the Voice for God speaking within me, speaking to my self of my Self, wooing me back into harmony with that vastness of Being to which I belong, gathering together the seeming fragments of the Sonship into one harmonious Whole. I am, indeed, still as God created me. Not just a body, not bound by the body, not characterized by the body, but "free of all limits, safe and healed and whole" (W-pI.97.7:2). I am that which God created, the holy Son of God Himself.

Lesson 212—July 31

"I am not a body. I am free. For I am still as God created me."
(192) "I have a function God would have me fill."
"I am not a body. I am free. For I am still as God created me."

PRACTICE SUMMARY

See the instructions on page 204 or the Practice Card at the end of the book.

COMMENTARY

What is the function God has for me? Lesson 192, which this lesson reviews, told me that, "Forgiveness represents your function here." I need to be reminded of that. My function is not some particular career or occupation. The content is what matters; the form will shape itself to that content, based on the circumstances of my life. Forgiveness is the content. If I am asking myself what my occupation should be, or what direction my life should take, let me ask myself this question: How does forgiveness best take form in my life right now? Or better yet, let me ask the Holy Spirit that question.

An "occupation" is what occupies most of my life. How, in form, can I occupy most of my life with forgiveness? How can I best serve to look upon illusions and see them disappear? How can I best serve to assist myself, and others, to let go of all guilt? How can I best reflect love in this world?

I work as a writer (you may do something quite different—fill in as you please). But that occupation is not my function; it is only one means of *expressing* my function, which is forgiveness—the same function God has given to all of us. The form may change or disappear; my function remains unchanged. A few years ago I was working as a computer consultant because, at that time, I felt that was the best means I had of fulfilling my function. Then, the form changed. But not the content.

Let me not seek any function in terms of form. Let me always seek the content. It is the content of forgiveness, of reflecting love in this world and releasing from guilt, that will set me free from illusions. No form can do that, since every form is itself part of the illusion. So all that I seek, and all that I lay claim to as mine, is the function God gave me (the content) and not any occupation, or job, or situation.

I am not a body (a form). I am free. I am formless, and I am therefore not tied to form of any kind.

Lesson 213—August 1

"I am not a body. I am free. For I am still as God created me."
(193) "All things are lessons God would have me learn."
"I am not a body. I am free. For I am still as God created me."

PRACTICE SUMMARY

See the instructions on page 204 or the Practice Card at the end of the book.

COMMENTARY

Every circumstance of life offers me the choice between a miracle and my own ego thoughts, which will hurt me. Or as the Text puts it, "The choice is miracles instead of murder" (T-23.IV.5:6). zThat is the lesson that all things have to teach me, today and every day. Which voice, ego or Holy Spirit, will I listen to in this moment, and the next, and the next? It's always one or the other, never neither, never both. "You will not make decisions by yourself whatever you decide. For they are made with idols or with God. And you ask help of anti-Christ or Christ, and which you choose will join with you and tell you what to do" (T-30.I.14:7–9).

In each situation I face today, this is what is going on. The ego offers its interpretation, and the Holy Spirit offers His; I choose which to listen to. I can choose the miracle, or murder. My choice determines my perception and my experience of the situation. Which will I choose today?

"When the temptation to attack rises to make your mind darkened and murderous, remember you *can* see the battle from above. Even in forms you do not recognize, the signs you know. There is a stab of pain, a twinge of guilt, and above all, a loss of peace. This you know well. When they occur leave not your place on high, but quickly choose a miracle instead of murder" (T-23.IV.6:1–5).

This choice is what sets me free. The Holy Spirit is always with me to help me make this choice. In each instant I can choose to learn the lessons God wants me to learn, and forget what I have been teaching myself. Let me not evaluate anything without His help.

If we could grasp just this one lesson, this habit of referring everything to the Holy Spirit, rather than trying to figure it out by ourselves (which always means *with the ego's help*), everything else would simply fall into place. This alone is enough to set us free.

One thing the Holy Spirit sees differently from the ego is my body. "The Holy Spirit does not see the body as you do, because He knows the only reality of anything is the service it renders God on behalf of the function He gives it" (T-8.VII.3:6). When I choose to protect the body, to make it the center of what I am doing, mistaking the body for myself, I am choosing murder. I am not a body. I do not exist for my body's sake; its purpose is to render service to God as I carry out the function He has given me in the world, and that is all. If I listen to the Holy Spirit, I have to be willing to see the body as meaningless in itself (W-pI.96.3:7), and useful only as a communication device with which to reach my brothers. Let me remind myself that I am not a body, as in each moment I seek to hear the Voice for God.

Lesson 214—August 2

"I am not a body. I am free. For I am still as God created me."
(194) "I place the future in the Hands of God."
"I am not a body. I am free. For I am still as God created me."

PRACTICE SUMMARY

See the instructions on page 204 or the Practice Card at the end of the book.

COMMENTARY

Accepting that the past is gone is simply common sense, because by definition, what is "past" is no longer here; it is gone. Only our mental attachment to things past, our insistence on regurgitating past incidents and chewing them over again, can have any effect on the present. The effects we feel are not of the past, but of our present thinking about the past.

Accepting that the future has not yet arrived is also common sense, because again by definition, what is future is not here now. It cannot have any effect on the present moment. Only our mental imagination of what the future might hold, and our thinking about what has not yet occurred, can have present effect.

In both cases, the effects that we imagine come from past or future come, in fact, from our present thinking. Therefore, only by changing our present thinking can those effects be altered. When I am able to mentally let go of the past and the future, placing the future in God's Hands, I am freed from their apparent effects. I am at liberty, in the now, to open myself to accept what God is giving me *now*.

The present circumstances in which I find myself may appear to be threatening. They may have come about, in my perception, because of past events. They may appear to lead inevitably to some unhappy future. Yet if I can open my mind to believe that, "What God gives can only be for good" (1:4), then that good will come to me. We cannot know all the factors involved in the events of our lives and their effect on everyone around us. But God knows. We can safely and confidently take our hands off, and place the future in God's Hands. We can look upon things that seem to bring evil and refuse the evil, accepting only what *God* gives as what truly belongs to us. In everything, there is a gift of God, if we look carefully enough. To place our future in God's Hands we must let go ourselves, and stop trying to orchestrate the events of our lives. Doing so is a constant lesson in trust. Trust is the key, an essential ingredient in placing the future into God's Hands.

In the Manual for Teachers, the fundamental stage in the process of development from "teacher of God" to "advanced teacher of God" is the development of trust. The full flowering of trust is not an overnight process. It goes through several stages, clearly set out in the Manual.

Most of those stages involve some discomfort, because until we have truly acquired trust, we keep trying to second-guess God. The pain comes not from the learning, but from what we have not yet learned. What we are learning will bring the removal of the pain, but pain along the way seems almost unavoidable. "Few teachers of God escape this distress entirely" (M-4.I.5:3). Yet when the lesson is learned, the peace will be like nothing we have ever known. We can only imagine what total freedom from all anxiety feels like, and yet, if we have wholly placed our future into God's Hands, what else could be the certain result?

Each effort we make in this direction is beneficial. Each moment we place into His Hands will lessen the burden of care we carry constantly for our lives. Gradually, we are learning to cast all our cares on Him, trusting in His caring for us.

Lesson 215—August 3

"I am not a body. I am free. For I am still as God created me."
(195) "Love is the way I walk in gratitude."
"I am not a body. I am free. For I am still as God created me."

PRACTICE SUMMARY

See the instructions on page 204 or the Practice Card at the end of the book.

COMMENTARY

Today's review adds a new note to the lesson. I walk in the way of love. As I walk, the Holy Spirit walks with me (1:3–4), and shows me the way to go.

Walking in the way of love is not always simple. Often, the "loving thing" to do is not obvious. If someone breaks into my home, and is arrested, do I press charges, or do I let them off the hook? Which action is "loving"? Or, to make it much more simple: A friend, prone to misuse of money, asks me for a loan. Do I give them the money, or refuse? Which is the way of love?

I do not know. Even if I think I know, I do not know. I cannot possibly know all the variables. I cannot evaluate the ego motivation of another. How could I possibly do that when I can't even evaluate my own ego motivations? I cannot judge when a person is open to a merciful action, or when the most loving thing would be to let them face the consequences of their mistakes. But the Holy Spirit does know all those things. He is my only Guide. My past experiences, no matter how extensive, are never enough to grant me perfect judgment. The Holy Spirit, however, knows every detail of every situation. He knows the ramifications of every possible outcome, and can guide me in the loving action I should choose.

How do I discern His Voice? Again, there is no guaranteed way. Learning to discern His Voice clearly is a life-long process. All I need do is to refer the situation to Him, consciously give it into His hands, and then act in whatever way seems best to me. Each day, and in each situation, I renew my resolve to never make a decision by myself. Sometimes I will sense an inner "nudge" in a certain direction, for no reason I can detect. Perhaps circumstances will occur that seem to point me in a particular direction. Serendipitous coincidences may occur that seem to be signs, directing me. Other times I will seemingly be left on my own. The Course promises us that if we make a mistake, He will correct us, if we have given the situation to Him. We will make mistakes, but we have His promise of correction.

One of the most important aspects of hearing His Voice, I have learned, is letting go of any investment in a particular outcome. The only outcome I seek is the outcome of forgiveness, the outcome of love, the outcome of peace of mind in all concerned. I cannot pick what external circumstances are best suited to this kind of outcome; only the Holy Spirit knows. A rebellious teenager threatens to leave home, or drop out of school. As a parent or friend I may believe that the best thing is that she stay at home, or stay in school. I do not know. Perhaps the lessons she needs to learn can only be found if she distances herself for a while from family and friends. So I lay the situation in the hands of the Holy Spirit, and ask that I be guided to say and do whatever best serves the way of love. Then, I keep my hands off. I trust that I *am* being guided, even if things begin to move in a way I, in my short-sightedness, do not like. My primary responsibility is simply not to interfere with Him.

Today, let me walk the way of love in gratitude, trusting the Holy Spirit to guide my every word and action. Let me remind myself that I am here only to be truly helpful, to represent Him Who sent me, knowing that I do not have to worry about what I will say or do, for He will direct me (T-2.V(A).18:2–6).

Lesson 216—August 4

"I am not a body. I am free. For I am still as God created me."
(196) "It can be but myself I crucify."
"I am not a body. I am free. For I am still as God created me."

PRACTICE SUMMARY

See the instructions on page 204 or the Practice Card at the end of the book.

COMMENTARY

The heart of the little summary today is the first sentence: "All that I do I do unto myself" (1:2). If we applied that one idea consistently, what a transformation there would be in our part of the world!

My own little personal list (you can make your own):

How do I greet people on the telephone?
How do I respond to interruptions?
How do I regard people serving me in stores and restaurants?
How do I react to snippets of talk I hear on the evening news?
How do I treat poor or homeless people I encounter?
How do I think about the very rich?
How do I think about other drivers?
What do I say to others about my friends when they are not present?

"All that I do I do unto myself." Is it any wonder I feel mistreated and misunderstood? All of these "little" examples are expressions of the ego's desire to crucify the Son of God. Each of them betrays the way I am treating myself, when I listen to my ego. This explains that wonderful saying in the Manual, "The teacher of God is generous out of Self interest" (M-4.VII.2:1).

Lesson 217—August 5

"I am not a body. I am free. For I am still as God created me."
(197) "It can be but my gratitude I earn."
"I am not a body. I am free. For I am still as God created me."

PRACTICE SUMMARY

See the instructions on page 204 or the Practice Card at the end of the book.

COMMENTARY

The salvation described by the Course is unique in the way it combines total responsibility for our own salvation with total dependence on God. My Self is what "saves" me, yet that Self is discovered only by recognizing that what I am is not any result of my own action, but the gift of God in creation.

There is a line in the Text that says, "Give thanks to every part of you that you have taught how to remember you" (T-13.VII.17:8). The gratitude we feel as we begin to awaken to what we are is due to the Self that we are discovering. I am the one who gives thanks; I am also the One to Whom thanks are being given.

It is very hard to understand all of this until you begin to experience it. I vividly recall one particular time in which it seemed to come to crystal clarity for me, for a few moments at least. I became aware of a loving part of myself that was continually moving me and motivating me in the direction of inner peace and Self acceptance. It was something that had always been there, more than a part of me, the reality of myself. I was simultaneously aware of another part of my mind that had begun to open up to that love, and in that moment, I felt a deep and unexpressible gratitude to myself for being willing to receive that love. I was aware both of being the giver of the love and the receiver of it, and in that moment the little self I had always thought was me felt swallowed up in this much larger, constantly moving, tide of love.

This peculiar gratitude to my Self can find expression in many little ways. Sometimes when I have taken the time for a quiet meditation, one in which I feel strongly renewed, I find the gratitude welling up, and I say, "Thank you." And I am not sure whether I am thanking God or myself. I am grateful to myself for having readied myself to receive this Course. I am thankful to myself for reading it, and continuing to study it and to apply it. When a line from the Course pops into my head at just the right moment, I can thank my Self for it.

The Course teaches that we all are already awake; the truth lives untarnished in our right mind. And it is this right mind, this Self that is the only part of us that has reality in truth, which is teaching us and calling us home. This right mind is the home of the Holy Spirit; He is part of us as well as part of God. His Voice is the Voice for God, yet it is also the Voice of my Self. It is my Self that brought the Course into the world. It is my Self that drew me to it. It is my Self that is bringing me to awareness. Everything that nudges me in the right direction is a gift from my Self.

Let me be grateful to my Self today. Let me recognize that I am deserving of my own gratitude. Instead of being annoyed with myself, impatient with myself, harsh on myself, discouraged with myself, or untrusting of myself, let me offer myself my own gratitude. And let me realize that my own gratitude is all I need and want. Let me understand that when I have learned fully to be completely grateful to my Self for what I am, I will have completed the journey, and will have learned, at the same time, to be fully appreciative and grateful to God for the gift He has given me: my Self.

Lesson 218—August 6

"I am not a body. I am free. For I am still as God created me."
(198) "Only my condemnation injures me."
"I am not a body. I am free. For I am still as God created me."

PRACTICE SUMMARY

See the instructions on page 204 or the Practice Card at the end of the book.

COMMENTARY

Condemnation does not injure the body. It reminds me of the old childhood chant, "Sticks and stones may break my bones, but names can never hurt me." I am not a body; what I am cannot be hurt by "sticks and stones." Only my own condemnation, my acceptance of those "names," can hurt me.

Haven't you called yourself names? I know I have. "You idiot!" "You are so stupid, Watson!" These self-mocking name-callings still, after all these years, pop into my head and out of my own mouth. They are only surface symptoms of a much deeper self-condemnation and mistrust of myself that is at the root of all my problems. Marianne Williamson hits the target when she says, "The ego is my self-loathing."

And when I realize that every other form of outward-directed condemnation—anger, prejudice, hatred, resentment, common dislike, even simple discomfort with someone—are all, every one, projections of my own self-attack, then I begin to realize just how deep and how far-reaching this self-condemnation really is. This condemnation injures *me*. I hurl my spears of attack out at the world, and every one returns to stab me in the back. "It can be but myself I crucify" (W-pII.216).

As long as I keep this war against myself going, my eyes are sightless to see my own glory. I cannot see the Christ in myself because of the dust storm of self-condemnation, whether it is directed inward or projected outward on illusions of myself I think are outside of me. It is the constant stream of judgment that blinds me.

Today, if I only choose to do so, I can see my own glory. All that I need is to accept Atonement for myself. Tune out the Judgment Channel. Tune in the Forgiveness Channel. Let me be quiet now, and sense the Love within: the love of God for me, His child; my love for Him; my Self's own love for me, and mine for my Self. And often, today, let me stop and remind myself that the only thing that *can* injure me is my own condemnation. And I am free to choose to let that go, assisted by the Holy Spirit, my inner Self, and all the angels of Heaven.

Whenever I feel a rush of judgment within, wherever it is directed, let me bring my case to Heaven's Higher Court, and hear the Holy Spirit dismiss the case against me (T-5.VI,4, 10).

Lesson 219—August 7

"I am not a body. I am free. For I am still as God created me."
(199) "I am not a body. I am free."
"I am not a body. I am free. For I am still as God created me."

PRACTICE SUMMARY

See the instructions on page 204 or the Practice Card at the end of the book.

COMMENTARY

Well, we don't get much choice today. We've got to take another look at the fact that we are not bodies.

The belief that I am a body, I think, is what put us here in this world, wearing a body. I may say I believe I am not a body, and that I understand what I am saying, but I'm still wearing a body. That shows that my words and the deep belief of my mind are not entirely in synch. The reason the Course has had us repeating this idea for the last twenty days (it started with Lesson 199) is certainly not because we already believe it and don't need it; obviously, the Course is recognizing that our belief that we are bodies is deeply imbedded in us, and the repetition is necessary to begin counteracting that belief. Remember that in Lesson 199, it suggested we make this idea a part of our practice *every day*. Our identification with our bodies is not an idea that will be easily dislodged.

The juxtaposition of the words "I am not a body" with the words "I am free" is interesting. If I had written the Course I would probably have said, "I am not a body. I am a spirit," or something like that. Why do you suppose Jesus put these two thoughts together?

The body is an enslaving thing. All of us are slaves to our bodies. Think how much time and energy of our so-called life in this world is devoted to caring for the body. We feed it, we work to house it and cloth it, we wash it, we devote entire rooms in our house to taking care of the needs for elimination and cleansing, we buy all sorts of gadgets to groom it. Every week or so we clip our nails. We make appointments for haircuts. Look at the cookbook section in a bookstore some time to get a feel for the thought and care that goes into just the feeding aspect. Look at our supermarkets, our clothing stores, shoe stores. Most stores in a mall have to do with caring for the body. Look at the expense we devote to health care and hospitals.

What if I am not a body? What if this great focus of effort and attention is all misdirected? What if we are majoring in minors? What if the center of gravity in our lives began to shift from caring for the body to caring for the spirit? What would my life and your life be like if that happened? What if I was as consistent in seeking holy instants as I am in feeding my face? What if I began stopping several times a day to feed my spirit as regularly as I do to eat, or go to the bathroom? We find it so easy to say to a friend, "Care for a cup of coffee?" What if it were just as easy to say, "Care to spend a few minutes in meditation with me?"

Just thinking about this makes it evident how unbalanced our lives are and how centered on our bodies. It makes me realize how far we have yet to go. And since change begins in the mind, just reminding myself as often as I can remember to do so, "I am not a body," is a good way to begin the great shift. Perhaps something as simple as letting my meals be a reminder to say a prayer can help, not because praying over food makes it any better, but because it helps me remember that I need my spiritual nourishment as much, or more, than I need physical food. Each time I become aware that I am taking time and effort to care for my body, let it remind me also to care for my spirit.

Think, too, of the freedom that will come to us when we realize that our body is no big deal. What I am is not something that wears out, grows old and dies. What I am is not something that is a "brief candle," as Shakespeare called it, but an eternal star shining forever in the heavens. The body is deserving of care because it is a useful tool for the situation in which we find ourselves, but no more than that. Like a car it is good for the purpose it serves. But the body is not "me" any more than my car is "me" (auto ads to the contrary). Think of all the anxiety and constant concern that would be lifted from our shoulders if we can think of our bodies in this way. Changing our mind in this respect is worth all the effort it will take.

Lesson 220—August 8

"I am not a body. I am free. For I am still as God created me."
(200) "There is no peace except the peace of God."
"I am not a body. I am free. For I am still as God created me."

PRACTICE SUMMARY

See the instructions on page 204 or the Practice Card at the end of the book.

COMMENTARY

To see ourselves as bodies is to be in conflict. Peace can be found only in God. Searching for peace in the realm of the physical is doomed to failure, because the body is an expression of conflict.

The prayer in this review lesson is about not wandering from "the way of peace." What might that mean? Obviously, it refers to any unpeaceful state of mind, any thought of antagonism, or anger, or attack, or hatred. The Course calls us to mental vigilance, watching our thoughts for anything that opposes peace, and, as soon as such a thought is detected, bringing it to the presence of the Holy Spirit for healing. We are told to think along these lines: "This is not what I want. I want the peace of God." So when we sense our thoughts moving into conflict mode, we respond. Perhaps we pray, "Let me not wander from the way of peace."

Wandering from the way of peace, however, includes more than overt attack. The ego can disguise attack very subtly; indeed the Course sees even our special love relationships, our false forgiveness, and our ego's attempts at empathy as veiled attacks. If there is no peace except God's peace, then to seek for peace in some other way is really a hidden attachment to attack. If there is only one road to my destination, and I choose not to follow the road, I am choosing my destination's opposite. It is really seeking peace through war, which is impossible. The ego, for instance, often seeks for illusory peace through force, attempting to physically or mentally overpower the situation. We cannot find peace by attempting to browbeat the world into submission. On any such road, we are not moving toward peace; we are lost.

The way to God's peace is through following the Holy Spirit, "Him Who leads me home." When we try to solve our problems on our own, we are not following the way to peace:

> The ego always tries to preserve conflict. It is very ingenious in devising ways that seem to diminish conflict, because it does not want you to find conflict so intolerable that you will insist on giving it up (T-7.VIII.2:2–3).

Trying to use our own ingenuity to resolve conflict, then, is another way we wander from the true road to peace.

When conflict seems to arise today, let me remember my lesson, that there is no peace except the peace of God. Let me instantly seek peace, but not in my own way. Let me turn to the Holy Spirit within and ask His direction.

> When you feel the holiness of your relationship is threatened by anything, stop instantly and offer the Holy Spirit your willingness, in spite of fear, to let Him exchange this instant for the holy one you would rather have. He will never fail in this (T-18.V.6:1–2).

A Workbook Companion
COMMENTS ON PRACTICE Part II

by Robert Perry

The crowning aspect of the Workbook

Part II of the Workbook was first mentioned in the Introduction to the Workbook, where we were told that Part I would be devoted to undoing our current perception and Part II would be devoted to acquiring true perception. Even there one can see the implication that Part I is the preparation for Part II—we undo false perception *so that* we can acquire true perception. This attitude has continued. By the time we reach Part II, we have been specifically preparing for it for eighty lessons, since Review IV (141–150). This preparation has had many aspects:

- Going beyond words
- Going beyond structure—getting fewer and fewer specific instructions
- Giving our practice into the hands of the Holy Spirit, Who will guide our practicing
- Putting together the Workbook's various kinds of practice into the overall four-fold framework of practice
- Acquiring more motivation, certainty, commitment and unified purpose
- Giving more time and effort
- Going beyond special blocks
- Having holy instants, experiences of what lies beyond our blocks
- Having direct experiences of God, tastes of the final step

In other words, in the last eighty lessons, the Workbook has been very specifically readying us for Part II. Part II, then, is the crowning aspect of the Workbook, what it all leads up to. Yet Part II seems like a let-down. It seems like all of the action was in Part I, where we read all of those interesting discussions, received all of those detailed instructions, and did all of those fascinating exercises. Now we get no instructions (after the Introduction to Part II), a few words of teaching for each lesson, and a brief prayer. It seems like the author just ran out of ideas, or got tired of making up new instructions and new teaching. Yet this is very deceptive. Part II *is* the crowning aspect, because we have supposedly moved beyond the need for all the instructions. We are (supposedly) practicing under our own power, practicing more than ever, practicing more deeply and effectively, and moving into a direct, experiential relationship with God. Let's look at some of the aspects of Part II's practice.

The structure changes dramatically

In Part II, the structure changes dramatically, largely because the previous structure falls away.

- There are no special instructions for each day, but instead one set of instructions for the entirety of Part II.
- All specific time requirements drop away.
- There is a brief paragraph of discussion for each day's lesson, instead of one to three pages of discussion.
- There is a prayer for each day's lesson, which was true of only occasional lessons in Part I.
- The function of giving daily teaching transfers from the daily lesson to a special "What is" section that is read every day for ten days.

The words, the lesson, the exercise, are mere introductions

Now, instead of focusing on various words and phrases throughout our practice period, we use the words given us only at the beginning. We use them merely as an opening invitation. Actually, there has been a pattern throughout the Workbook of having an active phase at the beginning of the longer practice periods, followed by a receptive phase. This tendency increases in Part II, where we begin the practice period by saying some simple words of welcome, and then we let go of words entirely.

Waiting on the direct experience of God, on His grace, on His final step

After those simple words of welcome, we wait for God to come and, in a sense, take over our practice time. In other words, the goal is that, after our words of welcome, all words and all mental activity will cease. This will allow God to come and give us the direct experience of His Presence. In this state, *we* are not doing anything, but merely being in Him. This focus on direct experience of God is the fulfillment of several trends in the Course:

- The focus on going beyond vision to experiencing God, which began in Lesson 157
- The focus on receiving grace and experiencing the final step, which began in Lesson 168
- The focus on holy instants, which also began in Lesson 157
- The focus on direct prayers to God, which began in Lesson 163 and shows up again in lessons 170, Review V (which begins on Lesson 171), 184 and 189. Also, Lesson 168, "Your grace is given me. I claim it now," is the only one in which the idea for the day is *itself*

a prayer to God. You could say that Part II is an extended version of this lesson.

- The promise, early in the Text, that some of the later steps in the Course would involve a more direct approach to God.

Clarification: When it says that we are to spend the latter half of the year waiting for God to take His final step, this can be very confusing. For the final step is supposed to be when God lifts us out of time and space permanently. So are we supposed to spend all of our practice periods expecting that God will come and swoop us out of time forever? I don't think so. From Lesson 169 I understand that the grace that lifts us out of time and into God forever is the *same* grace that lifts us out of time and into God *temporarily*. In other words, when we experience God directly, even for an instant, we are, in a sense, experiencing the final step. So I think that we are to spend the latter part of the year waiting for what the Text calls revelation, the experience of God, rather than specifically waiting for God to remove us from time and space permanently.

A daily prayer

As part of this theme of direct approach to God, we are given a prayer each day. This prayer, of course, is not meant to be simply read, but is meant to be said to God. It, in other words, constitutes those simple words of welcome we say to God. It is how we invite Him to come to us.

Use as much time as makes us happy

The instructions for the longer practice periods have now gone from at least five minutes and ideally thirty or more (153–200), to at least fifteen minutes (201–220), to as long as makes us happy. In other words, the time instructions for the longer practice periods have dropped away. Now we practice according to need, according to how long it takes us to achieve the result we desire.

Still have a central thought for each day

Part of the Workbook's structure that remains is that we are still being given a central thought to focus on each day. This remaining structure will itself fall away when we are done with the Workbook. At the end of the Workbook we will be told that no more daily lessons will be assigned.

Still have use for words of teaching: the "What is" sections

Even though the Workbook is going beyond words here in Part II, the Course never tires of teaching. Yet, as I mentioned earlier, that teaching is no longer found in the daily lessons, but rather in "instructions on a theme of special relevance" (11:2) that come before each set of ten lessons. Allen and I call these the "What is" sections of the Workbook (since the titles of all but one begin with those words); there are fourteen of them. We read each "What is" section each day for ten days. Each one is a gold mine of teaching and should be read very slowly and thoughtfully. If you think you have understood all that it has to say, simply ask yourself, "Why does this sentence follow the previous one? What is their connection?" Whole new meanings will open up to you.

Jesus speaks to us more frequently

In keeping with the theme of our practice deepening, becoming more experiential, and becoming more focused on direct approach to God, Jesus speaks to us more directly here in Part II. In Part I he showed up in Lesson 70 and in Review V. Now he directly addresses us in many of the lessons, including 221, 225, 231, 264, 288, 310, 313, 342, as well as in the Introduction, the final "What is" section ("What Am I?") and the Epilogue.

Part II, Introduction
Commentary

The Introduction to Part II of the Workbook is the last set of practice instructions we will receive for the next 140 days. The final instructions will be for the last five lessons, and do not really change much. So, since we will be following this set of instructions every day for the next five months, we need to pay close attention and fix them in our minds. I will mail out this set of comments from time to time, just to remind us all.

Remember that the Workbook is designed to train us in practicing, and to help us form a habit of daily practice that will endure until engaging with God in our lives has become a moment-to-moment way of life, with no need for any further practice. For a very few, this happy habit might be formed in a single year of doing the Workbook, although I know of no one for whom this is true. For most people, it seems, the pattern of practice being taught is still poorly formed and sporadically practiced after only one pass through the Workbook, and many find repeating the Workbook very beneficial, and its clear structure a necessary support in continuing to develop the desired habits.

Before we go over what the desired pattern of practice is, though, let me encourage you with a few observations from my own practice and that of several friends. Do not be discouraged if, on reading over the description of the daily practice, you realize that you are still far from "matching up" to the pattern. The form of daily practice described in this Introduction is the *goal*; being distressed because you don't match up to it right now is like being upset that you can't play Tchaikovsky's First Concerto after only a few weeks of practice. Forming habits takes a lot of time. Just do the best you can each day, and practice forgiving yourself when you don't measure up to your intentions. Whatever you do, keep at it! Don't allow the ego to kill your motivation to practice by pointing out how poorly you are doing it. Failure to follow the instructions fully is not a reason to stop practicing; it is a reason to return to practice with renewed vigor, as soon as you realize you have slipped.

The goal of our practice is to completely retrain our minds. It is to become so habituated to listening to the Voice for God that it becomes natural, something we do without even thinking about it, the first response to every temptation. The goal is to respond to every ego thought without fear, and instantly bring it into the holy place where we meet with God in our minds. The long-term goal of our practice is to arrive at the place where life becomes one continuous holy instant (W-pI.135.19:1), in which we never cease to think of God (W-pI.153.18:1). The short-term goal of Workbook practice is to form the habit of daily practicing that will take us to that long-term goal (W-pI.rIII.In.11:2; W-pI.194.6;2).

What, then, is the pattern of daily practice that is set forth for the next 140 days?

1. **Spending time with God each morning and night**, "as long as makes us happy" (2:6). The result we desire is "direct experience of truth alone" (1:3), or an experience of "rest" and "calm" (3:1), or experiencing the presence of God (4:1; 4:6). In sum, we desire to enter the holy instant; indeed, this Introduction twice refers to our morning and evening practice times as "holy instants" (3:2, 11:4), or "times in which we leave the world of pain, and go to enter peace" (1:4). These experiences of holy instants are called "the goal this course has set" and "the end toward which our practicing was always geared" (1:5).

   So every morning and evening practice period is meant to bring us to the holy instant, and "we will use as much [time] as we will need for the result that we desire" (2:8). The time is flexible, perhaps even a half hour or longer if we need or want that much time.
2. **Hourly remembrance** (2:9). Once each hour during the day we will pause to remind ourselves of the lesson for the day, using the thought for the day to "calm our minds at need" (3:1). But the hourly remembrance is not simply a repeating of the words; it is a brief time in which we "expect our Father to reveal Himself, as He has promised" (3:3). Ideally this will be two or three minutes in which we can be quiet, perhaps closing our eyes, to refocus on our goal and regroup our thoughts, bringing any grievance or upset of the past hour to the Holy Spirit for healing (see W-pI.153.17 and W-pI.193.12). When such an extended pause is impossible, briefly turning our thoughts to God and reaffirming our goal is sufficient.
3. **Frequent reminders** in between the hours, although not specifically mentioned in this introduction to Part II, were singled out in the Introduction to the review period we have just completed, and we can assume they are meant to be continued.
4. **Response to temptation.** Whenever we are "tempted to forget our goal" (2:9), we need to call to God. That the temptation mentioned is "to forget our goal" implies that all the rest of the time *we are remembering it*! So any time we notice our minds are about to wander from our goal, or have wandered, we call to God to help us return our minds to Him.

This is a rigorous spiritual practice. It demands considerable effort to form such habits. But the results are more than worth it. The goal of the Course, the whole purpose of Workbook practice, has been to bring us to this kind of direct experience of the truth. Without such direct experience, the concepts of the Text will be nothing more than empty concepts.

We are offered a little more detail about how to spend our extended morning and evening times. The specific words of the day's lesson, as it appears in the Workbook, are of diminishing importance. This is reflected in the fact that no more than a half page is given to them. The words of the lesson are not the focus any more (1:1); they are "but...guides on which we do not now depend" (1:2). The primary goal is direct experience of the truth, or the holy instant. Reading the daily lesson and repeating its main thought is only the beginning (2:1); having used the words to focus our minds, we spend our time waiting for God to come to us (3:3, 4:6). These times are called "periods of wordless, deep experience" (11:2). The bulk of our morning and evening times should be spent thus, in silent waiting and receptivity, without verbal thought.

If you look ahead at the lessons in Part II you will see that every one contains a short prayer to God the Father. There is no specific mention of these prayers nor how to use them, but I believe the following words give such instruction:

"We say some simple words of welcome, and expect our Father to reveal Himself, as He has promised" (3:3). "So our times with Him will now be spent. We say *the words of invitation that His Voice suggests*, and then we wait for Him to come to us" (4:5–6, my italics). Finally, the Introduction itself shifts into prayer with a sort of un-self-conscious naturalness, in 6:2–7:8; in 6:5 our prayers are called "little gifts of thanks" from us to God.

Those "words of invitation," suggested to us by God's Voice, are, I believe, the prayers given to us in each day's lesson. They are words suggested for our use, to invite God to speak to us, to offer welcome to Him. Actually speaking these prayers, praying them, can be a powerful tool in bringing us the direct experiences with God these lessons intend for us.

"Instead of words, we need but feel His love. Instead of prayers, we need but call His Name. Instead of judging, we need but be still and let all things be healed" (10:3–5).

So the morning and evening times are not intended to be spent in thinking about the concepts of the Course, nor in saying prayers for ourselves or for others, nor in making decisions about what to do or making judgments of how to solve our problems. They are meant to be times of *experience* and not thought. Simply feeling God's Love. Simply repeating His Name in our awareness of relationship with Him. Simply being still, letting go, *letting* all things be healed, like a patient lying still as the Healer does His work. "Sit silently and wait upon your Father" (5:5).

There are words of encouragement in this Introduction, assuring us that we couldn't have come this far if the goal were not our true will, if, in our hearts, we did not want God to come to us and reveal Himself.

This *is* our will, in case we are having any doubts, or looking at what is being asked of us and questioning whether or not we want it deeply enough. We do.

Jesus says, "I am so close to you we cannot fail" (6:1). "For now we cannot fail" (5:4). He reviews the way we have come, from our insane wish that God would fail to have the Son He created, to our recognition that illusions are not true. The end is near, he tells us. I think it is important to realize that he is speaking in the context of eons of time; "near" is a relative term, and probably is not referring to days or weeks or months. He says here that "the need for practice [is] almost done" (10:1). Yet in the Manual (Chapter 16) he makes it clear that some kind of practice is part of the life-long habit of the teacher of God. "Almost done," as well, is relative to the billions of years we have spent in separation. We *are* very near the goal, in that context!

One last item about our daily practice for the next five months, which should be carefully noted: we are supposed to read one of the "What is" sections *every day*, preceding either our morning or evening quiet time. Thus, each section will be read ten times. And each time we read it, we are asked to read it "slowly" and to think about it for a while.

Going along with this instruction, therefore, in the daily lesson comments that follow I will include my thoughts for that day about the current "What Is" section. I plan to comment, usually, on just a few sentences from the "What Is" section each day, covering the entire page over the period of ten days.

PRACTICE SUMMARY
Part II of the Workbook

Purpose: To take the last few steps to God. To wait for Him to take the final step.

Morning/Evening Quiet Time: As long as needed.

- Read the written lesson.
- Use the idea and the prayer to introduce a time of quiet. Do not depend on the words. Use them as a simple invitation to God to come to you.
- Sit silently and wait for God. Wait in quiet expectancy for Him to reveal Himself to you. Seek only direct, deep, wordless experience of Him. Be certain of His coming, and unafraid. For He has promised that when you invite Him, He will come. You ask only that He keep His ancient promise, which He wills to keep. These times are your gift to Him.

Hourly Remembrance: Do not forget.

Give thanks to God that He has remained with you and will always be there to answer your call to Him.

Frequent Reminder: As often as possible, even every minute.

Remember the idea. Dwell with God, let Him shine on you.

Response To Temptation: When you are tempted to forget your goal.

Use today's idea as a call to God and all temptation will disappear.

Reading: Preceding one of the day's moments of practice.

- Slowly read "What is" section.
- Think about it a while.

Overall Remarks: Now, in this final part of the year that you and Jesus have spent together, you begin to reach the goal of practicing, which is the goal of the course. Jesus is so close that you cannot fail. You have come far along the road. Do not look back. Fix your eyes on the journey's end. You could not have come this far without realizing that you want to know God. And this is all He requires to come to you.

Lesson 221—August 9

"Peace to my mind. Let all my thoughts be still."

PRACTICE SUMMARY

See the practice instructions on page 241, or the Practice Card bound into this volume.

COMMENTARY

As I emphasized in my comments on the Introduction to Part II, a large part of our two longer daily practice times are meant to be spent in wordless quiet. Receiving our healing, listening rather than talking. Today's lesson is a great one for inducing that state of mind. We begin by directing our minds to be peaceful, our thoughts to be still.

The opening prayer in the first paragraph speaks of coming in silence, and in the quiet of our hearts, waiting and listening for God's Voice. The words used—"quiet," "silence" (twice), "the deep recesses of my mind," waiting, listening, coming to hear His Voice—all these words are pointing us in the same direction, fostering the same attitude in us. An attitude of receptivity. A passiveness, we the feminine to God's masculine, the receiver to the Giver of Life. We still our own thoughts, and allow God's thoughts to come to us. We call to Him, and await His answer.

Jesus is with us as we quietly wait. He voices his confidence that God is with us, and that we will hear Him speak if we wait quietly with him. He asks us to accept his own confidence, telling us that his confidence is our own confidence. Often, I have found it helpful to realize that Jesus symbolizes the part of my own mind that is already awake. His confidence really *is* my confidence, a confidence I have denied so that I see it as outside myself.

We wait with only one goal: to hear His Voice speaking to us of what we are, and revealing Himself to us. In these times of quiet, this is what we are listening for: an awareness of the purity and perfection of our own being as He created us, and an awareness of His Love, His tender care for us, and His peace that He shares with us in these peaceful moments.

How can we hear a message without words? What we listen for is the song of love, eternally sung, forever thrumming its harmony throughout the universe. It is a song we hear wisps of in the eyes of our beloved, in the laughter of children, in the loyalty of a pet, in the expanse of a peaceful lake or the stately flowing of a river, and in the wonder of a well-told fairy tale. It is the song to which our hearts resonate, showing their true nature. It is our eternity calling us to dance. It is the Father sharing His Love with His only Son.

What is Forgiveness? (Part 1)

W-pII.1.1:1

"Forgiveness recognizes what you thought your brother did to you has not occurred" (1:1).

Forgiveness is a different way of seeing yourself.

I want to emphasize the words "you thought" and "to you" in that description of forgiveness. It does not say, "What your brother did has not occurred," but rather "What *you thought* your brother did *to you* has not occurred." It is not a denial that an event happened, but rather a different way of seeing yourself in relationship to the event. You thought that you were affected by it, hurt by it, damaged by it, whatever "it" was; in fact you were not affected by what your brother did at all! You are affected, so the Course tells us, only by your thoughts.

First and foremost, forgiveness means seeing yourself differently in relation to an event. It does not begin with seeing an event or another person differently. When you forgive, what happens first is that you recognize that you have not lost your peace or your love because of what happened; you lost it because you chose to lose it. You decided, at some point, to let go of the peace of God in your heart. The event then came along to justify your loss of peace. You projected the loss of peace onto the event and said, "That is why I am upset."

Therefore, once your thought in regard to yourself has been corrected, you now can see your brother is innocent in spite of his action. He may indeed have done something despicable. You don't have to approve of what he did, or like it, or put up with it like a doormat. However, his action or words did not hurt you. It was not what he did that took away your peace. He did not affect you, he did not injure you. You now can see that "sin" did not occur, and that he has done nothing that warrants guilt. He has perhaps made a grievous mistake, but that hurts only himself, not you.

So much of what the Course talks about is implied in this simple statement, "What you thought your brother did to you has not occurred." You think he injured you, your self, because you are identified with your ego feelings, with your body, with your possessions, with your family members and their bodies and possessions and feelings. The Course teaches that we have identified incorrectly. We are not our bodies. We are not our possessions. We are not the ego with all its hurt feelings. We are something much grander and vaster than that, something that cannot be touched in any way by external forces.

To fully forgive, our identification with our bodies has to be completely over. None of us has attained that, yet. That is why the Course so confidently implies that not one of us has ever, yet, completely forgiven anyone! That is why it says that if only one person completely forgave one sin, the world would be healed (M-14.3:7). (That is what Jesus accomplished, and because of it, the world is already healed. We just haven't been ready yet to receive it.)

A large part of my dealing with the Course has been in recognizing that, far from having no one to forgive, I have everyone to forgive.

If, in your picture of any situation, you still see yourself—or someone close to yourself—as having been in some way injured or hurt by the situation, you have not yet completely forgiven it in your mind. The Course teaches that if pain is real in your perception, you have not yet been completely healed.

Now, I haven't gotten past the first line on this page and probably I've got us all, including myself, feeling a little guilty about the fact that despite all our study of the Course we haven't yet learned to forgive. So I have to stop here, back off, and say: This is completely normal. Don't be surprised. And don't feel guilty about it! Before we can learn to forgive we have to admit that we are not forgiving! We need to recognize all the ways we still make pain real in our experience and belief, and just recognize that we are doing so. One lesson in forgiveness may be to forgive ourselves for being unforgiving.

"Forgiveness…is still, and quietly does nothing….It merely looks, and waits, and judges not" (W-pII.4:1,3). Treat yourself that way! Get in touch with the part of you that does not want to forgive, that does not want peace. Look at it, and do nothing, just wait without judging. It will disappear (in time) and peace will come of itself.

Lesson 222—August 10

"God is with me. I live and move in Him."

PRACTICE SUMMARY

See the practice instructions on page 241, or the Practice Card bound into this volume.

COMMENTARY

Again we are brought to the Presence of God, without words, in quiet. Our only awareness is of God, His Name upon our lips.

What does it mean to "live and move" in God? This is the message that the Apostle Paul brought to the Athenians, speaking of the "unknown God," and saying that, "In Him we live and move and have our being" (Acts 17:16–28). The lesson speaks of the omnipresence of God—that God is everywhere and "everywhen." In beautiful imagery, the lesson turns our thoughts to the all-pervading Presence, never apart from us, "closer…than breathing, and nearer than hands and feet," as Tennyson wrote.

This is imagery and not (in my opinion) literal. If the world is illusion, as the Course has so often said, God is not *literally* "the water which renews and cleanses me" (1:3). This is speaking of our spiritual reality, where we *really* are. God is the reality of all things in which we look to the world for sustenance, the true Source of our life. We think we live in the world, but we live in God. We think our body contains our life, but He is our life. We think we breathe air, but we breathe Him. God is our true food and our true drink, our true home. We do not live and move in the world; we live and move in God.

Reading this lesson aloud is an excellent exercise. Or turning the first part into a prayer: "You are the Source of my life…You are my home…." Use these words at the start of your practice period to set your mind into a consciousness of being immersed in and filled with God, kept in His loving care. Then, be still, and let yourself sink into that Presence, to rest with Him in peace a while.

✧

What is Forgiveness? (Part 2)

W-pII.1.2–7

"Forgiveness," it says, "does not pardon sins and make them real. It sees there was no sin" (1:2–3). This is the whole distinction between true and false forgiveness, which the *Song of Prayer* calls "forgiveness-to-destroy" (S–2.1:2). There is such a difference between seeing sin in someone and struggling to overlook it or to refrain from the desire to punish, and seeing not sin but a mistake, a call for help from a confused child of God, and naturally responding with love. When the Holy Spirit enables us to see the "sin" of another in this way, suddenly we can see our own "sins" in that same very different light. Instead of trying to justify our own errors, we can admit they are mistakes and simply let them go, without guilt.

Sin is simply "a false idea about God's Son" (1:5). It is a false self-appraisal projected onto everyone around us. It is the belief that we are truly separate, attackers of God's Love in our separation; it sees attackers everywhere.

Forgiveness is seen here (1:6–7) in three steps. *First*, we see the falsity of the idea of sin. We recognize that no sin has occurred; the Son of God (in the other or ourselves) is still the Son of God, and not a devil. He has been mistaken, but he has not sinned. *Second*, closely following on the first step and a natural consequence of it, we let the idea of sin go. We drop it. We relinquish our grievances, abandon our thoughts of attack. Only the first step depends on our choice; the second step follows as its inevitable result. When we no longer see attack, what reason is there to punish with counterattack?

The *third* step is God's part. Something comes to take sin's place; the Will of God is freed to flow through us unhindered by our illusions, and Love follows its natural course. In this we experience our true Self, the extension of God's own Love.

All we need do, then, if it can be called doing, is to be willing to see something other than attack, something other than sin. We need only to be willing to admit that our perception of sin is false. When we do, the Holy Spirit will share His perception with us. He knows how to forgive; we do not. Our part is merely to ask to be taught by Him. He does the rest, and everything flows out of that simple willingness.

Lesson 223—August 11

"God is my life. I have no life but His."

PRACTICE SUMMARY

See the practice instructions on page 241, or the Practice Card bound into this volume.

COMMENTARY

Our only mistake is thinking that we have some sort of life apart from God. We do not. God *is* Life. He is Being. He is Existence. He created all that there is, and there is nothing apart from Him. "Nothing can be apart from Him and live" (W-pI.156.2:9). "I do not exist apart from Him" (1:2).

Most of my time here on earth I have spent thinking of myself as someone or something apart from God. Most of my spiritual seeking has been a striving to "get back to God," as if He were unimaginably distant from me. He is not distant. He is not Something separate from my Self. "I have no life but His" (lesson title). There is a blessing often used in Unity churches which ends with the words, "Wherever I am, God is." Yes. My life is God's life. My thoughts are God's Thoughts. There is nowhere to go. There is nothing to do to find Him; He is here. He is with me. He is my life. If I live, I am participating in God.

There is a blessed relief that washes over us when we realize our unity with God. All the bitter struggle, all the fruitless longing, all the aching sense of being on the outside looking in—all of it ends. A thought of pure joy fills our minds. At times it bubbles over into laughter, a certain compassionate amusement at the ludricrous idea we have tormented ourselves with, that we could ever, in any remote or tiny way, be separated from Him. Can the sunbeam be separate from the Sun? Can an idea be separate from the mind that thinks it?

And so we turn again to the quiet place within, where all this is already known. We ask to "see the face of Christ instead of our mistakes" (2:1). We affirm that we no longer want to be lost in forgetfulness. We state clearly that we want to leave our loneliness and find ourselves, as we have always been, at home. And in the quiet, God speaks to us, and tells us we are His Son.

What is Forgiveness? (Part 3)

W-pII.1.2:1–2

The second paragraph is all about *un*forgiveness. The distinguishing characteristic of an unforgiving thought is that it "makes a judgment that it will not raise to doubt, although it is not true" (2:1).

The distinguishing characteristic of a forgiving mind, then, is that this mind *will* be willing to cast doubt on its own judgments! The unforgiving mind is saying, "My mind is already made up; don't confuse me with facts." The forgiving mind is saying, "Perhaps there is another way to look at this."

In the section discussing the ten characteristics of *advanced* teachers of God (Chapter 4 of the Manual for Teachers), the final characteristic is "open-mindedness." It says:

> As judgment shuts the mind against God's Teacher, so open-mindedness invites Him to come in. As condemnation judges the Son of God as evil, so open-mindedness permits him to be judged by the Voice for God on His behalf (M-4.X.1:3–4).

The willingness to let go of our own judgments and hear the judgment of the Holy Spirit is what makes forgiveness possible. An unforgiving mind "is closed, and will not be released" (2:2). The forgiving mind is open. Over and over the Course asks us simply to be *willing* to see things differently, simply to be willing to question what we think we know, simply to "do this:"

> Be still, and lay aside all thoughts of what you are and what God is; all concepts you have learned about the world; all images you hold about yourself (W-pl.189.7:1).
>
> With judgment set aside, "What then is free to take its place is now the Will of God (1:7).

Lesson 224—August 12

"God is my Father, and He loves His Son."

PRACTICE SUMMARY

See the practice instructions on page 241, or the Practice Card bound into this volume.

COMMENTARY

These lessons are helping us remember who we are: God's Son. Who we are is an Identity that is far beyond anything we can imagine, "so lofty...that Heaven looks to It to give it light" (1:1). In Lesson 221 we were silently waiting for God "speak to us of what we are" (W-pII.221.2:6). In 222, we learned that what we are exists in an environment of God. In 223, we recognized that we were not separate, but existed entirely in union with God. And now, we remember our true Identity: His Son. Our Identity "is illusion's end. It is the truth" (1:6–7).

The truth of what we are is the end of all illusions. Or, the flip side, a mistake about what we are is the source of all illusions. We have forgotten it, but in these times of quiet with God, we ask Him to remind us, to reveal that Identity to us. We are "lofty, sinless, glorious and great, wholly beneficent and free from guilt..." (1:1). Reading these words, notice how our conscious minds instantly question it, instantly recoil from the audacity of saying such things. It only shows how thoroughly we have deceived ourselves, how well we have learned our own lies. Yet something within, on hearing these words, begins to sing. Something within recognizes the melody of Heaven and starts humming along with it. Listen to that humming. Tune in to it. It is your Self, responding to God's Call. Say it! "God *is* my Father, and He *loves* His Son."

✧

WHAT IS FORGIVENESS? (Part 4)

W-pII.1.2:3–4

The unforgiving thought "protects projection" (2:3). Our minds, tormented with their own guilt, have projected the blame for our condition outside ourselves. We have found a scapegoat, as Adam did with Eve: "The woman gave me the fruit to eat. It was her fault." And so we cling to our unforgiveness, we *want* to find blame in the other, because to forgive, to let it go, would be to open the closet door that hides our guilt.

The more we cling to unforgiveness, the more we blind ourselves. The more solid our illusory projections seem to be, until we think it would be impossible to see in any other way. The distortions we impose on reality become "more veiled and more obscure" (2:3). Our self-deceptions become harder and harder to see through, "less easily accessible to doubt" (2:3). All we are being asked to do is to doubt them, to question our projections, to listen to a little reason. Unforgiveness blocks the way to this and tightens our own chains.

We see guilt in others because we *want* to see it there (2:4), and we want to see it there because it keeps us from seeing guilt in our own minds. Yet seeing the guilt in ourselves is the only way we can have it healed. If we deny we are wounded we will not seek the remedy. If we deny our own guilt and project it onto others, we will not bring ourselves into the healing Presence within, which is the only place it can be undone. If our mind is closed, if we are not willing to doubt our version of things, we are shutting the door to our own healing. Only in opening our mind, in loosening our determined grasp on finding others to be wrong, in allowing that "there must be a better way" (T-2.III.3:6), can we find our own release.

Lesson 225—August 13

"God is my Father, and His Son loves Him."

PRACTICE SUMMARY

See the practice instructions on page 241, or the Practice Card bound into this volume.

COMMENTARY

Love is reciprocal. We receive God's Love for us by returning it to Him; there is no other way to receive it, "for giving and receiving are the same" (1:1). This *exact* phrase occurs six times in the Course, and there are many others very much like it. We may think we understand what it means, but the Course assures us that no concept it teaches is more difficult for us to truly learn.

The way to know God's Love blazing in our minds is to return It to Him. If, in our times of quiet yesterday we focused on feeling His Love of us, let us today focus on our awareness of our love for Him. Donna Cary has a beautiful song I was listening to on tape just a day or two ago, which says, "I'll be forever in love with You." I wish I could send you all this song; it expresses so beautifully what I feel this lesson is saying. "I'll dance in the light of Your Love, forever in love with You."

What would it be like to have the Love of God "mine in full awareness, blazing in my mind and keeping it within its kindly light" (1:2)? Is this not what, in our heart of hearts, we all want? Let us cultivate this sense of love in our hearts today. Let simply this be our focus. Nothing complex, nothing even conceptual, just letting our hearts sing with love for God, basking in His Love for us. As the Song of Solomon in the Old Testament put it, "I am my Beloved's, and He is mine." To know God as the Beloved is one of the highest of spiritual expressions.

Have you ever sat in stillness with one you deeply love, simply gazing into his or her eyes, without words? That stillness of love is what this lesson is leading us to, a silent communion of love given and received, acknowledged and returned, flowing in an endless current that energizes and transforms our minds and hearts.

✧

WHAT IS FORGIVENESS? (Part 5)

W-pII.1.3:1–2

In contrast to the stillness today's lesson speaks of, an unforgiving thought is frantically active. It has to be. It must be frantic because it flies in the face of truth, and attempts to make real an illusion. Frenetic activity is often the sign of unrecognized unforgiveness. Things that seem to oppose what we want to be the truth keep popping up, like gophers in the silly kids' game of "bang the gopher," and we have to keep bashing them down to maintain our version of reality.

Stilling our mind and becoming quiet, in and of itself, is often enough to begin dissolving our unforgiveness. Unforgiveness cannot exist in quiet. You cannot be peaceful and unforgiving at the same time. "Peace to my mind. Let all my thoughts be still" (Lesson 221). One thing that can foster this peace and stillness is focusing on the very exchange of love that is the center of today's lesson. The power of our affection for God, and His for us, can quell the stormy thoughts and bring, even if only briefly, a moment of quiet peace, in which unforgiveness simply dissipates.

Lesson 226—August 14

"My home awaits me. I will hasten there."

PRACTICE SUMMARY

See the practice instructions on page 241, or the Practice Card bound into this volume.

COMMENTARY

Home. What an evocative word that is! "I'm going home." Sometimes just thinking about going home, even in an abstract sense, can cause deep emotions to rise up in us—happy ones, I hope, although for some an unhappy home life has tainted the word. Even then, when our "real" home was unhappy, most of us are still filled with a deep longing for home *as it ought to be*. Our real home is in God. Our longings for home find their roots in our longing for this spiritual home in God.

How can I "go home"? There are songs that convey the common idea that we go home to Heaven when we die: spirituals such as "Goin' Home." But the Course here is extremely clear. It speaks of departing this world, and says, "It is not death which makes this possible, but it is a change of mind about the purpose of the world" (1:2).

As long as we think that the purpose of the world lies within itself, that somehow happiness, freedom and contentment are to be found here, in the world, we will never leave it. Not even when we "die." The chains that bind us to the world are mental, not physical. Our valuing of the world is what holds us to it. If I value the world "as I see it now" (1:3, also 1:4), it will hold on to me even when my body crumbles. But if I no longer see anything in this world "as I behold it" that I want to keep or search for, I am free.

There is a world of meaning—literally!—in those phrases "as I see it now" and "as I behold it." In the ego's perception this world is a place of punishment and imprisonment, and simultaneously a place where I come to seek for what seems to be "lacking" in myself. As long as I somehow value that punishment and imprisonment, perhaps not for myself but almost always for others upon whom I have projected my guilt, I will be bound to the world, and I will not go home. As long as I think there is a lack in myself and continue to search for it outside myself, valuing the world for what I think it can give to me, I will always be bound to the world, and I will not go home.

"My home *awaits* me." Our home is not under construction. It is ready and waiting, the red carpet rolled out, everything is ready, and God's "Arms are open and I hear His Voice" (2:2). Home is available right now, if I only choose it. Let me be willing to look at what keeps me from choosing it, because those are the hindrances that keep me from finding it. Do I still wistfully long for my prince to come (or my princess)? Do I still have things I want to do before I am ready to go?

Do I still find secret pleasure when the "wicked" (in my sight) suffer? If this world could vanish an hour from now, what would I regret? Would I be ready to leave? If a shimmering curtain were to appear in the doorway and a Voice proclaim, "Pass this portal and you will be in Heaven," would I go through? Why not?

This is not a fantasy. The Voice *is* calling us, and Heaven is here and now. We can pass the portal any time we choose to. If we are not experiencing Heaven, we *must* be choosing not to do so, and finding out what holds us back is the work we are assigned to in this classroom. This is what the world is for—to teach us to let it go.

"What need have I to linger in a place of vain desires and of shattered dreams, when Heaven can so easily be mine?" (2:3)

✧

WHAT IS FORGIVENESS? (Part 6)

W-pII.1.3:3–4

We do not realize how much our unforgiving thoughts distort the truth (3:3). Unforgiving thoughts twist our perception of things which are not in accord with how unforgiveness wants to see things. They overlook any evidence for love, and find evidence of guilt. In "The Obstacles to Peace" and in the subsection on "The Attraction of Guilt," (T-19.IV(A).i), our unforgiving thoughts are compared to scavenging messengers "harshly ordered to seek out guilt, and cherish every scrap of evil and of sin that they can find, losing none of them on pain of death, and laying them respectfully before their lord and master." That is, we find what we are looking for, and the ego is looking for guilt.

But distortion is not only the *method* used by the ego; distortion is also the ego's *purpose*. Thus, the purpose of unforgiveness is to distort reality. Unforgiveness furiously aims "to smash reality, without concern for anything that would appear to pose a contradiction to its point of view" (3:4). Reality is the hated enemy, the intolerable presence, because our reality is still the Son of God, never in the slightest separated from Him. Reality exposes the ego as a lie, and cannot be tolerated. So the way our minds work, when dominated by unforgiving thoughts, is designed from the beginning to distort reality beyond all recognition.

In contrast to this, the Course asks us to dream of our brother's kindnesses instead of his mistakes, and to not brush aside his many gifts just because he isn't perfect (T-27.VII.15). It asks us to look for love instead of looking for guilt, and rather than finding fault, to try finding love instead. To begin with, we can simply start to question the way we see things, in awareness that our thought processes and our methods of making judgment have been severely impaired and simply are not reliable. It isn't that we *should not* judge, it's that we *cannot* judge (M-10.2:1). We are operating at diminished capacity; we need a healthy mind to judge on our behalf. And that mind is the Holy Spirit.

Lesson 227—August 15

"This is my holy instant of release."

PRACTICE SUMMARY

See the practice instructions on page 241, or the Practice Card bound into this volume.

COMMENTARY

Today's lesson is another reminder that these practice times are meant to be holy instants for us. Not every one will be a dramatic experience of wordless bliss, of course. Remember that simply being willing to turn your mind to God can be considered a holy instant, whether or not you consciously experience anything special. The seminal holy instant, from which the Course sprang, was simply a time when Bill Thetford said, "There must be another way," and Helen replied, "I'll help you find it." The mental shift into alignment with God's purpose is what really counts. If we faithfully practice, the direct experience of truth spoken of in the Workbook will come, not by our efforts, but by God's grace, when we are ready to receive it.

Consider the effect it has on our mind to focus on today's idea, "This is my holy instant of release," and then to sit in quiet stillness, open and receptive to whatever is given to us. We should enter each such time expectantly, waiting to hear what God's Voice will speak.

I am already free; now, today. My thought of separation had no effect on my reality, so the imprisonment I have imagined never happened. "Nothing I thought apart from You exists" (1:3). How wonderful to know that the thoughts I believed were apart from God don't exist! How healing it is to give them up, lay them down at the feet of truth, and to have them "removed forever from my mind" (1:5). This is the healing process of the Course: to take each thought that seems to express a will separate from God's, and bring it into this Presence to be removed from my mind, with God's own assurance that it has affected nothing. I am still His Son.

This is how my mind is restored to me. This is how my awareness of my Identity is returned to my awareness.

✧

WHAT IS FORGIVENESS? (Part 7)

W-pII.1.4:1–3

"Forgiveness, on the other hand, is still, and quietly does nothing" (4:1). If we can understand these first few sentences we will have a clear grasp of what forgiveness really is. The words, "on the other hand," refer to the preceding two paragraphs which described an unforgiving thought, especially to 3:1: "An unforgiving thought does many things." Forgiveness, on the other hand, does nothing. Unforgiveness is highly active, anxiously trying to make things fit into its picture of reality; forgiveness does nothing. It does not rush to interpret or to attempt to understand. It lets things be as they are.

Notice once again the heavy emphasis on stillness and quiet. The practice of the holy instant, as the practice of forgiveness, is practice at being still, being quiet, doing nothing. Our usual state of mind is the product of the ego's training—habitually active, constantly working. We need *practice* at being still and doing nothing. It takes a lot of practice to break the habit of frantic activity and form a new habit of being still and quiet.

One trick of the ego I notice, frequently, is that it will try to make me guilty about being still and quiet! When I try to take ten minutes to sit in stillness, my ego floods my mind with thoughts of what I ought to be doing instead.

The mental state in which forgiveness occurs is one in which we simply allow all of reality to be as it is, without judging anything. "It offends no aspect of reality, nor seeks to twist it to appearances it likes" (4:2). The appearance my ego usually likes is some form of, "I am right and they are wrong." Or, "I am good and they are bad." Or simply, "I am better than he/she is." Even more simply, "I am not like him/her." All of these thoughts share one theme: I am different from others, and therefore separate from them. Any such thought is twisting reality, because the reality is that we are the same, we are equal, we are one. Forgiveness stills such thoughts and abandons all efforts to mash reality into a "more desirable" shape.

"It merely looks, and waits, and judges not" (4:3). It does not deny what it sees, but it puts no interpretation on it. It waits to be told the meaning by the Holy Spirit. "My mate is having an affair." Forgiveness looks, and waits, and judges not. "My child is sick." Forgiveness looks, and waits, and judges not. "My boss just fired me." It looks, and waits, and judges not. We are so quick to think we know what things mean! And we are wrong. We do not know. We leap to an understanding based on separation, and such understandings understand nothing.

The most salutary thing we can do when any such upsetting event occurs in our lives is—nothing. Simply to let our minds become still and quiet, and to open ourselves to the healing light of the Holy Spirit. To seek a holy instant. Let this become the ingrained habit of our lives, and we will see the world in an entirely different way, and Love will flow through us to bring healing instead of hurt to every situation.

Lesson 228—August 16

"God has condemned me not. No more do I."

PRACTICE SUMMARY

See the practice instructions on page 241, or the Practice Card bound into this volume.

COMMENTARY

It takes great courage to let go of our self-condemnation. We are so afraid that if we stop condemning ourselves we will go berserk, the evil in us will be unchecked and will break out in some terrible disaster. But what if there is no evil in us? What if God is right? Is it so very likely that He is wrong and we are right? What God knows, the lesson says, makes sin in us impossible; "Shall I deny His knowledge?" (1:2)

The lesson is asking us, quite simply, to "take His Word for what I am" (1:4). Who knows what something or someone is better than its Creator? And what does God know about me? "My Father knows my holiness" (1:1). Every time I read such statements I watch my mind struggle to oppose the idea, cringing in a pseudo-humility that cries out, "Oh, no, I can't accept that about myself." If I dare to ask myself, "Why not?", my mind immediately comes up with a whole list of reasons: My flaws, my lack of total dedication to the truth, my addiction to this or that pleasure of the world. Yet every one of those things, brought into the light of the Holy Spirit, can be seen as nothing more than a misdirected prayer, a cry for help, a veiled longing for God and for Home.

"I was mistaken in myself" (2:1). That is all that has happened. I forgot my Source, and what I must be, coming from that Source. My Source is God, and not my dark illusions. My mistake about myself is not a sin to be judged but a mistake to be corrected; it needs, not *condemnation*, but the healing of love. "My mistakes about myself are dreams" (2:4), that is all, and I can let these dreams go. I am not the dream; I am the dreamer, still holy, still a part of God.

Today, as I still my mind in God's Presence, I open myself to receive His Word concerning what I am. I brush aside the dreams, I recognize them for what they are, and let them go. I open my heart to Love.

✧

WHAT IS FORGIVENESS? (Part 8)

W-pII.1.4:4–5

In the last two sentences of this paragraph, notice that a contrast is made between judging and welcoming the truth exactly as it is. The opposite of judgment is the truth. Judgment, then, must always be a distortion of the truth. This section has already pointed out that unforgiveness has distortion as its purpose. If I do not want to forgive, I must distort the truth; I must judge. Judgment here clearly carries the meaning of condemnation, of seeing sin, of making something wrong. Forgiveness does not do that; forgiveness makes right instead of wrong, because "right" is the truth about all of us.

None of us is guilty. That is the truth. God does not condemn us. If I do so, I am distorting the truth. Judgment is always a distortion of the truth of our innocence before God. When I judge another, I do so because I am trying to justify my unwillingness to forgive. I have gotten very good at it. I always seem to find some reason that justifies my unforgiveness. But what I do not realize is that every such judgment twists the truth, hides it, obscures it. It "makes real" something that is not real.

Furthermore, in obscuring the truth about my brother or sister, I am hiding the truth about myself. I am substantiating the basis of my own self-condemnation. That is why the last sentence of the paragraph switches from my unforgiveness of another to the forgiveness of myself: "He who would forgive himself" (4:5). If I want to learn to forgive myself, I must abandon my judging of others. If their sin is real, so is mine. Instead I must learn to "welcome truth exactly as it is" (4:5). Only if I welcome the truth about my brother or sister can I see it for myself. We stand or fall together. "In him you will find yourself or lose yourself" (T-8.III.4:5).

To a mind habituated to seeing itself as a separate ego, abandoning all judgment is frightening. It feels like the rug is being swept out from under our feet; we don't know where to stand. How can we live in the world without it? We literally do not know how. Judgment is how we have ordered our lives; without it, we fear chaos. The Course assures us this will not happen:

> You are afraid of this because you believe that without the ego, all would be chaos. Yet I assure you that without the ego, all would be love (T-15.V.1:6–7).

When we let go of judgment, when we are willing to welcome the truth exactly as it is, love rushes in to fill the vacuum left by the absence of judgment. It has been there all along, but we have blocked it. We don't know how this happens, but it happens because love is the reality, love is the truth we are welcoming. Love will show us exactly what to do when our judgment is gone.

Lesson 229—August 17

"Love, Which created me, is what I am."

PRACTICE SUMMARY

See the practice instructions on page 241, or the Practice Card bound into this volume.

COMMENTARY

Many of these lessons in Part II of the Workbook may seem to be expressing a state of mind that is beyond where I am as I read them. In reality, they express my *true* state of mind, the state of my right mind. It is this state of mind we can reach in the holy instant. Right-mindedness is not some future state I am trying to reach. There is an aspect of my mind that already knows these things and already believes them. It is this part of my mind that is leading me home. "Now need I seek no more" (1:2), is the truth right now. It is the part of my mind that doubts this, that denies it, which is unreal.

Love *is* what I am; It is my Identity. Let me look honestly at what I believe I am instead, because it is in discovering what Love is not that I will come to know Love.

> Love is not learned. Its meaning lies within itself. And learning ends when you have recognized all it is *not*. That is the interference; that is what needs to be undone (T-18.IX.12:1–4).

Love waited for me, "so still" (1:4). Love is still because that is what forgiveness does; it is "still, and quietly does nothing" (W-pII.1.4:1). My own Love waits to forgive me all I think I have done, all that I have believed I was other than Love. I actually "sought to lose" my Identity (1:5), but God has kept that Identity safe for me, within me, as me. "In the midst of all the thoughts of sin my foolish mind made up" (2:1), my Father kept my Identity untouched and sinless. Let me turn to that Identity now. Let me give thanks, and express my gratitude to God that It has never been lost, even when I was sure it was. I cannot be anything other than what God created me to be. "Love, Which created me, is what I am."

In my heart, in my mind, in the still and tranquil core of my being, lies everything I have ever been seeking for. Let me now remember.

✧

WHAT IS FORGIVENESS? (Part 9)

W-pII.1.5:1–2

Faced with this stark contrast between forgiveness and unforgiveness, what then are we to do? "Do nothing, then" (5:1). We are not called upon to *do*, we are called upon to cease doing, because there is nothing that need be done. To the ego, to do means to judge, and it is judgment we must relinquish. If we feel there is something that must be done, it is a judgment that affirms lack within ourselves, and there is no lack. That is what we must remember. To believe that something must be done is a denial of our wholeness, which has never been diminished.

"Let forgiveness show you what to do, through Him" (5:1). To forgive ourselves means to take our hands off the steering wheel of our lives, to stop trying to "make things right," which only affirms that something is wrong. To forgive others means we stop thinking it is our job to correct them. The Holy Spirit is the One Who knows what we should do, if anything, and His guidance will often surprise us. Yes, there may still be something for us to "do," but we will not be the ones to determine what that is. Our doing is so often deadly, quenching the spirit instead of affirming it, imparting guilt instead of lifting it.

The Holy Spirit is my Guide and Savior and Protector. In each situation where I am tempted to do something, let me stop, remember that my judgment is untrustworthy, let go, and give it into His hands. He is "strong in hope, and certain of your ultimate success" (5:1). How often in a time when I am judging, whether myself or another, am I certain of my ultimate success? Let me then give the situation into the care of One Who is certain. He will show me what to do.

"He has forgiven you already, for such is His function" (5:2). Each time I bring Him some terrible thing I think I have done, let me remember: "He has forgiven you already." I do not need to fear entering His Presence. His function, His reason for being, is to forgive me. Not to judge me, nor to punish me, nor to make me feel bad, but to forgive. Why would I stay away an instant more? Let me fall gratefully now into His loving arms, and hear Him say, "What you think is not the truth" (W-pI.134.7:5). He will still the troubled waters of my mind, and bring me peace.

Lesson 230—August 18

"Now will I seek and find the peace of God."

PRACTICE SUMMARY

See the practice instructions on page 241, or the Practice Card bound into this volume.

COMMENTARY

"In peace I was created. And in peace do I remain" (1:1–2). Jesus, in his Course, never tires of reminding us that we remain as God created us. He repeats it often because we so obviously do not believe it. We may believe that God created us in peace. How, indeed, could we believe otherwise? Would a God of Love have created us in pain and agony, in turmoil and confusion, in conflict and strife? So the first sentence isn't really a problem to us; we can accept that God created us in peace.

The problem arises, in our minds, with the second sentence: "In peace do I remain." Quite simply we don't believe it. In fact we are firmly convinced that we know otherwise. Perhaps this morning I am distraught by something that happened yesterday, or worried about what may happen today, or next week. I can look back on a lifetime that, in my experience, has had very little, if any, peace. Some days it seems as though life is conspiring against me to rob me of peace. It seems as though, in most of my busy days, that I rarely have a moment of peace. So how can I accept this statement: "In peace do I remain"?

It seems incredible to us, unbelievable, when the Course insists that since God created me in peace, I must still be in peace. God's creation of me took place, the lesson says, "apart from time, and still remains beyond all change" (2:2). It tells me, "It is not given me to change my Self" (1:3). My experience of life in this world tells me otherwise.

The question is, which one will I believe? God's Voice, or my experience? One of them must be false. And it is earth-shattering, mind-blowing, even to consider that my entire experience of this world has been a lie, a mistake, and an hallucination. Yet what is the alternative? Shall I believe, instead, that God is a liar? Shall I believe that His creation was flawed, and capable of corruption? Shall I believe that what He willed for me was overcome by my own independent will? Yet this is what I *must* be believing if I insist that I am not at peace, in this very moment.

If God is not a liar and His creation is not flawed, then what must be true is that my own mind has deceived me and has manufactured an entire lifetime of false experience. If I am willing to listen, this is not as far-fetched as it sounds at first. In fact, if I simply watch my mind, I can catch it in the act of doing that very thing. I can watch and observe how I see what I expect to see. I can notice how different people perceive the same events quite differently. I can remember times when I was quite sure I understood things clearly, only to have the whole situation turned on its head by some new fact that I had been unaware of. I need only watch the sun rise, move across the sky, and set, to realize that my perception is faulty. It is not the sun that moves; it is me, as the earth turns. When night comes and the sun is "gone" in my perception, the sun shines on; it is my world that has turned its face from the light.

What if my apparent lack of peace does not mean what I think it means? What if the peace of God has never left me, but shines on, while I have turned my face from it? In the holy instant I can find that this is the truth. Simply by turning my mind away from its mad belief in unrest, I can discover the peace of God shining in me now.

✧

WHAT IS FORGIVENESS? (Part 10)

W-pII.1.5:3

There is another part to forgiveness. Since the Holy Spirit has already forgiven me, carrying out His only function, I now "must...share His function, and forgive whom He has saved" (5:3).

Consider what we have said about the way the Holy Spirit interacts with us, how we can come to Him with our darkest thoughts and find them absorbed and dissipated in His Love. The utter lack of judgment. His gentleness with us, His acceptance of us, His knowledge of our sinlessness, His honoring us as the Son of God, unchanged by our foolish thoughts of sin. Now, we are to share His function in relation to the world. Now, we are to be His representatives, His manifestation in the lives of those around us. To them, we offer this same gentle kindness, this same conviction of the inner holiness of each one we deal with, this same quiet disregard for thoughts of self-condemnation in everyone we see, or speak to, or think about. "It is the privilege of the forgiven to forgive" (T-1.I.27:2).

What we reflect to the world is what we believe in for ourselves. When we judge, condemn, and lay guilt on those around us, we are reflecting the way we believe God is towards us. When we experience the sweet forgiveness in the loving Presence of the Holy Spirit, we reflect that same thing to the world. Let me, then, enter into His Presence, allowing Him to look upon me, to find Him quietly doing nothing, but simply looking, and waiting, and judging me not. Let me hear Him tell me of His confidence in my ultimate success. And then, let me turn and share this blessing with the world, giving what I have received. Only as I share it will I know, for sure, that it is mine.

Lesson 231—August 19

"Father, I will but to remember You."

PRACTICE SUMMARY

See the practice instructions on page 241, or the Practice Card bound into this volume.

COMMENTARY

This lesson is talking about our will. When the Course uses the word "will" in this way, it is talking about a fundamental, unchanging part of us, the permanently fixed goal of our Self. It isn't talking about our wishes and our whims, but our *will.* Jesus speaks to us directly in the second paragraph and says, "This is your will, my brother" (2:1). It is a will we share with Him, and also with God our Father.

What is our will? To remember God; to know His Love. And that is all. Not many of us, as we began reading this Course, would have answered the question, "What do you want out of life?" with the words, "To remember God and know His Love." A lot of us probably don't feel those words fit us even now. The lesson recognizes that: "Perhaps I think I seek for something else" (1:2).

What is the "something else" you are seeking? It might be wealth, or fame. It might be some form of worldly security. It might be romance. It might be hot sex. Or a good time. Or a quiet family life, in the tradition of the American dream. We've called it by many names. We *think* these things are what we are seeking for. Yet no matter what we may think, these things are not what we truly will for ourselves. They are all forms, forms that we believe will give us something. It isn't the form we are really seeking, it is the content, it is what we believe these things offer to us.

And what is that? Inner peace. Satisfaction. A sense of completion and wholeness. A sense of worth. An inner knowing that we are essentially good; lovable and loving. A feeling of belonging, of being valuable. Ultimately these things come only from remembering God and knowing His Love. They are something inside of us, not something outside of us. Only when we remember the truth about ourselves, only when we remember our connectedness to Love Itself, will we find what we are seeking. And we will find that we *are* what we have been seeking, and always have been.

"To remember Him is Heaven. This we seek. And only this is what it will be given us to find" (2:3–5). Remembering God is the *only* thing I am really looking for. Let me then, today, spend time, morning and evening, reminding myself of this fact: "Father, I will but to remember You." Let me stop briefly every hour to recall it to my mind. And each time I find myself thinking that I want "something else," let me gently correct myself: Remembering God is all I want.

WHAT IS SALVATION? (Part 1)

W-pII.2.1:1–3

To begin with, it will help to realize that the Course does not attach the same meaning to this word as does traditional religion. "Salvation" carries, for most of us, the connotation of some impending disaster from which we are "saved." From hell, for instance. From some terrible punishment. From the consequences of our wrongdoing. The picture often used in traditional Christianity is of a drowning man being thrown a life-preserver; "Throw out the life-line," the old Gospel hymn says. The Course directly refutes this idea:

> Your Self does not need salvation, but your mind needs to learn what salvation is. You are not saved *from* anything, but you are saved *for* glory (T-11.IV.1:3–4).

Salvation in the Course *is* a "life preserver," but not in the same sense. It does not save us from death; it preserves us in life. It is a guarantee that death will never touch us: "Salvation is a promise, made by God, that you would find your way to Him at last" (1:1). We are not in danger of destruction, never have been, never will be. The Course's version of salvation does not reverse a disaster; it prevents the disaster from ever happening.

Before time began, God made His promise, a promise that "cannot but be kept" (1:2). That promise guaranteed that time, and all the mess we appear to have made in time, would have an end, and ultimately be without any effect at all. It guaranteed that life cannot end, that holiness cannot become sin, that Heaven cannot become hell. It guaranteed that there could never be more than an *illusion* of separation and a *dream* of suffering and death. It promised that the ego could never become real, that no will independent of God could ever arise. It defined the end from the beginning, and made it perfectly secure. We *will* find our way to God at last, because God has promised that it will be so.

Lesson 232—August 20

"Be in my mind, my Father, through the day."

PRACTICE SUMMARY

See the practice instructions on page 241, or the Practice Card bound into this volume.

COMMENTARY

When I wake, God is in my mind; His Presence is with me and in my awareness. His Love, and the joy and peace of knowing God are with me; they take precedence over any other thoughts. Physical discomfort and concerns about scheduling the day arise, but none of these displace the peace of God; it is my bedrock, my foundation, and my first concern. It is a constant awareness, like the background hum of an air conditioner, always there, often unnoticed, but ready to be noticed any time I turn my attention to it.

"Let every minute be a time in which I dwell with You" (1:2). Here *is* my desire! To dwell with God every minute of the day. It reminds me of John 15 in the New Testament: "Abide in me, and I in you." Or the Old Testament expression of the same idea: "The eternal God is a dwelling place, and underneath are the everlasting arms" (Deut. 33:27, NASB). Let me remember today, each hour, to say, "Thank You for being with me today. Thank You for *always* being with me."

> As evening comes, let all my thoughts be still of You and of Your Love. And let me sleep sure of my safety, certain of Your care, and happily aware I am Your Son (1:4–5).

Sure of my safety. Thus, free of all fear. For the most part, our lives are run by fears of various kinds; the ego is driven by fear. Peace is the absence of fear. And since fear is only the absence of love, peace and love are interdependent. When I am loving, I am peaceful. When I am peaceful, I am loving. Where I am sure of my safety, knowing the Presence of God in every moment, I am at peace and love flows through me.

"This is as every day should be" (2:1). This is the goal for life in this world: to live every day with God in my mind. To wake in His Presence, to walk in His shining Love, and to sleep in His care and protection. To so live that His Presence becomes my foreground and all else, the hum and bustle of the world, becomes background.

What is a day like for someone who has learned what the Course is teaching? Simply this: To constantly practice the end of fear. To walk with faith in Him Who is my Father, trusting all things to Him, letting Him reveal all things to me, and in everything to be undismayed because I am His Son (paragraph 2).

WHAT IS SALVATION? (Part 2)

W-pII.2.1:4

How does salvation work? The essence of it is stated here in a single sentence: "God's Word is given every mind which thinks that it has separate thoughts, and will replace these thoughts of conflict with the Thought of peace" (1:4). The instant our mind had a thought of conflict, God's Word was implanted in our mind as well. Before disaster could even begin, the Answer was given.

You and I, who think of ourselves as separate entities, are such minds, which think that they have separate thoughts. But God's Word has been implanted in us; the Truth lies beneath all our self-deception. From within, the Thought of God is quietly working, waiting, moving to replace all our thoughts of conflict. The thoughts of conflict are myriad, taking thousands of forms, each in conflict with the universe and most in conflict with each other. The Thought of peace is one. It is the one remedy to every thought of conflict, whether it be hatred, anger, despair, frustration, bitterness, or death. The Thought of God heals them all.

The remedy lies within me, now. This is salvation: To turn within to the Thought of peace, and find it there within myself.

Lesson 233—August 21

"I give my life to God to guide today."

PRACTICE SUMMARY

See the practice instructions on page 241, or the Practice Card bound into this volume.

COMMENTARY

One thing I find very interesting about the Course is that it is not terribly picky about its theology. There are places in the Course that make it quite clear that God does not even hear the words of our prayers, and that, knowing only the Truth, He does not know of our errors. "Technically," then, prayers "ought" to be addressed to the Holy Spirit or to Jesus, who are specifically spoken of as intermediaries between truth and illusion, or a bridge between us and God. Yet here in the second half of the Workbook we have 140 lessons, each of which contains a prayer addressed to "Father."

In today's lesson, the Father is asked to guide us. Yet elsewhere, being Guide is defined as the function of the Holy Spirit. So I get the feeling that Jesus (the author) isn't particularly concerned with strict theological correctness. I think he is a good example for all of us to follow. Would he be teaching us to pray to the Father if it were some sort of substandard spiritual practice?

If we gleaned nothing more from the Course than the practice of daily giving our lives over to God's guidance, we would be quickly taken home. We can ask Him to replace our thoughts with His own, and to direct all our acts during the day, all we do and think and say. To act or think on our own is, literally, a waste of time. His wisdom is infinite, His Love and tenderness are beyond comprehension. Could we ask for a more reliable Guide?

The first step in following God's guidance is a stepping *back*, releasing our tight hold on our lives and deliberately placing them under His control. The guidance will come. Sometimes, perhaps rarely, we will hear an inner Voice. In my personal experience this is very rare. Other times, things will happen around us that make our way plain. Or an inner conviction will build for no apparent reason. We will "just happen to notice" something someone says, or a song on the radio, or a line in a book. If we are *listening* for it, we will hear it.

Another key is giving our day to Him "with no reserve at all" (2:2), that is, holding nothing back. Sometimes we are so fixated on what we think we want or need that we are not willing to hear any guidance to the contrary. And if we aren't willing to hear it, we won't. We're like a broken shopping cart that always wants to steer left or right; we just don't respond well to guidance. We have to be willing to let go of all our preferences, all our investment in the outcome, and become completely malleable, completely open to whatever direction He wants to give to us. An old Christian hymn says:

Have Thine own way, Lord,
Have Thine own way.
Thou are the potter,
I am the clay.
Mold me and make me,
After Thy will,
While I am waiting,
Yielded and still.

That is what stepping back means. That is how we give our lives to God to guide. He guides. We follow, without questioning (1:7).

WHAT IS SALVATION? (Part 3)

W-pII.2.2:1–3

The Thought of peace that is our salvation "was given to God's Son the instant that his mind had thought of war" (2:1). No time intervened at all between the thought of war and the Thought of peace. Salvation was given instantly when the need arose. In a beautiful image, the Text says that "not one note in Heaven's song was missed" (T-26.V.5:4). The peace of Heaven was completely undisturbed. And having been answered, the problem was resolved for all of time and all eternity, in that timeless instant.

Our discovery of salvation, however, takes time. Or at least seems to. A poor analogy: Imagine that you are suddenly burdened with a $10,000 tax bill for a hitherto unexpected reason, but at that very instant, someone deposits $1 million in your checking account. You could spend a lot of time trying to raise the needed money if you didn't know about the deposit, but actually all you need to do is nothing, because the problem is already solved. Your only need, then, is to stop trying to solve the problem, and learn that it has already been answered.

Before the thought of separation (or war) arose, there was no need for a "Thought of peace." Peace simply *was*, without an opposite. So in a certain sense we could say that the problem created its own answer. Before the problem, there was no answer because there was no need of one. But when the problem arose, the answer was already there. "When the mind is split there is a need of healing" (2:3). It is the thought of separation that makes the thought of healing needful, but when the healing is accepted, or when the thought of separation is abandoned, healing is no longer needed. Healing is a temporary (or temporal, related to time) measure. There is no need of it in Heaven.

As the Course says of forgiveness, because there is an illusion of need, there is need for an illusion of answer. But that "answer" is really simple acceptance of what has always been true, and always will be. Peace simply is, and salvation lies in our acceptance of that fact. Salvation, as the Course sees it, is not an active divine response to a real need. It is, instead, an apparent response to a need that, in truth, does not exist.

This is why the Course calls our spiritual path "a journey without distance" (T-8.VI.9:7) and, indeed, "a journey that was not begun" (W-pII.225.2:5). While we are in it, the journey seems very real, and often very long. When it is over, we will know that we never left Heaven, never travelled anywhere, and have always been exactly where we are: at home in God. The journey itself is imaginary. It consists in learning, bit by bit, that the distance we perceive between ourselves and God is simply not there.

Lesson 234—August 22

"Father, today I am Your Son again."

PRACTICE SUMMARY

See the practice instructions on page 241, or the Practice Card bound into this volume.

COMMENTARY

This lesson is about anticipating heaven.

"Today we will anticipate the time when dreams of sin and guilt are gone, and we have reached the holy peace we never left" (1:1).

That is what we do each day as we draw near to God in these times of quiet and stillness. We are giving ourselves a foretaste of Heaven. Just in this moment, just for now, imagine that all your dreams of sin and guilt are gone. Imagine that all fear has ended—all fear! Imagine that every thought of conflict is past. Imagine that there is nothing and can be nothing ever again that will disturb your perfect rest.

What you are imagining is real—the true state of things.

"Nothing has ever happened to disturb the peace of God the Father and the Son" (1:4).

The dreams of sin and guilt, the dream of fear, the dream of conflict, the dream of any disturbance at all is just that. Nothing more than a dream. Let it go, let it float away, meaningless and without significance. Just a bubble in the stream.

> Merely a tiny instant has elapsed between eternity and timelessness. So brief the interval there was no lapse in continuity, nor break in thoughts which are forever unified as one. Nothing has ever happened to disturb the peace of God the Father and the Son. This we accept as wholly true today (1:2–5).

In these moments of remembrance, these holy instants we set aside each day, we are anticipating the time when our bad dreams are wholly absent. No, I am not there yet, nor are you, not in our experience—although in reality, as the lesson states so clearly, we never left. There has never been a "lapse in continuity," and not one note in Heaven's song was missed. We, however, are still living most of the time in the dream. But we can experience moments of anticipation, direct experiences of the truth. It is that we seek right now. A moment of anticipation. A sense in the core of our beings, something we identify with the word "peace," something that words cannot capture.

These are practice times in which we deliberately stretch ourselves above the level of our normal, mundane experience. We choose to "accept as wholly true" the fact that the peace of God, Father and Son, has *never* been disturbed. Just for the moment, just for now, we allow ourselves to experience believing that. We don't worry that in fifteen minutes we may not believe it. We don't worry about what will happen to our lives if we believe it. We don't consider all the evidence to the contrary our senses have brought us in the past. We just let all that go, and breathe deeply of the rarified atmosphere of Heaven. This is my Home. This is what I really am. This is what is really true. This is all that I want.

If thoughts of sin, or of guilt, or of fear, do arise in our minds, we gently dismiss them. "This is not what I want to experience right now. Right now, I want the peace of God. Right now, I have the peace of God."

Jesus, our Elder Brother, joins us and leads us in prayer, praying with us:

> We thank you, Father, that we cannot lose the memory of You and of Your Love. We recognize our safety, and give thanks for all the gifts You have bestowed on us, for all the loving help we have received, for Your eternal patience, and the Word which You have given us that we are saved (2:1–2).

✧

WHAT IS SALVATION? (Part 4)

W-pII.2.2:4–5

To our mind, the separation is real. "The separation is a system of thought real enough in time, though not in eternity" (T-3.VII.3:2). "The mind can make the belief in separation very real…" (T-3.VII.5:1). The mind experiences itself as split, separated from God, and with one fragment of mind separated from other fragments. This is our experience in time, and it is "real enough" in time, although it is not real in eternity. In truth, the mind is not actually split; it is simply failing to recognize its oneness (2:4). But within that one mind, the experience of separation *seems* real.

Think of nearly any dream you have had in which you are interacting with other people. You are yourself in the dream, and there are other characters. Perhaps someone is making love to you. Perhaps you are arguing with someone, or being chased by a monster. Within the dream, every character is distinct and separate. The other people in the dream may say or do things that surprise you, or that you do not understand. And yet, in fact, every one of those "other characters" exists only in your one mind! Your mind is making them up. In the dream there is separation between the characters. In reality, there is only one mind, and different aspects of that mind are interacting with one another as if they were separate entities.

This, according to the Course, is exactly the case with this entire world. It is one mind, experiencing different aspects of itself as if they were separate beings. Within that dream the separation between the different characters seems to be clear and distinct, unbridgable. And yet the mind is still one. The one mind does not know itself; it believes that "its own Identity was lost" (2:5). But the Identity was not lost in fact, only in a dream.

And so, within each fragment of the mind that is failing to recognize its oneness, God implanted the Thought of peace, "the Thought that has the power to heal the split" (2:4). This "part of every fragment" (2:4) remembers the Identity of mind. It is a part that is shared by every fragment. Like a golden thread running through a piece of fabric, it binds us all together, and draws the seemingly separated fragments constantly toward their true oneness. This Thought within us knows that "Nothing has ever happened to disturb the peace of God the Father and the Son" (W-pII.234.1:4).

This Thought, implanted within us by God, is what we seek when we become still within the holy instant. By quieting all the separated thoughts, we listen for this Voice within us, speaking of our oneness, our wholeness, our eternal peace. This Thought has power to heal the split, to dissipate the seeming solidity of our illusions of separation, and to restore to the Sonship the awareness of its unity. "Salvation…restores to your awareness the wholeness of the fragments you perceive as broken off and separate" (M-19.4:2).

Lesson 235—August 23

"God in His mercy wills that I be saved."

PRACTICE SUMMARY

See the practice instructions on page 241, or the Practice Card bound into this volume.

COMMENTARY

If we look at our own thoughts honestly we will be able to see many ways in which we believe the direct opposite of today's lesson. We think, "God in His anger wills that I be punished." Somewhere in each of us is a pathetic voice telling us that we must deserve whatever we get in the way of pain, or that what joy we have may be taken from us because we are undeserving of it.

To those who begin to list their complaints about the world and how it mistreats them, the Course has very abrupt advice: "Give up these foolish thoughts!" (M-15.3:1) It is in my power to reverse these things. All I need to do is to assure myself, "God wills that I be saved from this" (1:1). God does not will my pain, my sadness, or my loneliness. By changing the way I think of all this, I can change the world.

We think our hurt and sadness is caused by the events of the world; the Course is teaching us that it is the other way around. Our belief in God's anger is what brings us suffering; our belief in His mercy and love can transform our lives. What needs changing is not out there in the world, but here, in my own mind. Let me today remember, Father, that I am "safe forever in [Your] arms" (1:3). Let the thought that You will my happiness fill my mind today. If You are Love, if you love me, what else could You want for me?

✧

WHAT IS SALVATION? (Part 5)

W-pII.2.3:1–3

> Salvation is undoing in the sense that it does nothing, failing to support the world of dreams and malice. Thus it lets illusions go (3:1–2).

To participate in salvation is not the addition of a new activity, but the letting go of our ancient drama of dreams and malice. To be saved is to *stop* supporting our illusions, to cease adding fuel to the fire of anger, attack, and guilt that has ravaged our minds for eons. Salvation is not a doing but an undoing. It is to end our resistance to the flow of love, both the flow from God to us, and the flow from us to God and to our brothers. Salvation means we stop inventing excuses not to love. It means we stop inventing reasons why we are not worthy of it.

"The ego has no power to distract you unless you give it the power to do so" (T-8.I.2:1). The only power the ego has is what we give to it; it uses our own power against us. All ego illusions are funded by our investment in them. When we withdraw that power, and stop our support of the ego's illusions, they "quietly go down to dust" (3:3). How is the ego undone? By our choice to no longer support it.

"The secret of salvation is but this: That you are doing this unto yourself" (T-27.VIII.10:1).

Lesson 236—August 24

"I rule my mind, which I alone must rule."

PRACTICE SUMMARY

See the practice instructions on page 241, or the Practice Card bound into this volume.

COMMENTARY

If the "secret of salvation" is that "I am doing this to myself" (T-27.VIII.10:1), the reason that is "salvation," or good news, is that it means there are no inimical external forces imposing themselves on me. It's just my own mind screwing up. And if that is true, there is hope. Because nobody is running my mind but me! Therefore, I can turn things around. My mind is my kingdom, and I am king of my mind. I rule it; nobody and nothing else does.

Yes, it's true that, "At times, it does not seem I am its king at all" (1:2). At times! For most of us it seems more like most of the time. My "kingdom" seems to run me, and not the other way around, telling me "what to think, and what to do and feel" (1:3). *A Course in Miracles* is a course for kings; it trains us how to rule our minds. We've been letting the kingdom run wild instead of ruling it. We've made the problem, projected the image of the problem, and then we've blamed the image for being the problem. As the Text says, we've reversed cause and effect. We are the cause, we made the effect, and now we think the effect is causing us (T-28.II.8:8). So we need a course in "mind training" that teaches us we are the rulers of our minds.

The mind is a tool, given to serve us (1:4–5). It does nothing except what we want it to do. The problem is that we have not been watching what we've asked the mind to do. We've asked for separation, we've asked for guilt, and being guilty, we've asked for death, and the mind has delivered as asked. We've given it over to the wild insanity of the ego, and the result is the ego's world we live in. So we need to see that, stop doing it, and give the mind's service to the Holy Spirit instead.

That raises a question for me. If I am supposed to rule my mind, how is giving it to the Holy Spirit doing that? To give the mind to the service of the Holy Spirit is said, here, to be the way "I direct my mind" (1:6–7). The answer is actually quite simple. There are only two alternatives: ego or Holy Spirit, fear or love, separation or union. The Holy Spirit is not a foreign power ruling over me, He is the voice of my own Self, as well as the Voice for God. He is the Voice of both Father and Son because Father and Son are one, with one will. The call to rule my mind is not a call to total self-reliant independence, the king as me-all-by-myself. That is the *ego* version of ruling the mind. The call to rule my mind is a call to total dependence, to total *Self* reliance; reliance upon the Self that is shared by us all.

I have the choice between the illusion of independence, in which my mind is actually enslaved by its effects, and real freedom, in which my mind is given to its divinely intended purpose, serving the will of God. Who can deny that our experience of being independent minds is actually an experience of slavery, with our "kingdom" telling us what to think and do and say? Let us today realize there is an alternative, and gladly give our minds to God. Let us enter with willing hearts into the process of retraining our minds to think with God.

WHAT IS SALVATION? (Part 6)

W-pII.2.3:4

When we stop supporting the mind's illusions, and they fall down into dust, what is left? "What they hid is now revealed" (3:4). When illusions are gone, what remains is the truth. And the truth is a wonderful reality within ourselves. Instead of the malice, pettiness and evil we fear to find within us, we find "an altar to the Holy Name of God whereon His Word is written" (3:4). The truth that lies behind all the masks, the misdirection, the subtle deceptions of the ego, is an altar to God within my own heart, a sacred place, an ancient and eternal holiness.

There are treasures lying before this altar. And they are treasures I have put there! They are the gifts of my forgiveness. And it is only a short distance, a moment of time, from this place to the memory of God Himself (3:4).

The discovery of the holy altar to God within my mind is the result of doing nothing; of failing to continue my support of the ego's illusions, of refusing any longer to give my mind to the ego and its purposes. The discovery of what is true about me, and the memory of God that follows from it, all grow out of my willingness to question the illusions and let them go. I do not need to build the altar or rebuild it; it is there, behind the mists of self-deception. The way to truth is through the exposure of the lies that hide it. Deep within me, communion with God continues uninterrupted, waiting only that I turn from the lies that tell me otherwise. I can turn to that altar now. I can brush past the curtains that hide it, and enter God's Presence, and find my Self waiting there.

Lesson 237—August 25

"Now would I be as God created me."

PRACTICE SUMMARY

See the practice instructions on page 241, or the Practice Card bound into this volume.

COMMENTARY

These lessons in Part II all seem to be about realizing Who or What I really am. As the Introduction says,

> The workbook is divided into two main sections, the first dealing with the undoing of the way you see now, and the second with the acquisition of true perception (W-In.3:1).

So the emphasis in this entire last section of the Workbook, the last 145 lessons, is on true perception. The assumption is that the reader has at least become aware of the ego thought system in his life, although by no means is it supposed that the ego is entirely undone. If that were the case, additional lessons would not be needed.

What we are doing in these last lessons is putting the positive side of the Course into practice, and attempting to bring it into application. "Now I would be as God created me." The goal is not just to understand the idea and file it away under "Facts: human nature, true," but *to be* the Son of God, by bringing that truth to my awareness throughout the day, and living accordingly.

"I will arise in glory" (1:2). Each day can begin in glory. Radiance, bright outshining. Glory, according to my dictionary, means "majestic beauty and splendor; resplendence." It is not a word we easily associate with ourselves. Today I can make a conscious effort to be aware of my glory. I am a radiant being. The light of love and joy shines out from me to bless the world. Let me sit a moment in silence, just picturing that, being aware of my own shining.

As I go through the day, let me

> ...allow the light in me to shine upon the world. I bring the world the tidings of salvation which I hear as God my Father speaks to me (1:2–3).

This has more to do with being than with doing. It has more to do with radiating than with speaking. We teach peace by *being* peaceful, not so much by talking about it. If I am joyful, restful, loving, and accepting of those around me, my attitude will speak louder than my words.

So in this day, as I work and visit with friends, let me be radiant. I am as God created me, so I *am* radiant; I don't need to do anything to become radiant. All that is needed is to notice what my thoughts would do to dim that radiance, and to choose otherwise.

In a certain sense this supersedes the earlier lesson where I ask the Holy Spirit where to go, what to do and what to say. Now the emphasis is on what I am. It really doesn't matter so much where I go, what I do, or what I say, as long as I am acting as the being whom God created rather than my independent self.

I come to see "the world that Christ would have me see" (1:4), and I see it as "my Father's call to me" (1:4). Seen through the eyes of Christ the world can become a constant call to be who I am, to shine, to radiate His Love, to be His Answer to the world.

✧

WHAT IS SALVATION? (Part 7)

W-pII.2.4:1

If the altar to God is within me, yet remains largely hidden from my habitual awareness, what I need to do is to "come daily to this holy place" (4:1). This is the practice of the holy instant recommended by the Text (T-15.II.5,6; T-15.IV), a premeditated turning aside from our routine activities to bring our minds into this holy place, with Jesus at our side ("Let ***us*** come...and spend a while together" (4:1)). If you are open to it, it seems to me that Jesus is here asking us to spend some time, daily, with him, in God's presence. If the figure of Jesus is somehow discordant for you, picture an anonymous spiritual guide, perhaps representing your higher self. With him or her, you enter this temple, stand by the altar, and spend time there in communion with God.

We need to form this habit of bringing our minds into the holy instant, reminding ourselves of the presence of Jesus (or the Holy Spirit), remembering this altar to God within ourselves, with His Word written on it (3:4). That Word, I think, is the Word of salvation, the promise He made that we would find our way to Him (1:1). It is the Thought of Peace, which will replace our thoughts of conflict. This meeting place is where we experience the unbroken communication between ourselves and God. This is where we bathe in the flow of love that streams constantly between the Father and the Son.

Chapter 14, Section VIII, of the Text describes this holy meeting place, and says:

> All this is safe within you, where the Holy Spirit shines. He shines not in division, but in the meeting place where God, united with His Son, speaks to His Son through Him. Communication between what cannot be divided cannot cease. The holy meeting place of the unseparated Father and His Son lies in the Holy Spirit and in you. All interference in the communication that God Himself wills with His Son is quite impossible here. Unbroken and uninterrupted love flows

> constantly between the Father and the Son, as Both would have it be. And so it is (T-14.VIII.1:10–16).

And so it is. This is what I want to know and experience daily, in coming to this place. Here I bring my guilt and fear and lay it down, accepting Atonement for myself. Here my mind renews its contact with its Source. Here I rediscover the unending communion which is mine, my inheritance as God's Son. Here my nightmares are all banished, and I breathe the fragrant air of Heaven and of home.

Lesson 238—August 26

"On my decision all salvation rests."

PRACTICE SUMMARY

See the practice instructions on page 241, or the Practice Card bound into this volume.

COMMENTARY

In Lesson 236 I saw that I alone rule my mind. God has created me free to choose to listen to His Voice, or not to listen. Salvation thus rests entirely on my decision. The message of today's lesson is that, if this is true, God must have a great deal of trust in me. As humankind is typically pictured, it is weak, vacillating, or downright rebellious. Sinners at the core, and totally untrustworthy. But if God "placed [His] Son's salvation in my hands, and let it rest on my decision" (1:3), that dark picture cannot be the truth. If I was such an untrustworthy being, if humankind were so unreliable, God would never have put such enormous trust in us. Therefore, "I must be worthy" (1:1). "I must be beloved of You indeed. And I must be steadfast in holiness as well" (1:4–5). In sum: If God trusts me, I must be worthy of that trust.

It isn't just my own salvation that rests on my decision; "all salvation" rests on it., because the Sonship is one. If one part remains separate and alone, the Sonship is incomplete. Yet God "gave [His] Son to me in certainty that He is safe" (1:5). If God is certain that the Son is safe in my hands, He must know something about me that I have forgotten. He knows me as I am (1:2), and not as I have come to believe I am. The trust He displays is amazing, because the Son is not simply His creation, the Son is "still part of" Him (1:5). God has entrusted part of His very Being to my care, in confidence of what my decision will be: To freely, willingly, choose to join with and enter into His Love and His Will. He knows that in the end I will not choose otherwise and cannot choose otherwise, for He formed me as an extension of His own Love.

Let me, then, today, reflect often on how much God loves me; how much He loves His Son; and how God's love for His Son is demonstrated by entrusting all salvation to my decision. Let me rest assured that the outcome is as inevitable as God. Let me take confidence in God's confidence in me.

✧

WHAT IS SALVATION? (Part 8)

W-pII.2.4:2-5

When we come daily to this holy place, we catch glimpses of the real world, our "final dream" (4:2). In the holy instant we see with the vision of Christ, in which there is no sorrow. We are allowed to see "a hint of all the glory given us by God" (4:2). The goal of the Course for us is to come to the place where we carry this vision with us always; where our minds are so transformed that we see nothing but the real world, and live a life that is one, continuous holy instant. That time may seem far off to me, but it is much nearer than I believe, and in the holy instant I experience it as *now*. It is by repeatedly coming to the holy instant, repeatedly immersing our minds in the vision of the real world, that this world becomes the only reality to us, the final dream before we waken.

In this happy dream, "Earth is being born again in new perspective" (4:5). The images of grass pushing through the soil, trees budding, and birds coming to live in their branches speak to us of Springtime, of a rebirth after a long winter. The images stand for the new perception we have of the world, in which our spiritual night is gone, and all living things stand together in the light of God. We look past illusions now, past what has always seemed like solid reality to us, and see something more firm and sure beyond them, a vision of everlasting holiness and peace. We see and hear "the need of every heart, the call of every mind, the hope that lies beyond despair, the love attack would hide, the brotherhood that hate has sought to sever, but which still remains as God created it" (W-pI.185.14:1).

Here, in the vision of the real world, we "hear the call that echoes past each seeming call to death, that sings behind each murderous attack and pleads that love restore the dying world" (T-31.I.10:3). We see that the only purpose of the world is forgiveness. "How lovely is the world whose purpose is forgiveness of God's Son!" (T-29.VI.6:1)

"How beautiful it is to walk, clean and redeemed and happy, through a world in bitter need of redemption that your innocence bestows upon it!" (T-23.IN.6:5)

Lesson 239—August 27

"The glory of my Father is my own."

PRACTICE SUMMARY

See the practice instructions on page 241, or the Practice Card bound into this volume.

COMMENTARY

"Let not the truth about ourselves today be hidden by a false humility" (1:1).

One thing I am aware of as I have not been before while doing the Workbook is that when it uses the words, "we," "us," and "ourselves," it is not referring to just us students of the Course. The "we" includes Jesus. After all, it is Jesus who is speaking throughout the book. This is no ordinary, generic "we" that any author might use. Jesus is identifying himself with us, and us with him, each time a third-person pronoun is used.

The "truth about ourselves" is the truth about you, me and Jesus. In recognizing that, I get a sense of his joining with me that I've never quite had before. And I see in his use of the terms a purpose, to focus my attention on the sameness of himself, myself and my brothers.

When I see traces of sin and guilt "in those with whom He shares His glory" (1:3), I am seeing them in myself. That is a false humility! When I see my brother as guilty or sinful it is because I am putting myself in that same class, and thus hiding the truth about myself. Guilt can take a seemingly saintly form: "We are all just poor students of the Course, weak and frail and constantly failing." And that guilt, that false humility, obscures your glory and my own.

It is true that we are all just students, that we are on the lower rung of the ladder and just beginning to be aware of all we really are. It is false spirituality to pretend to what we do not experience. But it is false humility to constantly emphasize our weakness by judging or focusing on failures. We all have egos, but we also all share the same glorious Sonship. We need to spend time, from time to time, giving thanks for "the light that shines forever in us...We are one, united in this light and one with You, at peace with all creation and ourselves" (2:1,3).

What I dwell on in my brothers is what I am seeing and dwelling on in myself. How I view my brothers only reflects my view of myself.

> Perception seems to teach you what you see. Yet it but witnesses to what you taught. It is an outward picture of a wish; an image that you wanted to be true (T-24.VII.8:8–10).

"How can you manifest the Christ in you except to look on holiness and see Him there?" (T-25.I.2:1) In other words, you manifest the Christ in you only by looking on your brother and seeing the Christ in him.

> Perception tells you *you* are manifest in what you see (T-25.I.2:2).
>
> Perception is a choice of what you want yourself to be; the world you want to live in, and the state in which you think your mind will be content and satisfied....It reveals yourself to you as you would have you be (T-25.I.3:1,3).

If I would not hide the truth of my own glory, I cannot hide that of my brother. "What is the same can have no different function" (T-23.IV.3:4). If I deny the truth in my brother, I am denying it to myself. I am denying it in him *because* I am denying it about myself. When I mentally separate myself from someone, and make him or her less than myself by judging, I am seeing only what my mind is doing to myself. I am hiding my own glory, and therefore judging another, projecting the guilt outside. My judgment of another can then become a mirror to show me that I have forgotten who I really am. It can remind me, cause me to remember, and to choose again, to remember my status as Son of God, "at peace with all creation and [myself]" (2:3).

✧

WHAT IS SALVATION? (Part 9)

W-pII.2.5:1–2

We turn from the world to the holy place within; we enter the holy instant, where our illusions fall because we no longer support them, and we begin to see with the vision of Christ, seeing the real world. And *then we return to the world.* "From here we give salvation to the world, for it is here salvation was received" (5:1). This movement is repeated again and again in both Workbook and Text: Away from the world of dreams—into the holy instant—returning to give salvation to the world. The Course does not plan for us to retreat from the world, but to save it. It does not urge us into a withdrawn, contemplative life, but urges us *from within the state of mind we find in contemplation* to offer what we have found to the world.

"The song of our rejoicing is the call to all the world that freedom is returned" (5:2). Our inner healing bubbles over in a "song of rejoicing," and that song, that ebullient joy, becomes the very thing that calls the world back to its freedom. Nothing is so healing as a person whose face is radiant with joy. It is not so much that we come to the world preaching a new religion (W-pI.37.3:1,2), but that we transform it by our joy. We represent a new state of mind. As the Manual puts it, we "stand for the Alternative" (M-5.III.2:6). We save the world by being saved.

Lesson 240—August 28

"Fear is not justified in any form."

PRACTICE SUMMARY

See the practice instructions on page 241, or the Practice Card bound into this volume.

COMMENTARY

"Fear is deception" (1:1). When we are afraid, we have been deceived by some lie, because given what we are (Sons of God, a part of Love Itself) (1:7–8), nothing can ever harm us or cause us loss of any kind. Therefore when fear arises, we must have seen ourselves as we could never be (1:2). The reality of what we are is never in danger: "Nothing real can be threatened" (T-Int.2:2). All the things in the world that appear to threaten us are simply impossible, because we cannot be threatened. "Not one thing in this world is true" (1:3). "Nothing unreal exists" (T-Int.2:3).

All the threats of the world, whatever their forms, witness only to one thing: our illusions about ourselves (1:4–5). We are seeing ourselves as something vulnerable; a body, a fragile ego, a physical life-form that can be snuffed out in an instant. That is not what we are, and when we fear, that is what we are thinking we are. In order for us to come to believe that we are something else—the eternal Son of God, forever secure in God's Love, beyond the reach of death—we must be willing to learn the unreality of all that the world seems to witness to. Eventually we must come to see that to attempt to hold on to the reality of this world is to hold on to death.

If we insist on making the world real, today's statement, "Fear is not justified," will never seem true to us. *Everything* in this world is vulnerable, changeable, and will ultimately pass away. If we try to hold on to it, fear is inevitable because the end of what we are holding on to is also inevitable. The only way to be truly free from fear is to cease to value anything but the eternal.

This does not mean that we cannot enjoy what is temporary, that we cannot, for instance, pause to appreciate the beauty of a sunset which passes in minutes. But we come to understand that it is not the sunset we value, but the beauty it mirrors for a moment. It is not the touch of a body we value, a body which withers and is gone, but the eternal love it catches and expresses in the moment. Not the form, but the content. Not the symbol, but its meaning. Not the overtones, the harmonics, or the echo, but the eternal song of love (Song of Prayer-1.III.3:4).

Let me practice, then, today, by repeating, "Fear is not justified in any form." And when fears arise, let me remember they are foolish (2:1). Let me recall there is no real reason for them. Let my very fears remind me that the truth of what I value *never* passes away.

WHAT IS SALVATION? (Part 10)

W-pII.2.5:2

Salvation results, not in a perfect material world, but in a state in which "eternity has shined away the world, and only Heaven now exists at all" (5:2). As we enter more and more fully into the holy instant, and the vision of the "real world" it brings, we are literally hastening the end of time itself. The phrase "the real world" is in actuality an oxymoron, a self-contradictory pair of words, for the world is not real. (See T-26.III.3:1–3.) The real world is the goal of the Course for us, and yet, when we have attained it fully, we will barely have time to appreciate it before God takes His last step, and the illusion of the world vanishes into the reality of Heaven (T-17.II.4:4). The nightmare is gradually translated into a happy dream, and when all the nightmares are gone there is no longer any need for dreaming; we will awake.

Salvation, then, is the process of translating the nightmare into the happy dream, the process of undoing the illusions, the process of removing the barriers we have built to love, the process, in short, of forgiveness. The experience we are now in is our classroom. The reason we are here is to learn the truth, or rather, to unlearn the errors. The Course urges us to be content with learning, and not to be impatient. We will not be, and cannot be, "abruptly lifted up and hurled into reality" (T-16.VI.8:1–2). It would terrify us, like a child in kindergarten abruptly being made President, or a first-year piano student being forced to do a solo recital in Carnegie Hall. Each of us is exactly where we belong, learning just what we need to learn. Let us, then, enter whole-heartedly and joyously into the process, practicing our holy instants, receiving our little glimpses of the real world, each one assuring us of the reality of our goal, and the certainty of its attainment.

Lesson 241—August 29

"This holy instant is salvation come."

PRACTICE SUMMARY

See the practice instructions on page 241, or the Practice Card bound into this volume.

COMMENTARY

When the lesson says that today "is a time of special celebration" (1:2), I rather suspect it is using the word "special" in the same way it uses it in one place in the Text, where Jesus says, "All my brothers are special" (T-1.V.3:6). Today is special because, in the holy instant, salvation has already come. And yet, "You can claim the holy instant any time and anywhere you want it" (T-15.IV.4:4). Whenever you claim the holy instant, it is a special time! A day of joy!

This is just like telling a child that they can have Christmas every day if they want it. And indeed the Course tells us exactly that, in the section titled "The Time of Rebirth," written at Christmas. It tells us that Christmas is the time of Christ, and the time of Christ is the holy instant (T-15.X.2:1); and then it tells us, "It is in your power to make the time of Christ be now" (T-15.X.4:1).

And so, why not today? Why not every day? Why not now? Any time I want to, I can make it a time "when sorrows pass away and pain is gone" (1:4). The practice of the holy instant offers me this. Within my mind I can, at any instant, open a window onto the real world, and breathe its fragrant atmosphere. I can experience a united world, drawn together by my forgiveness.

I do not yet find that I experience bliss the moment I close my eyes and say, "This holy instant is salvation come." The reality I have experienced, from time to time, is always here; I am certain of that. Yet my awareness of it remains spotty. (*Very* spotty!) But once you have tasted it, and in that instant *known* that what you are experiencing is eternal, you can never fully doubt its eternal presence. There are still many barriers blocking my awareness of it. I am still holding on to quite a few of those barriers. My grievances are still, most of the time, hiding the Light of the world from me. But it is there. My forgiveness can release it (1:7–2:1).

Every time I pause to remember, every time I attempt to claim the holy instant, another barrier falls, another drop of willingness is added to my reservoir. What better way could I possibly spend my time? As Lesson 127 said: "There is no better use for time than this" (see paragraphs 7 and 8).

One aside: Notice that in 1:8, Jesus speaks of our forgiving *him*. Let me examine myself today, to see if there is something I still hold against him; something in him I mistrust; some way in which I still fear him, or blame him, or resent him. Even if I respect him as my teacher, it is very easy to feel resentful of one's teachers.

✧

WHAT IS THE WORLD? (Part 1)

W-pII.3.1:1-4

The first sentence answers the question: "The world is false perception" (1:1). The rest of the page is the explanation of this summary statement. Some of us, on first reading the Course, think that perhaps the Course is not saying that the world is unreal, but that our perception of it is false. Yet here, quite clearly, Jesus is saying that the world and false perception are the same thing. The world is an hallucination; we are perceiving something that isn't there.

In my perception, "I" am inside my head, looking out at a world that is not me. Separate. And that is simply not the truth. There is no world outside my mind (T-18.VI.1:1; T-12.III.6:7). "What is projected out, and seems to be external to the mind, is not outside at all" (T-26.VII.4:9).

The world was "born of error" and it has not left our minds which sourced it (1:2). As the Course so often says, "Ideas leave not their source." The world is the mistaken idea of separation in our minds (1:4), and it has never left our minds. When our mind (the one mind we all share) no longer cherishes the idea of separation, the world which represents that idea will simply disappear.

Many who were raised in a religious tradition which taught that God created the world have gone through a lot of distress and confusion, wondering how God could ever have created such a mess! If He was responsible for this, we weren't sure we wanted to know Him. What a relief it is to realize that He did *not* create it; it was born of the error of our mind, from our mistakenly entertaining the idea of separation. The misery of this world only reflects the misery brought to our mind by the thought of separation. It is as if we wondered, "What if we were separate?" and were instantly given a virtual reality tour of what would result.

An early lesson said, "I can escape from this world by giving up attack thoughts" (Lesson 55, reviewing Lesson 23). The thought is the same. Heal the attack thoughts, the thoughts of separation which I still cherish, and I can leave the world behind. The Course is helping us to do just that; to let our attack thoughts go, and solve the problems of the world at their source.

Lesson 242—August 30

"This day is God's. It is my gift to Him."

PRACTICE SUMMARY

See the practice instructions on page 241, or the Practice Card bound into this volume.

COMMENTARY

"I will not lead my life alone today" (1:1).

In a day that seems rushed and over full with things to do, it is a relief to remember that I need not lead my life alone. I can burden myself with a thousand little decisions, or I can relax into His hands. I may list what needs to be done, but I can let go of all attachment to doing any of them. In each moment, I can trust that I will know what to do next, and that my choice will be perfect.

What is important, however, is not the guidance of the Holy Spirit, but His companionship. I will not be alone today, although I may have no other human presence with me. I can consciously be with God, and God with me. Instead of talking out loud to myself, why not talk out loud to Jesus? He is a much wiser companion than my limited mind.

"I do not understand the world, and so to try to lead my life alone must be but foolishness" (1:2).

There is such resistance in me, in us all, to realizing that we do not and cannot understand the world. I understand nothing. My awareness of what is going on is about one five-billionth of just our physical planet and its people. I know nothing of other planets and galaxies, and I am nearly totally unaware of the numberless realms beyond the physical—spirit beings, angels, ascended Masters, whatever there may be. I don't know that the clerk in the laundry may need a smile, or whatever else is going on in minds apparently separated from me. How can I even think of rationally deciding what to do, where to go, what to say, all on my own?

Some event occurs, such as an appointment being juggled around from one time to another and finally settling on the time I least wanted (by my preferences). If I think I understand what is going on, if I think my preference is all that matters, I could be upset. If I realize I don't understand the world, I let go, I accept, I trust. And I show up at my friend's door minutes after she has heard the news about a friend's sudden death, present to comfort her when she needs it. And, not coincidentally, prepared by an afternoon of discussing death with another friend, when I had no idea why I agreed to take time for that discussion when I had other things I thought important to do. How foolish not to let Him lead me!

So today, again, I resign as my own teacher and settle a bit more deeply into the awareness that I do not know, I do not understand, and knowing that is wisdom. I release this day into God's hands; "It is my gift to Him." This is a really good deal! I let go of my day, and He makes it full of miracles! That's what He wants it for. It takes great effort, at first, to let go of wanting to understand. But when I do, nothing but joy follows.

> But there is One Who knows all that is best for me. And He is glad to make no choices for me but the ones that lead to God. I give this day to Him, for I would not delay my coming home, and it is He Who knows the way to God (1:3–5).

"Best for me" doesn't necessarily mean that I will get done all I think I have to do, or that everything will work out perfectly (in my eyes) in form. Often it does mean that, but sometimes not. "Best for me" means the things "that lead to God." It means "coming home" and making progress on "the way to God." Because that is all that life in this world is for. "The healing of God's Son is all the world is for" (T-24.VI.4:1), and nothing else. If I give my day to God, to the Holy Spirit, I will end the day closer to God, nearer home; that is my goal every day of my life. Nothing else. All other events are stage props for this one unfolding drama.

No matter what else may happen, if I spend this day more conscious of Jesus' companionship, a little more often at peace, a little more joyful in every minute or a few more minutes spent joyfully, it is a success.

> And so we give today to You. We come with wholly open minds. We do not ask for anything that we may think we want. Give us what You would have received by us. You know all our desires and our wants. And You will give us everything we need in helping us to find the way to You (2:1–6).

"Wholly open minds." No preconceptions about what should take place. "Wholly" means totally, completely open. As for what we expect to come, anything can fail to happen and we are not distraught. As for what we do not expect, anything can come, and we are not dismayed. I recognize that my mind does not want to be wholly open. For instance, I think if I did not finish writing my article before lunch I might be upset. If I have that thought let me see it is only my thought. Not a fact. What other things am I attached to today? Jesus, I want to be wholly open. And it isn't easy.

How can I let go of my wants and needs? By remembering that "You know all our desires and wants." He knows what I think I need, and I do not need to ask Him for those things. He knows. And if the day does not bring what I think I want, it is not because He did not know, or that He lost my case file, or that He is punishing me for some imaginary guilt. It is because what I thought I wanted was not best for me. The Holy Spirit is not inconsiderate nor forgetful. He "will give us everything we need in helping us to find the way to" God. Let me let down the defenses of my planning mind, and follow this advice: "Let no defenses but your present trust direct the future, and this life becomes a meaningful encounter with the truth that only your defenses would conceal" (W-pI.135.19:2).

✧

WHAT IS THE WORLD? (Part 2)

W-pII.3.1:4–5

If the world is simply the effect of the thought of separation in my mind, then obviously it is true that:

"When the thought of separation has been changed to one of true forgiveness, will the world be seen in quite another light, and one which leads to truth..." (1:4). The antidote for the thought of separation is true forgiveness. If the Course is a course in changing our thoughts, the thoughts that are being changed are separation thoughts, and they are being changed into thoughts of true forgiveness. The "wall" that keeps us separate is our unforgiveness, our grievances, our judgment upon one another as undeserving of love. The result of changing those thoughts to thoughts of forgiveness is that we see the world very differently. Instead of a world of judgment we see the real world. Instead of enemies we see brothers. And the vision of this real world "leads to truth," beyond perception to knowledge; beyond the real world to Heaven.

This light "leads to truth, where all the world must disappear and all its errors vanish" (1:4). In other words, as we've already seen, the progression is from "the world" (the result of the thought of separation) to "the real world" (the result of the thought of forgiveness); and then to "Heaven" (the truth), where there is no world at all.

The process we are going through in the world is the healing of our thoughts of separation. As those thoughts are healed, we begin to see the real world more and more, a world in which only love is reflected. But when the thought of separation is *entirely* healed in every part of every fragment of the mind, the world will not simply be seen differently; it will disappear. "Now its source [the thought of separation] has gone, and its effects [the world and all its errors] are gone as well" (1:5).

Lesson 243—August 31

"Today I will judge nothing that occurs."

PRACTICE SUMMARY

See the practice instructions on page 241, or the Practice Card bound into this volume.

COMMENTARY

If attempting to practice today's lesson does nothing else, it will show me just how constantly my mind *is* judging. The eventual goal, of course, is to truly relinquish all judgment, and to allow the Holy Spirit to judge everything for us. Letting go of judgment is a key to transcending the ego: "The ego cannot survive without judgment, and is laid aside accordingly" (T-4.II.10:3).

"I will be honest with myself today" (1:1). The Course teaches us that letting go of judgment is simply learning to be honest with ourselves. This lesson is paralleled in the Manual:

> It is necessary for the teacher of God to realize, not that he should not judge, but that he cannot. In giving up judgment, he is merely giving up what he did not have. He gives up an illusion; or better, he has an illusion of giving up. He has actually merely become more honest. Recognizing that judgment was always impossible for him, he no longer attempts it (M-10.2:1–5).

So giving up judgment is simply being honest about the fact that I *cannot* judge. To judge accurately I would have to know many things that "must remain beyond my present grasp" (1:2). I would have to know "the whole" just from what my limited perception is telling me. And I can't do that. So any judgment I make has to be an illusion, no more valid than a wild guess.

Still—just watch yourself doing it! Our minds automatically categorize every person we see. We evaluate their clothes, their grooming, their sexual attractiveness, the appropriateness of their behavior, the way they walk, and on and on. We get up, see the sunshine, and say, "What a nice day!" or we see rain and say, "What miserable weather!" We read a book and tell a friend what a "great book" it is. We take a bite of food and instantly judge it. The ego mind seems to do little else but judge. Just watch yourself.

That isn't going to stop overnight, if ever. What we can do, however, is to become aware of these judgments constantly going on and realize that they are without any real meaning. We can tell the ego, "Thank you for sharing," and choose to realize that we don't really know what anything means or how to react to it, despite what the ego is telling us. We can turn instead to our inner guidance. We can "leave creation free to be itself" (2:1) without our constant interference. We can bring our judgments to the Holy Spirit and ask Him to heal our minds. And, perhaps most important of all, we can simply *desire* that judgment be undone. In the end, that desire is all it takes:

> Vision would not be necessary had judgment not been made. Desire now its whole undoing, and it is done for you (T-20.VIII.1:5–6).
>
> Undoing is not your task, but it is up to you to welcome it or not (T-21.II.8:5).

Don't worry about *how* your judgments can be undone. Don't try to undo them yourself. Just desire that they be undone; just welcome the undoing. That is all, and the Holy Spirit will do it for you.

✧

WHAT IS THE WORLD? (Part 3)

WpII.3.2:1–3

"The world was made as an attack on God" (2:1). That is probably one of the most shocking statements in *A Course in Miracles*. It puts to bed any idea that perhaps the world was, at least partly, created by God; God would not create an attack on Himself. The world is the ego's attempt to replace and displace God, and to provide us with an alternative satisfaction.

In Chapter 23, Section II, the Text speaks of "The Laws of Chaos," the ego's laws. It tells us that these laws are what make the world real; it says, "These *are* the principles which make the ground beneath your feet seem solid" (T-23.II.13:5). The ego's laws are what made the world.

What of the world's beauty? What of the glitter of the stars, the fragile beauty of a flower, the majesty of an eagle in flight? Nothing but glitter, a shiny surface hiding the death-rot underneath. "Kill or be killed" is the law of this world. Beneath the lovely, glittering surface of the ocean lies a world of sharp teeth, cruel deception, and constant warfare, where life consists of eating some things and avoiding being eaten by others.

"Can you paint rosy lips upon a skeleton, dress it in loveliness, pet it and pamper it, and make it live?" (T-23.II.18:8) "There is no life outside of Heaven" (T-23.II.19:1).

The world symbolizes fear, which is the absence of love. "Thus, the world was meant to be a place where God could enter not, and where His Son could be apart from Him" (2:3). The ego made the world as a place to hide out from God, to get away from Him. Yes, we can find symbols of God in nature, and we should; true perception sees nothing but love in all things. But that means we see him in tornadoes and earthquakes as well as in flowers and birds. It means we see Him in everything because He is in our minds. But at its root, this world is a "place where God is not." That is why the ego made it. That is our purpose in coming here, as egos. And we egos did a pretty good job; people have been trying to "prove" the existence of God within the context of this world for millenia, and nobody has ever done so except, perhaps, to the satisfaction of a few who were already inclined to believe. Finding God *in* the world is quite a stretch. The world does a far better job of hiding God than it does of demonstrating Him.

What is the message in all of this for us? Remember, "The world is false perception" (1:1). It is not the truth. The picture of the world, symbolizing fear and attack, is the picture of the ego's thoughts. "It is born of error" (1:2). This world is not what we want. We cannot attempt to cling to its "better" parts and forget about the horror all around us. We take it whole or let it all go. And so, we can learn to look upon the world with love—all of it. Loving it gives it the only value it has (T-12.VI.3:1–3). With forgiveness, we look past the messages of hate and fear it constantly tries to give us, and see there, as well as in the more "pleasing" aspects, the universal call for love.

> You do not want the world. The only thing of value in it is whatever part of it you look upon with love. This gives it the only reality it will ever have. Its value is not in itself, but yours is in you. As self-value comes from self-extension, so does the perception of self-value come from the extension of loving thoughts outward. Make the world real unto yourself, for the real world is the gift of the Holy Spirit, and so it belongs to you (T-12.VI.3:1–6).

Booklets in this Series Based on *A Course in Miracles*

by Robert Perry and Allen Watson

1. **Seeing the Face of Christ in All Our Brothers** *by Robert.* How we can see the Presence of God in others. $5.00.
2. **Special Relationships: Illusions of Love** *by Robert.* Explains the unconscious motives that drive our seemingly loving relationships, and describes methods for transforming them into something holy. (Limited quantities available. Revised and updated in #18.) $5.00.
3. **Shrouded Vaults of the Mind** *by Robert.* Draws a map of the mind based on ACIM, and takes you on a tour through its many levels. $5.00.
4. **Guidance: Living the Inspired Life** *by Robert.* Sketches an overall perspective on guidance and its place on the spiritual path. $5.00.
5. **Holy Relationships: The End of an Ancient Journey** *by Robert.* No longer in print. Revised and updated in #18.
6. **Reality & Illusion: An Overview of Course Metaphysics, Part I** *by Robert.* Examines the Course's vision of reality. With Booklet #7, forms a comprehensive overview of ACIM's metaphysical thought system. $5.00.
7. **Reality & Illusion: An Overview of Course Metaphysics, Part II** *by Robert.* Discusses the origins of our apparent separation from God. $5.00.
8. **A Healed Mind Does Not Plan** *by Allen.* Examines our approach to planning and decision-making, showing how it is possible to leave the direction of our lives up to the Holy Spirit. $5.00.
9. **Through Fear To Love** *by Allen.* Explores two sections from *A Course in Miracles* that deal with our fear of redemption. Leads the reader to see how it is possible to look upon ourselves with love. $5.00.
10. **The Journey Home** *by Allen.* Presents a description of our spiritual destination and what we must go through to get there. $5.00.

Booklets in this Series Based on *A Course in Miracles*

by Robert Perry and Allen Watson

11. **Everything You Always Wanted to Know About Judgment but Were Too Busy Doing It to Notice** *by Robert and Allen.* A survey of various teaching about judgment in ACIM. $5.00.
12. **The Certainty of Salvation** *by Robert and Allen.* How we can become certain that we will find our way to God. $5.00.
13. **What is Death?** *by Allen.* The Course's view of what death really is. $5.00.
14. **The Workbook as a Spiritual Practice** *by Robert.* A guide for getting the most out of the Workbook. $5.00.
15. **I Need Do Nothing: Finding the Quiet Center** *by Allen.* An in-depth discussion of one of the most misunderstood parts of the Course. $5.00.
16. **A Course Glossary** *by Robert.* 158 definitions of terms and phrases from *A Course in Miracles* for beginning students, more experienced students, and study groups. $7.00.
17. **Seeing the Bible Differently: How *A Course in Miracles* Views the Bible,** *by Allen.* Shows the similarities, differences, and continuity between the Course and the Bible. $6.00
18. **Relationships as a Spiritual Journey: From Specialness to Holiness,** *by Robert.* Describes the unconscious motives that drive our special relationships, describes the shift from special to holy relationships, and traces the stages of the holy relationship. (Replaces #2 & #5.) $10.00.
19. **A Workbook Companion, Volume I,** *by Allen,* with Robert. Daily readings to aid in the understanding and practice of the lessons in *A Workbook for Students.* Covers Lessons 1 to 121. 320 pages, $16.00.

Booklets in this Series Based on *A Course in Miracles*

by Robert Perry and Allen Watson

If your local bookstore does not carry these books, they may be ordered directly from:

The Circle of Atonement
Teaching and Healing Center
P.O. Box 4238
West Sedona, AZ 86340
(520) 282-0790, Fax (520) 282-0523

http://nen.sedona.net/circleofa/

Please include your check or money order for the price of the books, plus $2.00 for postage and handling for the first one or two books, and $1.00 more for each additional book.

A Workbook Companion

PRACTICE SUMMARIES CARD

Lessons 153–170 and 181–200.

Morning/Evening Quiet Time: Five minutes, at least; ten is better; fifteen even better; thirty or more, best.
Hourly Remembrance: As the hour strikes, for more than one minute (reduce if circumstances do not permit). Sit quietly and wait on God. Thank Him for His gifts in the past hour. Let His Voice tell you what He wants you to do in the coming hour. (Suggestion for 181–200: Do a short version of morning/evening exercise.)
Remarks: At times the business of the world will allow you only a minute or less, or no time at all. You may forget. Yet whenever you can, do your hourly remembrance.
Frequent Reminder: Remind yourself of the thought for the day.
Remarks: In time you will never cease to think of God, not even for a moment, not even while busy giving salvation to the world.
Overall Remarks: Your practice will begin to be infused with the earnestness of love, keeping your mind from wandering. Do not be afraid, you will reach your goal. God's Love and strength will make sure of it, for you are His minister.

REVIEW V (Lessons 171–180)

Purpose: To prepare for Part II of the Workbook. To give more time and effort to practicing, that you may hasten your slow, wavering and uncertain footsteps, and go on with more faith, certainty and sincerity. Make this review a gift to Jesus and a time in which you share with him a new yet ancient experience.
Central Thought: "God is but Love, and therefore so am I." This thought should start and end each day and each practice period, and be repeated before and after each thought to be reviewed. Each of these thoughts, in turn, should be used to support this central thought, keep it clear in mind, and make it more meaningful, personal and true.
Morning/Evening Quiet Time: Five minutes, at least; ten, better; fifteen, even better; thirty or more, best.

- Repeat the central thought (*"God is but Love, and therefore so am I."*). Then repeat the first review thought, followed by the central thought. Then repeat the second review thought, followed again by the central thought.
- Let go of the words, which are only aids. Try to go beyond their sound to their meaning. Wait for experience, place your faith in it, not the means to it. If your mind wanders, repeat the central thought.
- Close with the central thought.

Hourly Remembrance: As the hour strikes, for over one minute (reduce if circumstances do not permit). Suggestion: Do a brief form of the morning and evening practice. Repeat the review thoughts, surrounding them with the central thought. Then try to go beyond the words into experience. Close with the central thought.

REVIEW VI, Lessons 201–220

Purpose: To carefully review the last 20 lessons, each of which contains the whole curriculum and is therefore sufficient for salvation, if understood, practiced, accepted and applied without exception.

Morning/Evening Quiet Time: Fifteen minutes, at least. Repeat: "I am not a body. I am free. For I am still as God created me." Then, close your eyes and relinquish all that clutters the mind; forget all you thought you knew. Give the time to the Holy Spirit, your Teacher. If you notice an idle thought, immediately deny its hold, assuring your mind that you do not want it. Then let it be given up and replaced with today's idea. Say: "This thought I do not want. I choose instead (today's idea)."

Remarks: We are attempting to go beyond special forms of practice because we are attempting a quicker pace and shorter path to our goal.

Hourly Remembrance: Repeat: "I am not a body. I am free. For I am still as God created me."

Frequent Reminder: As often as possible, as often as you can, repeat: "I am not a body. I am free. For I am still as God created me."

Response To Temptation: Permit no idle thought to go unchallenged. If you are tempted by an idle thought, immediately deny its hold, assuring your mind that you do not want it. Then let it be given up and replaced with today's idea. Say: "This thought I do not want. I choose instead (today's idea)."

PART II, Lessons 221-360

Purpose: To take the last few steps to God. To wait for Him to take the final step.

Morning/Evening Quiet Time: As long as needed.

- Read the written lesson. Then use the idea and the prayer to introduce a time of quiet. Do not depend on the words. Use them as a simple invitation to God to come to you.
- Sit silently and wait for God. Wait in quiet expectancy for Him to reveal Himself to you. Seek only direct, deep, wordless experience of Him. Be certain of His coming, and unafraid. For He has promised that when you invite Him, He will come. You ask only that He keep His ancient promise, which He wills to keep. These times are your gift to Him.

Hourly Remembrance: Do not forget. Give thanks to God that He has remained with you and will always be there to answer your call to Him.

Frequent Reminder: As often as possible, even every minute, remember the idea. Dwell with God, let Him shine on you.

Response To Temptation: When you are tempted to forget your goal.

Use today's idea as a call to God and all temptation will disappear.

Reading: Preceding one of the day's moments of practice.

- Slowly read "What is...?" section.
- Think about it a while.

Overall Remarks: Now, in this final part of the year that you and Jesus have spent together, you begin to reach the goal of practicing, which is the goal of the course. Jesus is so close that you cannot fail. You have come far along the road. Do not look back. Fix your eyes on the journey's end. You could not have come this far without realizing that you want to know God. And this is all He requires to come to you.